Themes in British Social History

Leisure and Society

1830-1950

James Walvin

Leisure and Society
1830–1950

Themes in British Social History

edited by Dr J. Stevenson

*already published

Leisure and Society
1830–1950

James Walvin

WITHDRAWN

Longman
London and New York

Longman Group Limited London

Associated companies, branches and representatives throughout the world

Published in the United States of America by Longman Inc., New York

First published 1978

British Library Cataloguing in Publication Data

Walvin, James
 Leisure and society, 1830–1950. –

 (Themes in British social history).
 1. Recreation – Great Britain – History
I. Title II. Series
301.5'7'0941 GV75 78–40045

ISBN 0 582 48681 5
ISBN 0 582 48682 3 Pbk

Set in Compugraphic Baskerville 10 on 11pt
and printed in Great Britain by
Richard Clay (The Chaucer Press) Ltd,
Bungay, Suffolk

Contents

Acknowledgements

I am grateful for the help and the facilities provided by the staffs of the public libraries at Blackpool, Scarborough, Southport and York, the Manchester Central Library and the library of the Bognor Regis College of Education. Other material was gathered in the British Museum, the University of London library and the Institute of Historical Research, London University. The New York Public Library once again proved a rewarding and exciting place to work. The books in the library of the Football Association proved extremely useful, and I was greatly helped by collections in the Borthwick Institute and the Institute of Architectural Studies, both in York. My greatest debt however is to the University of York library and particularly to the friendly cooperation and expertise of David Griffiths. Parts of this book were delivered initially at seminars at Waterloo and McMaster Universities in Canada. But it is to my own university, and to the Department of History, that I am more especially indebted, for the substance of this book first appeared in the form of two lecture series at York. Numerous ideas and corrections from colleagues and students have ultimately found their way into the finished text.

Department of History
University of York
January 1978

Cover illustrations: Radio Times Hulton Picture Library

Introduction

The place of leisure in modern western society is a common source of intellectual and political discussion. In societies which appear to be affording ever more free time and purchasing power to a growing proportion of their people, the ways in which those people choose to spend their free time is clearly of importance to government, industrialists, unions, planners and the nation at large. Commentators now frequently speak of the 'problem' of leisure; of the need to retrain people who have been accustomed over generations to the idea that work, not rest, is and ought to be the mainstay of everyday life. Now, it is said, there is a need to convert people to the different and apparently conflicting view that leisure in its varied forms will soon involve the most difficult of personal decisions. One need not take a revolutionary view of the future to appreciate that even in one's own lifetime (for those say, with memories going back thirty years) the leisure activities of the English people have changed fundamentally. Yet even that perception can be misleading, for many of today's major recreations – football, cricket, cinema, radio, reading, seaside holidays – existed in recognisably the same form in 1945. But while an increasing number of critics interest themselves in predictions about future trends there has not been a correspondingly fruitful study of the history of leisure.

It is significant that the most important studies of leisure have been undertaken by sociologists and equally significant that few of them have been English. Yet from Karl Marx onwards, sociologists have been regularly drawn to the problem (and the definition) of leisure. Marx for instance was particularly concerned about the relationship between leisure and work. Nevertheless it was not until the publication of Veblen's *Theory of the Leisured Classes* (1899) that the theoretical and empirical study of leisure was fully launched. From that day to this, the most important analysts in this area have been Europeans and North Americans. David Riesman in the USA (*The Lonely Crowd*, 1950; *Individualism Reconsidered and Other Essays*, 1954) has more recently attempted to state the case for the academic study of leisure. But it is perhaps the work of the French sociologist Joffre Dumazedier (*Towards a Society of Leisure*, 1967) which has given the subject its most important theoretical and empirical exposition.

The English sociological tradition has tended to be much more concerned with empirical findings, often on a very narrow front. English historians, however, have been much less interested in the problem of leisure, though those who have, notably E. P. Thompson and J. H. Plumb have, through their own works and through a remarkable influence on their students, produced immeasurably formative work. The historical study of (in this case English) leisure is attractive at a number of levels. In the first place it is interesting in itself and affords a rich and relatively untapped field. Secondly, the historical study of leisure goes some way towards clarifying a number of presentday leisure preoccupations. But perhaps most important is the way the study of leisure throws a great deal of light on a wider range of English social history over the past century and a half. This book is not designed as a contribution towards any theoretical discussion, nor the sociology, of leisure. Its more modest ambition is to tell a previously neglected story. And by leisure I simply mean the ways in which people voluntarily chose to spend their non-working hours of rest.

It has been argued that leisure is itself a product of industrial society and this book is concerned primarily with the leisure pursuits of the first industrial nation. As England became a highly populated, urban and industrially dominated society, the way people chose (and were encouraged) to spend their free time changed dramatically. Indeed even the existence of time free from work was a major preoccupation throughout the nineteenth century, for the march of industry came to demand of growing numbers of people an unremitting commitment to work. What follows is, in essence, the story of the way the first industrial nation conceded non-working leisure hours to the great bulk of the English people and how those people chose (or were urged) to spend their free time and, later, their spare cash.

It is of course a complex phenomenon, differing greatly from place to place and between social groups. In the peak years of that first phase of industrialisation armies of working people were denied any effective leisure time, whereas their betters (known, significantly, as 'the leisured classes') could, if they so wished, devote themselves uniquely to the search for pleasure. Yet the leisure pursuits of most people were slowly changed, often out of all recognition, by the joint forces of industrialisation and urbanisation, though these changes were less marked in rural life and in the world of children's recreations. This book is an attempt to describe, in very broad outline, the development of the modern leisure habits of the English people in the years between the emergence of an industrial society and the years of material prosperity in the 1950s and 1960s. There is, inevitably perhaps, a certain concentration on particular forms, but the purpose is not to examine the developments of any particular leisure occupation, to tell the story of specific games or customs, so much as to illustrate the changing relationships between a society and the opportunities it created.

No work of this kind can hope to be comprehensive – to explain all the leisure pursuits of all the people over a period of a century and a half. It will be obvious to any reader that a wide range of local, trade, class and temporal differences are absent, but it is hoped that any such omissions will not detract from the strength of the overall theme. It will also be clear that this book is informed and guided by two of my earlier books, *The People's Game: a social history of English football*, and *Beside the Seaside: a social history of the popular seaside holiday*. Moreover, in studying so broad a topic over such a long period it is inevitable that, in places, there must be great reliance on the work of other historians. No one concerned with nineteenth-century social history can avoid an indebtedness to Brian Harrison whose *Drink and the Victorians* is a model piece of social history, much wider in its implications than its title suggests. Similarly the work of E. P. Thompson and Asa Briggs, different as they are, have shaped our understanding of the historical development of modern English society and their influence permeates this book. More specifically, my ideas about Victorian music have been directed by the research of David Russell whose work on popular music in the West Riding promises to add considerably to our wider understanding of the role of music in Victorian society.

I am deeply indebted to the sharp, critical eye of John Stevenson whose editorial work greatly improved my original manuscript. Finally, I dedicate this book to my friend Michael Craton whose love of cricket is matched only by his commitment to history.

James Walvin
University of York
January 1978

Part One

Leisure and industrial society 1830–1870

1 Leisure in an urban society 1830–1870

Visitors to England in the 1830s and 1840s were often struck by the paucity of recreational facilities for the common people; the country seemed to offer a sharp contrast to the more abundant leisure pursuits of Europe and North America. And the contrast was great even closer to home, for the English middle and upper classes were as notable for their pursuit of pleasure as their inferiors were generally devoid of it. Such differences were not surprising, for the country was passing through that first painful period of major urbanisation which was drawing a growing proportion of the expanding population into the towns and cities. It was in the urban areas that recreational changes were at their most startling. A German visitor, Frederick von Raumer, commented in 1835 that 'the working people . . . have generally no means of excitement or amusement at command during the week [and] . . . even Sunday, stern and rigid as it is here, brings no recreation or enjoyment.' Writing about the people of Manchester in that same year, Alexis de Tocqueville painted an equally grim picture. 'Never the gay shouts of people amusing themselves, or music heralding a holiday. You will never see smart folk strolling at leisure in the streets, or going on innocent pleasure parties in the surrounding country.' Manchester was exceptional, but to contemporaries it represented in a particularly acute and unpleasant form many of the urban problems which were slowly engulfing the nation's cities, one of which was the change in recreations. Time and again commentators remarked on the lack of proper urban recreations, in the absence of which working people turned to drink. Frederick Engels claimed in 1844 that for the working men of Manchester, 'Liquor is almost their only source of pleasure, and all things conspire to make it accessible to them.'

Such views were not confined to foreign observers but were frequently repeated by Englishmen concerned about the decline in popular culture, and by others who felt themselves deprived of the pastimes of their youth. Speaking about Sheffield to a parliamentary committee in 1843 John Wardle, a local cutler, recalled that 'Thirty years ago it had numbers of places as common land where youths and men could have taken exercise at cricket, quoits, football and other exercises. . . . Scarce a foot of all these common wastes remain for the enjoyment of the industrial classes.' Much the same story, though with local, regional and trade variations, was presented to parliamentary committees from towns and cities throughout the country. Dr Kay, whose work yielded abundant information on the state of Manchester, told a Select Committee of 1833 that 'the entire labouring population of Manchester is without any season of recreation, and is ignorant of all amusements, excepting that very small portion which frequents the theatre. Healthful exercise in the open air is seldom or never taken by the artizan of this town.' A similar story was told of Birmingham where, it was alleged, 'the want of some place of recreation for the mechanic is an evil which presses very heavily upon these people, and to which many of their bad habits may be traced.' Edwin Rice, an English engineer who had worked in France, Germany and Switzerland, noticed the sharp contrast between the English and the continental Sunday;

> there, people going out to dances and games, and having different recreations at the places where they go, such as cards and dominoes, can cheerfully enjoy themselves, drinking but little. But here a man can do nothing at a public house, if he goes there, but drink and he can go nowhere else on a Sunday.

Many of these claims, advanced as political arguments, were inevitably exaggerated, partial and sometimes unrepresentative. But their central theme was consistent and can be found wherever contemporaries spoke or wrote about the condition of the English urban people. And these early commentators were generally united in tracing the roots of the recreational changes to the social and economic transformation which had been reshaping the face of the country since the last years of the eighteenth century. These complex, interrelated forces of urbanisation and industrialisation had produced a society which, by the 1840s, was qualitatively different from any previous human society. England was becoming urban and industrial; few aspects of social life remained unaffected. Changes in recreations seen in their most acute form in the cities, were but one manifestation of deeper economic changes.

One of the most distinctive features of the new cities was their lack of open spaces. Land in the new urban environment was costly and in demand, and much available space was devoured for houses, streets and the hardware of the new urban society. The lack of open spaces, common land and parks, did as much as anything to deprive the poor of their old recreations. A Select Committee on Public Walks reported in 1833,

> During the last half century a very great increase has taken place in the population of large Towns, more especially as regards those classes who are, with many of their children, almost

continually engaged in manufacturing and mechanical employments. During the same period, from the increased value of Property and extension of Buildings many inclosures of open spaces in the vicinity of the Towns have taken place, and little or no provision made for Public Walks or Open Spaces, fitted to afford means of exercise or amusement to the middle and humbler classes.

Men of social conscience in the country's major towns sought to impress on their neighbours the importance of providing the poor with land for recreation. In December 1853 Joseph Sturge addressed his fellow Birmingham ratepayers to the effect that 'on no side of the town is there a green field within a moderate distance, on which even a child can play or walk without being liable to prosecution. . . . The want of places of outdoor recreations is universally admitted.'

What had happened was clear enough; the cities were using up available land, and with it the working people's right and access to open recreations. Commenting on Birmingham in 1842 it was noted that:

Within the last half century the town was surrounded by land which was divided into gardens, which were rented by the mechanics at one guinea or half a guinea per annum. Here the mechanic was generally seen after his day's labour spending his evening in a healthy and simple occupation to his great delight. This ground is now for the most part built over.

Football, a traditional game in pre-industrial society and played in town and country since time immemorial, withered in the new, restrictive conditions of the early nineteenth-century city. It was difficult to play football in the confines of urban areas where the new local authorities, taking upon themselves more and more powers to control the expanding population, legislated effectively against the more turbulent and unsociable forms of behaviour, particularly recreations. But the problem of popular recreations in the new cities was not simply a question of space or amenities. Equally important was the question of free time.

The Short Time Committee complained in 1844 that 'Schools and libraries are of small use without the time to study. . . . Parks are well for those who can have time to perambulate them, and baths are of little use to dirty people as do not leave work until eight o-clock at night.' The new industrial conditions had effectively eroded the industrial population's free time, while mechanisation had simultaneously imposed a punative working week on the labour force. Clearly not everyone, even by mid-century, worked in the new industries, but for those living in the shadow of the factory or the pit-head, life was now dominated by the place, and the pace, of work. Nevertheless this picture is pitted by a myriad of local and trade exceptions, where the peculiarities of local life enabled the old recreational pursuits to survive well into the century.

Such exceptions apart, the formula was simple; the more mechanised an industry and the heavier the capital investment, the more unwilling were the owners and managers to release the work-force from the time-consuming demands of the machines. Time was money and free time meant idle machinery which was hence unprofitable. Of course the progress of industry was made possible not simply by the mechanical changes but also by the evolution of a new sense of individual and collective work discipline which demanded – and got – a commitment and a regular rhythm of performance from the workforce. Work discipline was undoubtedly a concept devised and perfected by a new class of industrialists, but like paternalism in the slave societies of the New World it was useless and ineffective without the acceptance and participation of the labour force. New generations of industrial workers succumbed to, and then perpetuated, the growing duty of an industrially based work discipline which looked to the clock for directions. Industry, in the words of Eric Hobsbawm, 'brings the tyranny of the clock, the pace-setting machine, and the complex and carefully-timed interaction of processes.' New industries, led by the pioneering textiles trades, worked the labour force as never before (though this is not to deny the harshness and rigours of pre-industrial trades or rural work). Working hours were long and unremitting; free time was scarce and inadequate to compensate for the exhaustions of work: holidays became ever rarer. Monday through to Saturday was devoted to work; Sunday was a hiatus between bouts of work. Furthermore the pre-industrial calendar of frequent and varied holidays was simply consumed by the encroaching national commitment to useful toil. When, asked early Victorians, did working people get the time to enjoy themselves?

Industrial workers suffered dramatic deteriorations in their working lives and few of the early industrialists were as enlightened as Robert Owen or Sir Robert Peel, who sought to protect their workers, and others, from the worst excesses of overwork. Parliament, the only body capable of providing the necessary protection on a national basis, was slow to respond, and initially only did so on behalf of the most exposed groups: first of all for pauper children. Under pressure from Owen, Parliament undertook a series of investigations into working hours and child labour, but until the 1830s the results were both marginal and difficult to enforce. Not until 1833, for example, were children's working hours effectively controlled. The hard years of the 1840s revealed the continuing and growing exploitation of factory labour and, more horrifically, of child and female labour in the mines. Not until 1847 was a Ten Hour Act carried through Parliament. Modified in 1850 and 1853, it insisted on a 10½ hour working day, from 6 a.m. to 6 p.m., with 1½ hours for meals. Such Acts, even allowing for the difficulties of enforcement, constituted great improvements for many working people, but even such advances left armies of people – men, women and children – tied to a time-consuming regime which dominated their waking hours and left precious little time, and even less energy, for enjoyment.

The results of the Ten Hours Bill were disputed by contemporaries as J. T. Ward has shown. Lord Shaftesbury wrote that Manchester operatives 'are morally and physically improved. The children look lively and *young*; a few years ago they looked weary and aged *old*.' Others felt that the Act made little impression.

> The working classes of Blackburn and its neighbourhood have few amusements. . . . They run to foolish singing rooms . . .
> where depravity prevails and morality is at a low ebb; after which both parents and children retire to the beer shop and thus spend their hard-earned weekly wages. Their very bodies are poisoned with smoke and drink, ribaldry and obscenity.

The campaign for free time for industrial workers involved more than the question of excessive working hours for it also raised the wider question of the provision of national holidays. The years of industrialisation had witnessed a rapid decline in the number of rest days to which people were legally entitled. Official holidays had contracted dramatically since the mid-eighteenth century when the Bank of England, for instance, closed on forty-seven holidays: by 1808 this had declined to forty-four, to forty in 1825, eighteen in 1830 and, by 1834, it stood at a mere four – Good Friday, Christmas Day and the first of May and November. There was of course an infinite variety of local holidays, festivities, fairs and wakes which people enjoyed, though often *in spite* of an employer's resistance. Frequently, however, employers found it much easier to concede free time at a local holiday period (enabling them for example to overhaul the machinery). But they bitterly resisted, and did their best to root out, their workers' addiction to many of the regular and undisciplined holiday breaks of pre-industrial life. In those towns where industries were organised in a series of workshops rather than in factories, old customs died hard. In both Birmingham and Sheffield the ancient break of 'St Monday' was commonplace well into the nineteenth century. Led by the better-paid workmen, Monday was treated as a holiday, located primarily in local ale-houses and embracing a variety of games and recreations. Indisciplined and often drunken workmen were the bane of Birmingham employers' lives long after the labour force in the textile trades, for example, had been tamed and drilled in the virtues of a tight work discipline. A correspondent to the *Birmingham Journal* as late as 1840 informed the readers 'that the Birmingham mechanic will not in general, if ever, work more than five days a week'. Furthermore, when business was good, 'and labour abundant, it is not an uncommon occurrence to find him but four days only at his customary employment'. Such pre-industrial work patterns and recreations could not exist in areas where the workforce was regimented into wholesale employment, and day and week dictated by the clock and their work rhythms measured out by machines. Yet in both cases the patterns of recreation were shaped by the demands of the working life.

Among early industrialists it was a fundamental belief that leisure for their workforce was both unnecessary and costly, and it was to be many years before both master and man came to accept that rest and recreation were economically important. Sunday alone remained untouched by the determination to squeeze the maximum effort from the workforce; sometimes even the free Sunday was resented. 'A Sunday's holiday is looked upon as a heinous sin by so many worthy and respectable people [commented one man in 1852] that it cannot be indulged in with impunity.' The result of this encroachment of the industrial working week was that the labour force had free time on Sundays and on the rare national or local holiday for its leisure and recreations. But in the cities there were few places (drink places apart) where they could even enjoy such breaks from work.

Although Sunday was generally free, the powerful, and growing, Sabbatarian feeling in early nineteenth-century England made organised and mass Sunday recreations virtually impossible. There was of course nothing new about Sabbatarianism which had since the seventeenth century formed a trenchant and powerful opposition to the people's enjoyments on Sundays. Strict observance of the Sabbath involved, in the eyes of the nation's godly, a dogged resistance to those recreations which in the sixteenth and seventeenth centuries had inevitably taken place on Sunday. As early as 1571 a preacher complained that although 'the Lord God hath commanded that the Sabbath should be kept holy . . . the multitude call it there revelynge day, whiche day is spent in bulbeatings, bearebeatings, bowlings, dicyng, cardyng, dauncyng, drungeness, and whoredome'. Two hundred and fifty years later very similar complaints issued from towns and villages throughout the country. A Sunday school teacher in Fulletby, Lincolnshire, complained in 1826 that

> the sabbath day in our village was awfully desecrated. The
> young men and youth, and some of the married men too,
> usually spent the chief part of the day in playing games of
> chance, football, nurspell, etc. by which the rising generations
> were allured to sabbath-breaking; and were brought under the
> demoralising influence of wicked pursuits, and evil company.

In that same year a letter reached Peel in the Home Office from a Manchester man, complaining that St George's church 'is beset by many Irish men and Boys playing a Ball against the said Church even on Sunday mornings and evenings'. The problem was not easily resolved, for, until the granting of free Saturday afternoons (in the 1860s), when else could ordinary working people relax and play? In the cities moreover the freedom of the Sabbath contrasted with the demands and disciplines of the rest of the week to such an extent that many workers simply did not know how to spend their free time. Dr Kay reported that 'on Sunday the entire working population sinks into a state of abject sloth or listless sensibility'. It was a common complaint: 'The whole Sunday is too frequently lost in either drinking or inactive idleness.' It was, in large measure, perfectly understandable that a system which dictated people's working lives in such fine detail should equally entail the denial of individual and collective initiative. Again much the same situation could be seen among slaves in the New World.

English Sundays were depressingly dull (or drunken), and the irony was that the very forces of sabbatarianism which sought to exclude Sunday recreations, propelled many towards the one institution which remained open throughout – the pub, tavern or beer shop. There seemed to be two alternatives. One, impossible in the climate of early Victorian England, was to open up the sabbath to normal recreations. The other, more immediately realistic, was to make provision for leisure in other parts of the week. 'If games and sports are right on Sunday afternoons [wrote Lord John Manners] then they ought to be restored; if they are wrong and Sundays are to be kept as strictly religious festivals, then it must be right . . . to provide for their celebration on other days.' Growing numbers of enlightened men and labour organisations came to see that the interests of the nation would best be served by agitating for more free time in the working week. Saturday was the obvious day for such concessions and it was thus on Saturday afternoons that the nation's weekly time for non-devotional leisure was slowly conceded. *La semaine anglaise* thus gradually came into being.

The repressive forces which worked to deny the right of recreation to working people were similarly at work in shaping and controlling those sports and pastimes which managed to survive into the machine age. The need for an industrial work discipline also ensured that the recreations of the labour force would be equally disciplined. Turbulence, violence and unpredictability had characterised many of the collective pastimes of pre-industrial people, but these qualities were totally at variance with the need of a new society which demanded, and got, individual and collective restraint. An urban society in which the Metropolis was no longer the sole major centre of expanding population, could not survive the social weaknesses of a pre-industrial community. Until the coming of the industrial revolution, the English common people, in both town and country, had seized whatever rare recreational opportunities punctuated their lives, investing them with a vigour and intensity which were, in their superiors' eyes, as unrestrained as they were undesirable. Popular leisure activities were hard won and hence all the more important, and the rowdiness which heralded the breaks from work were often feared by their social betters. Not surprisingly it was often felt that leisure itself ought not to have a place in the lives of the poor. 'For gentlemen [R. W. Malcolmson reminds us] recreation was a natural and legitimate part of their culture; for labouring men it was (and could easily become) a dangerous temptation, a distraction from their primary concerns.' Indeed the history of popular recreations before the late eighteenth century could be written in terms of the attempts made to curb and forbid them by men in authority. Yet such pastimes could not be wished away or dispelled by acts of legislation, and the fact that these recreations survived for generations in the teeth of recurring opposition suggests the degree to which they were unshakeably rooted in popular culture. Football is perhaps the best example of a rowdy pre-industrial game which survived for centuries despite opposition to it.

Nonetheless, in the course of the eighteenth century the attacks against the people's recreations intensified and became more and more effective, most noticeably against blood sports. Opposition to cock-fighting, bull-baiting, and throwing at cocks reached a peak in the late eighteenth century with a series of effective local Acts against these sports. By 1801 Joseph Strutt felt confident enough to claim that bear-baiting 'is not encouraged by persons of rank and opulence in the present day; and when practised, which rarely happens, it is attended only by the lowest and most despicable parts of the people; which plainly indicated a general refinement of manners and prevalency of humanity among the moderns'.

Blood sports and cruel treatment of animals had been popular for centuries and the growing revulsion of the late eighteenth century was drawn from a complexity of changing attitudes which embraced, on the one hand a theologically inspired opposition to unnecessary cruelty and on the other a social awareness that, in changing times, cruel sports might undermine social morality. Blood sports and other turbulent pastimes showed 'a greater tendency to undermine social discipline'. Football, boxing, bull-baiting, cock-fighting – these and others were objected to on moral grounds; they were also distrusted because of their intrinsic appeal to violence and their attraction for large and potentially dangerous crowds. In a society which lacked effective means of social control – a problem appreciated by the authorities – volatile crowds, often drinking heavily and inflamed with the natural passions and tensions of gambling, quite apart from the partisan support for the contestants, all these added up to a social force replete with intimidating potential. In the last resort, it was because traditional recreations tended to attract such crowds that the pastimes themselves became undesirable and unsuited to a changing society. At much the same time, and for similar reasons, popular wakes, fairs, festivals and holidays came to be feared.

It was in the urban, and particularly the industrialising areas, that opposition to the people's enjoyments were most clearly expressed and most effectively acted upon. In rural parts, the old pastimes and customs died hard and could still be found in a thriving state towards the end of the nineteenth century. In the towns and cities of early Victorian England, however, there seemed no place for many of the traditional recreations, though some survived despite dogged resistance. The new urban society required new games for a new type of people, just as it needed new attitudes to work. It was no accident that the recreations spawned by industrial society were to be disciplined, controlled and orderly, regimented by rules and timing, characterised by a greater degree of orderliness among the spectators and encouraged by men of substance and local position. It was, for example, symptomatic that the brand of football which emerged in its new disciplined form from the public schools in the 1860s was as disciplined as its pre-industrial forebear had been lawless, and was played and encouraged, in the first instance, by men of superior social station.

The campaigns against the violent and bloody recreations of the poor were often led by men whose own recreations were equally cruel. While it was thought to be wrong for the lower orders to enjoy the pleasures of blood sports, there was rarely a hint that such pursuits were unsuitable for their betters. To modern eyes such inconsistencies, not to say hypocrisies, are startling. Cock-fighting was wrong; fox-hunting right. Bear-baiting was cruel but shooting, hunting and fishing were thought to be morally neutral – the unquestioned, legitimate pursuits of gentlemen. Those who pointed to such inconsistencies were exceptional and generally unheeded. In 1809 an article in the *Edinburgh Review* remarked that

> A man of ten thousand a year may worry a fox as much as he pleases, may encourage the breed of a mischievous animal on purpose to worry it; and a poor labourer is carried before a magistrate for paying sixpence to see an exhibition of courage between a dog and a bear! Any cruelty may be practised to gorge the stomachs of the rich, none to enliven the holidays of the poor.

Field sports were of course among the best known and most obvious of upper-class recreations and the hunting and shooting which lay at the heart of their rural enjoyments (and which are well documented in an abundance of contemporary prints) were made possible both by the material wellbeing and by the sportsmen's undisputed access to and control of vast tracts of the countryside. Throughout the eighteenth century a battery of legislation was introduced to safeguard the hunting rights of the propertied while simultaneously forbidding the dispossessed from enjoying similar rights. Game laws which dispensed legal immunity for the landed hunter prescribed death, transportation, imprisonment and fines for the hapless poor who dared to trespass on this distinctive leisure of the English upper classes. Levels of material prosperity inevitably dictated that there would be major differences between the recreations of different social classes; legislation and local deference ensured that the poor crossed the recreational divide only at risk to life and limb.

The pleasures of the fields were however only among the most obvious of upper-class pleasures, and the difficulty in describing their wider recreations in the early nineteenth century is to know where to begin for, unlike the poor, theirs was a world created for pleasure and enjoyment. They were after all the leisured classes, their wealth usually secured by the ownership of land, sometimes through colonial or overseas trade and also, as industrialisation created unprecedented wealth for the enterprising sections of the growing middle classes, through wise investment in the nation's burgeoning industry, trade or banking. But the end result was much the same and new industrialists were swift to follow the ancient traditions of their aristocratic superiors by sinking some of their capital into land and property. In their rural retreats, surrounded by acres of land, there existed a never-ending cycle of pleasure seeking and enjoyment which consumed a substantial proportion of their income.

While the poor struggled to resist the erosion of their leisure, many in the upper classes were able to devote their attention more-or-less full-time to pleasurable diversions. The very style and construction of their town and country houses (the two places indicative of their weekly and seasonal programmes) provide telling evidence of their commitment to pleasure. These large homes housed not merely a man's family but the armies of retainers essential to and commensurate with his station and his need to feed and entertain his batches of guests. Close to the house were the ranks of animals vital for both transport and pleasure. With dozens of rooms, these buildings were intended for more than mere accommodation and were used equally for entertainment. The number of guests' rooms, extra wings, libraries, concert rooms, elaborate dining rooms, vast kitchens and food stores stand as testimony to the multitude of recreational purposes grouped under one roof. Some of these stately homes provided the combined facilities of hotel, ballroom, assembly and pump room, library, concert and games rooms while also providing a base for the more vigorous pursuits of the field. Such houses were in effect the pleasure centres of the rich where, among friends and acquaintances, they could enjoy the delights of London or other provincial centres, or of the spas. Indeed it is very striking that many upper-class recreations were home-based; lower-class recreations (with the obvious exception of sex) were not to become domesticated until the size of dwellings increased, families got smaller and material comforts improved.

When the upper classes entertained, they did so at home, although similar entertainments could also be found in more commercial and concentrated form in the spa towns which, were, in effect given over to upper-class pleasures. Since the sixteenth century the English spas had developed to cater for the varied recreational and medical needs of the English leisured classes. Located wherever natural spring water issued from the ground, the spas, with counter-parts throughout Europe, could trace their cultural roots back to the classical and medieval world, often becoming the centres of religion and cults. But it was in the eighteenth century that the English spa reached its peak of social importance. Inspired by royalty and goaded by their medical advisers, aristocrats – and those who aped them – found in the spas all those refinements of upper-class recreation which they expected: the soirées, concerts, balls, rounds of entertainment and assignations, to say nothing of the alleged medical virtues of taking the waters. Bath was pre-eminent among English spas; its matchless architecture remains to this day as a monument to the quality and style of upper-class pleasures.

The fame of the spas soon spread, and their popularity swiftly percolated down the social ladder. Indeed it became a matter of concern to the most privileged visitors that the *nouveaux riches* were, in the course of the eighteenth century, lured to the spas in great numbers for rest and enjoyment. Smollett's Squire Bramble in *Humphrey Clinker*, expressed this dislike perfectly:

> Every upstart of fortune, harnessed to the trappings of the mode, presents himself at Bath. . . . Clerks and Factors from the East Indies, loaded with the spoil of plundering provinces; planters and negro drivers and hucksters from the American plantations, enriched they know not how; agents, commisaries, and contractors, who have fattened on two successive wars, on the blood of the nation; usurers, brokers and jobbers of every kind, men of low birth and no breeding, have found themselves translated into a state of affluence, unknown to former ages . . . and all of them hurry to Bath, because here, without any further qualifications, they can mingle with the princes and nobles of the land.

Although it was clearly the case, as contemporary cartoonists vividly and frequently showed, that the 'men of low birth' had lowered the social tone of the spas, the watering places nonetheless remained, into the early nineteenth century, the preserve of the wealthy. Bath and other spas were 'the natural magnet for the *beau monde*, foreign grandees, the new rich, country squires, for the gamesters and adventurers, and of course for invalids'.

The spa towns were a distinctive type, of which the later nine-teenth century was to see many throughout the western world. They were major urban areas whose prime function, design and cultural institutions were, almost uniquely, to cater for leisure. Most towns, and even huddles of rural buildings, had some focus for the pleasure of local people, if only a church or a tavern. But the spas, like seaside and skiing resorts of later years, existed primarily for recreation, and their architecture (like the style and size of their patrons' homes) was revealing both of the kind of leisure on offer and of the social groups catered for.

By the early years of the nineteenth century urban England was changing radically: not only were there towns given over to the pursuit of leisure, but well away from the spas there were towns whose sole function and rationale was work. The industrial towns of the nineteenth century, which in their formative years denied leisure of most kinds to their labour force, were as characteristic of the new century as were the spas of the eighteenth; the one built for work, the other for rest. As the new century advanced, however, the new towns and cities slowly came to terms with the need to create space (and free time) for local people. Substantial numbers of city dwellers began to turn to nearby seaside towns for an escape, however brief, from the cities. Yet the seaside towns were themselves major urban areas. In all cases, the leisures of the English people were evolving within the limitations and requirements of an urban environment.

The popular drift to the seaside had become noticeable by the late eighteenth century and in common with the earlier history of the spas it was partly stimulated by the joint example of royalty and medical opinion. Doctors came to regard sea water as having the medical properties they had previously proclaimed for mineral waters, and their anxious clients gradually gravitated to the small towns and villages in Essex, Kent and Sussex and Dorset which were within tolerable distance of the capital. From such small beginnings the seaside resorts began to emerge as rivals to the spas, largely by copying the spas' most attractive and successful features. The recreations, buildings, design and daily routines of the new resorts mirrored the style and life of the spas. Slowly the resorts usurped the recreational position of the inland spas. By the early years of the nineteenth century, Brighton, not Bath, had become the fashionable centre of the summer season, and it is significant that the cartoonists and caricaturists began to turn their graphic satire against the resorts rather than the old spas.

In the north of England the spa town of Scarborough, by the happy accident of having a mineral spring by the edge of the sea, was able instantly to transmute from a spa into a seaside resort, catering for those of the landed and wealthy whose centre of social gravity was York. In the south, however, the prosperous had greater variety, although the cost and inconvenience of coach and horse travel made the south coast more expensive and inaccessible than the Essex and Kent resorts (Southend, Margate, Ramsgate and Broadstairs), which were conveniently reached by boat down the Thames. From an early date the resorts on the Thames became more 'common', less aristocratic, despite their claims. Cowper in a letter of 1779, had no doubts about the lowness of the company ferried down the river to Margate: 'The hoy went to London every week, loaded with mackerel and herrings, and returned, loaded with company. The cheapness of the conveyance made it equally commodious for dead fish and lively company.' Despite the obvious social distinctions between and within the new resorts, they were frequented by those with free time and plenty of spare money. The only visitors of the lowest social orders were those who, in growing numbers, worked in the resorts, or those working people who lived close by.

The resorts stimulated a popular interest in swimming, frequently in the nude, with a complicated medically approved timetable which involved 'dippers', bathing machines and an expanding ancillary industry. Of course swimming need not be so elaborate or costly, and it had for centuries been a familiar enjoyment, particularly among men and boys, on the coast and beside rivers and lakes. But the fashionable cult of the late eighteenth century undoubtedly generated wider interest than ever in swimming even among those unable to afford a visit to the resorts. In 1795, John Aiken reported from Liverpool that

> It is the custom with the lower class of people, of both sexes, for, many miles up the country to make an annual visit to Liverpool, for the purpose of washing away (as they seem to suppose) all the collected stains and impurities of the year. Being unable to afford a long stay, or to make use of artificial conveniences, they employ two or three days in strolling along shore, and dabbling in the salt-water for hours at each tide, covering the beach with their promiscuous numbers, and not so much embarrassing themselves about appearances.

In 1813 Richard Ayton found much the same phenomenon at the small village of Blackpool:

> crowds of poor people from the manufacturing towns, who have a high opinion of the efficacy of bathing, maintaining that in the months of August and September there is physic in the sea - physic of a most comprehensive description, combining all the virtues of all the drugs in the doctors shop and of course a cure for all varieties of diseases.

For the poor such visits to the coast could only be for those living close to the sea, and on those rare days when they were freed from their labours. But it is interesting that by the turn of the century the social customs of their superiors had undoubtedly become influential among the poor. In the case of the spas and, later, the seaside resorts, there was a clear process of assimilation at work through which the forms of leisure of the aristocratic and propertied minority influenced, first the *nouveaux riches* and middle classes, and later, in much diluted form, the lower orders. The nineteenth and twentieth centuries were to see an accentuation of this process, but in the early years, of the nineteenth century few people below the level of the middle classes had sufficient time or money to devote much time to thoughts of leisure. And where the interests of different social classes tended to converge – more especially in the case of hunting – the propertied defended their bailiwick and their privileges by punitive legislation. Even in those areas of recreation where they could not legislate to preserve their dominance, their economic power enabled them in the last resort to maintain their isolation. Put simply, if the lower orders or even the middle orders came too close, the aristocrats could always move elsewhere. Characteristically perhaps, the royal family quit Brighton when the trains arrived in 1841.

Before the coming of the railways travel was expensive, slow and often painful, and recreations which depended on travel were clearly primarily, though not uniquely, within the compass of the well-to-do. This was the case with both spas and resorts and, of course, with the domestic entertainments of the English gentry and aristocracy. Travel for its own sake was to become a characteristic of the age of machines. led by the trains and steamboats, and later extended by motor and air transport. Yet despite its formidable discomforts, travel was becoming a major recreation before the arrival of the railways. The Grand Tour had long been regarded as a finishing school for the sons of the English ruling class, although 'Milord', with his tutors and servants in tow, was as likely to return from his two or three years in Europe with little grasp of the languages and culture of, and even less sympathy for, the inhabitants south of Calais. The Grand Tour often became, not the finishing school for an internationally sophisticated person, but the confirmation of xenophobic prejudices.

By the turn of the century the idea that European travel was merely educational had been replaced by the belief that Europe could be enjoyed as a holiday experience. In part this was a result of early romanticism, in part the heady excitement of the first years of the French Revolution. It was also a more extravagant parallel to the growth of travel in England itself.

The French Revolution, the wars, naval blockades and general wartime disruption, put large areas of Europe beyond the pale for the English visitor. It is worth remembering, however, that when the brief peace was signed in 1802 there was an amazing rush of British visitors across the Channel. War soon intervened again, although France was now firmly established in the aristocratic imagination as a worthwhile place to visit, its attractions enhanced during the war by the Napoleonic cult and the very real physical improvements in Paris carried out by the Emperor, and by the links forged between the English people and French *emigrés* in the years of the Revolution.

In the post-war years, the growing numbers of visitors to Europe were no longer primarily aristocratic. John Bull – the English middle-class visitor – replaced the English aristocrat. Those same people, replete with the personal confidence brought about by economic prosperity, who had secured the popularity of Margate, now turned their attention to Europe and while they clearly lacked the finesse and polish of the aristocrats they were able to enjoy such aristocratic delights because of their prosperity. Cross-Channel travel became swifter, thanks to the steamboats after 1825, and more widely used. Similarly, travel within England produced some remarkable recreational changes. The new improved roads, better coaches and infinitely better Royal Mail coach routes led to a rapid expansion in road travel, most noticeably from London to Brighton. Coaches to Brighton in the 1820s were frequent, swift and cheap. Consequently, more of the growing middle class made their way to the formerly aristocratic preserve by the sea. 'I cannot boast of much good company which formerly we abounded with at this season', complained Mrs Fitzherbert to Creevey in 1818. The old order, in prints and public correspondence, regularly bemoaned the encroaching middle-class tide into old leisured preserves. There was of course much to complain about, for the rapid growth of the population and the expanding size and prosperity of the middle class, meant, at its simplest, many more 'newcomers' anxious to enjoy themselves in the traditions of aristocratic enjoyment. Their single- (and often simple-) minded determination to put themselves on an equal footing with their superiors was a constant source of ridicule among those who despised middle-class pretensions. Their clothes, accents, attitudes and leisure occupations were often absurd replicas of the class above, and were to be the objects of derision throughout the nineteenth century from the lampoons of Cruickshank through to Dickens's dismissiveness. They can be found late in the century in the form of Mr Pooter's ridiculous pretensions. The emergent middle class was to be seen in its most caricatured form when embarking on the leisures of their betters – at the hunt, at the fashionable ball, on the cross-Channel steamer, with glazed eyes in front of the wonders of Paris, or simply parading their new-found wealth on the front at Brighton or, worse still, Blackpool.

Contemporaries were in no doubt that the middle classes were moving into areas of leisure which in the not-so-distant past had been reserved for the upper reaches of society. The war years had seen both a significant growth in their ranks and a swelling of their economic strength (largely through wartime economic growth). And the post-war years saw the emergence of a strident middle-class political voice and power. While it was true that the working class was born in these painful years of wartime and after, the middle class was also emerging, less painfully, but more assertively. Landed and aristocratic England, perfectly represented by the excesses of George IV, had enjoyed a peak of wealth and leisure in the years up to the end of the war and it was significant that their 'Palladian and neo-classical country houses multiplied, more than at any time before or since except the Elizabethan'. But by 1830 it was the middle class, now recognising itself *as* a class, and not as a rank or order, which stood pre-eminent as representing the new industrial and business prosperity. Often rooted in dissenting traditions, more at home in Manchester than

London, and speaking unashamedly with pronounced rounded accents, the class which saw its creed best expressed by the *Manchester Guardian* could stand financial comparison with most of the aristocracy. It was their unhappy lot to find their way barred into many aristocratic preserves. But they could match their betters when it came to enjoying themselves. Furthermore, from the mid-1830s onwards they were given the means of extending their leisure activity further when the railways – the fruit and cause of industrial change – began to produce dramatic transformations in the nation's social life.

2 The railway age

Early Victorians were deeply impressed by the profound changes, and the potential for further change, brought about by the railways. Older men divided their memories between pre- and post-railway years. Thackeray wrote in 1860, 'Your railroad started a new era, and we of a certain age belong to the new time and the old one. . . . We elderly people have lived in that prae-railroad world, which passed into limbo and vanished from under us.' Dr A. B. Granville, who in 1841 published a comprehensive account of the nation's spas and seaside resorts, was able to embark on such an undertaking largely because of the railway system. Not surprisingly, he prefaced his remarks with the acknowledgement that 'the great, the enormous sum of benefit that must accrue to mankind from the establishment of a means of conveyance which seems to level all topographical distinctions, and not only brings distant cities, but remote countries nearer to each other, and annihilates time and distance, is not to be questioned, and becomes every day more manifest'. The economic consequences of the railways were incalculable. Equally far-reaching were the results which relatively swift, cheap and nationwide rail communications had on leisure pursuits. Travelling time and costs shrank, as did the serious logistic difficulties of travelling long distances. The countryside seemed to shrink perceptibly, as the iron rails swiftly formed connections between cities, linking town and country, city and coast, and bringing together the far extremities of the land.

The railways heralded a new phase in the history of the national economy, one consequence of which was further changes in the way people were able to enjoy their leisure. Railways, and related mechanisation, completed the process begun in the previous century of shaping both the people and the economy to the dictates and needs of an industrial society. And it also ensured that many of the pre-industrial leisure pursuits were either destroyed or transformed to accommodate the peculiarities of a mechanical society. Few aspects of life escaped the impact of mechanisation. Many pre-industrial workers, for example, had enjoyed, and needed, regular supplies of alcohol to see them through a hard working day, but the demands of safety and efficiency of the railway age put a premium on sobriety and attentiveness. A drunken agricultural labourer was relatively harmless, but a drunken railway driver or signalman was potentially (and often actually) disastrous. The railways and all they entailed thus drove a wedge between leisure and work, ensuring the separation of the two and producing a firmer commitment to work discipline.

Victorians were convinced that the railways were a force for democracy, by bringing strangers and different classes into close, uncomfortable compartments, and by exposing the hidden recesses of the country to the travellers' gaze. Whether this belief was justified or not, it is indisputable that the trains produced a greater 'nationalisation' of British society (if not a greater unity within Britain).

The simplest and most obvious revolution in leisure was in travel itself. The road to Brighton was, thanks to the pre-eminence of Brighton as a seaside town, among the best in the country. But even that short distance involved a journey of six hours in the 1820s, at a cost of twelve shillings for an outside seat. Nonetheless in 1835 some 117,000 people travelled to Brighton along that road. The change following the opening of the railway in 1841 was dramatic; by 1850, 73,000 rail passengers arrived at Brighton in one week alone; in 1862 on Easter Monday, 132,000 visitors descended on the town in a single day, the travel time having been reduced to a mere two hours, and the cost lowered by one-third.

Much of the inspiration behind the initial development of the railways in the late 1830s was the belief that economic wellbeing lay in transporting goods. In the event, the upsurge in passenger travel was even more remarkable, particularly when the railway companies began to provide special excursion fares for poorer passengers and at holiday periods. From the early days, the railway companies appreciated the economic benefits of excursion travel and a multitude of private organisations came to see that the excursion was a way of providing their members with cheap, mass travel. Time and again, the opening of a new railway line was swiftly followed by the arrival of excursionists from nearby towns; they were perfected, but not pioneered, by Thomas Cook's famous temperance excursions from Leicester to Loughborough on 5 July 1841 (costing one shilling return). In September 1842, 2,364 Sunday school scholars and teachers left Preston for an excursion to Fleetwood, in a train twenty-seven coaches long; 'the whole multitude were engaged in singing hymns'. By 18 August 1844 the *Preston Chronicle* reported that 'cheap trips and pleasure excursions are now all the go and fashion'. A week before, thirty-eight coaches left Preston with 1,700 passengers 'chiefly of the working classes' on an excursion to Fleetwood.

The ability to transport such large numbers of people for a day by the sea had great attractions for the paternal philanthropists who wished to reward their workers – or local children – with a healthy, wholesome trip away from the industrial cities. To celebrate the repeal of the Corn Laws, Richard Cobden arranged an excursion for

1,000 of his employees in Chorley. The first excursion from a mill in Swinton to the new railway station at Blackpool in 1846, cost a shilling for the fare, and a penny for the band; the workers were woken for the trip by two soldiers playing drum and fife going through the town at 3 a.m.

Working men and their families, dressed in their best clothes and headed by a band became a regular sight on the railroutes of Lancashire in the summer throughout the 1840s. In August 1848 1,200 workpeople from Blackburn, many of whom 'had never seen a sea-bathing place, been on a railway or passed through a tunnel', took an excursion to Blackpool. According to the *Blackburn Standard*:

> Fares were 1/- there and back; and to those in worst circumstances tickets were given or sold at reduced prices. A band was provided by Messrs Hopwood; and about two hundred loaves and from two to three hundredweight of cheese were stored in the horse box for those who were unable to comply with the injunction to provide themselves with refreshments.

Charitable excursions soon became a delightful treat for the urban poor; inevitably of course many less deserving cases managed to secure free or cheap tickets.

The numbers involved were often enormous. At Whitweek 1848, 116,000 passengers left Manchester on cheap excursions. A year later the number had risen to 150,000 and by 1850 had reached 202,543. There was of course an initial fascination both to sample the dubious delights of the early trains and to see parts of the country, and more especially the coast, which had previously been inaccessible. And while it is true that cheap, and sometimes charitable, excursions brought travel within the compass of many thousands of city dwellers, it is equally clear that the excursions required both free time and spare cash. It is impossible to know how representative of their social class these travellers were, but it is certain that many more working people remained at home as the trains left for the coast. Stories about the excitement of the train and the thrill of the seaside doubtless permeated discussion and aspirations in working-class communities. But economic uncertainties, large families and low income ensured that many – perhaps most – working people were left simply to day-dream about travel to the seaside or elsewhere.

The story was much the same whenever a new railway line forged a link between an industrial city and the coast in the 1840s and 1850s. The initial train, bearing dignitaries and officials in comfortable first-class carriages, was very soon followed by lines of third-class excursion coaches. Twelve days after the Scarborough line had been opened in July 1845 the first excursion train arrived carrying 1,000 people from Wakefield. Some days later another train arrived from Newcastle. In both cases the passengers were thought to be 'the pale, emaciated inhabitants of murky and densely populated cities seeking to restore their sickly frames to health and vigour by frequent immersions in the sea'.

The railway system which emerged through a series of booms and slumps, over-optimistic expansion and collapse, transformed the nation's communications. In 1835 there were only 471 miles of track in England and Ireland; ten years later it had risen to 3,277 and by mid-century stood at 13,411. And still the railway expansion continued, so that by 1885 30,843 miles of railway track snaked around the country. And whenever a new line was opened to the coast or into the country it generated an abundance of excursion travel among low income groups. Churches ushered their flocks into coaches for a day by the sea; the Newcastle and Carlisle Railway carried members of the local Mechanics Institute. In 1840, 40,000 school children were transported from Manchester to avoid the unpleasantness of the local races. Demand seemed to be insatiable and just as the numbers of excursion trains grew, so did the length of the trains themselves. Five engines hauled 1,500 people to Edinburgh to see Queen Victoria; in May 1844 six engines pulled fifty-seven carriages to Brighton (whence the Queen had fled to the Isle of Wight as a result of the arrival of the railway).

Throughout the 1840s, excursion trains, despite their well-known discomforts and dangers, had proved their unique value in providing a swelling army of customers with the excitement of travel and visits to strange and exotic places. But it was the Exhibition of 1851 which finally confirmed the excursion train as the greatest single force in the democratisation of English leisure. By 11 October when the Exhibition closed, some six million people had visited the Crystal Palace, large numbers of them on excursions from around the country. If the Exhibition stood as proof of the Victorians' self-confident belief that theirs was the peak of industrial and civilised development, much of their success was due to the impressive railway network which not only deposited large numbers of visitors at the Exhibition but also helped to make possible the mechanical achievements of the Exhibition itself.

The trains were also instrumental in the massive urban development of seaside resorts. Of course the phenomenal rise in population and the growing concentration of people in towns and cities was characteristic of the nineteenth century. But the seaside towns grew more rapidly than any other urban group, partly to cater for holiday makers and day trippers (many of the new hotels were financed by the railway companies) and also as coastal residential towns, where the middle and upper classes could escape - for the summer or permanently - from the grime and bad health of the cities. Southend, Margate, Ramsgate and Broadstairs, and the southern resorts in Kent and Sussex, drew on London for their population. Liverpool businessmen could, after the coming of the railways, commute from their homes in Southport. Retired families quit the grubbiness of Manchester and the nearby textile towns for the Blackpool area or the new resort of Morecambe. On the east coast, Scarborough held similar attractions for the wealthier classes from the West Riding.

Sometimes, the emergence of a resort was a direct, though often accidental, by-product of a railway line. Rhyl and Morecambe were cases in point. In other instances a line was deliberately sought to foster the creation of a new resort. Skegness was a good example later in the century. Such links between the railways and the development of resorts continued well into the century; Skegness developed quite late, as did resorts in the West Country, simply because the railways themselves were late in penetrating their regions. Thereafter however the pattern was familiar, for there followed a rapid urban development, with middle- and upper-class families settling in the resorts and enjoying their natural and manmade attractions. In some towns they were rapidly followed by trainborne hoards of less prosperous day trippers. Sometimes this pattern was repeated in the inland spa towns. Buxton, for example, had since the Romans boasted of its spa waters, and its decline as a spa was arrested by the coming of the railways in 1867 and the subsequent development of the town's facilities.

Railway lines came relatively late into Devon, but much the same story was repeated. While the seaside towns in that county flourished, the inland market towns – the county's oldest – withered and decayed. Devon's rural people drifted to the new local resorts of Plymouth, Exeter and Devonport, where they could find work in the complexity of service industries catering for the retired professional people, the invalids in search of a better climate and the middle-class visitors resting for the summer. Late in the century these 'residential' groups were to be joined by trippers and day excursionists. In the West Country, as in the south, Lancashire and Yorkshire coasts in the first wave of railway development, the railways were directly responsible for the transformation of small fishing villages into large urban areas which were significant towns in their own right and, increasingly, the leisure centres for urban people who sought relief and enjoyment beside the sea.

The impact of the railways can best be seen in the physical growth of the resorts, which was remarkable enough to catch the attention of the 1851 Census. 'Seaside resorts have expanded more rapidly than any other group of town.' Brighton (with more than 65,000) had by far the largest population, and of the ten largest, six – Brighton, Hastings, Ramsgate, Margate, Weymouth and Torquay – were in the south. Scarborough, at that time the biggest of the northern resorts – Whitby, Southport and Blackpool included – had a population of only 12,915. In all of them, urban growth was the order of the day. New lines of private houses mushroomed along the coast, around the boundaries of the resorts, into the interior and along the once-virgin land bordering the railway lines. Hotels and boarding houses were built in the central areas, and the sea front was gradually built over by breakwaters and promenades which, in their turn, provided space for leisure facilities and walking. The resorts were in effect becoming highly distinctive urban areas; major towns and cities perched on the water's edge, and offering unique facilities to residents and visitors.

The railways created a new industry in the form of visitors and residents, often for towns which had not existed before. In 1800 there were only two buildings at Rhyl, but with the coming of the railway in 1848 a large town emerged on the site. The transformation was equally dramatic in Bournmouth, where the first buildings were only erected in 1812; even as late as 1841 there were still fewer than thirty. Although the town was well promoted by Dr Granville in 1841 Bournemouth had to wait till 1870 for its railway line; thereafter its population tripled in a decade to 16,859. Historians have often noted that the years of industrial progress in England saw the development of industrial towns where natural resources, climatic conditions or communications were most suitable. It is equally remarkable, and just as characteristic of Victorian society, that a new type of town designed for pleasure, relaxation and enjoyment rapidly developed where the railway lines from the cities stopped on the coast. Indeed the most remarkable feature of the new resorts is that their rate of growth was greater than that of the industrial cities and even of London. While mid-Victorian England is best remembered by its dirty cities and industrial areas – the Mecca for curious foreign observers and commentators – it was no less epitomised by seaside resorts whose basic industry was the provision of pleasure.

Not all excursion trains carried their trippers to the coast, for the railways revealed wide areas of previously unexplored countryside to the Victorian traveller. Sheffield workingmen 'took their families to Grimsby, to the Dukeries, to Wharncliffe Crags or into Derbyshire by special trains'. The Newcastle and Carlisle Railway ran trips to Hadrian's Wall. Even villages with few real claims to fame found themselves inundated with visitors from the cities once a railway line was opened through the village. In September 1839, on the new Manchester–Leeds line,

> the little village of Littleborough experienced on Saturday last a considerable accession of company. They were mostly clerks, warehousemen, and the decenter sort of operatives, with some females and children – the two latter fewer in number, probably in consequence of the broken weather. The day passed off without the least irregularity or disturbance, and not a small proportion of the visitors attended service in the afternoon at the church.

Rail travel remained, to modern eyes, uncomfortable and dangerous. But the slow improvements in rolling stock and safety helped to overcome the unease about rail travel and in any case those legions of trippers who travelled so rarely generally forgot the discomforts and hardship in the excitement of the journey. Indeed the swelling thousands who took to the trains on their infrequent holidays bear testimony not merely to the growing consumer power of the lower reaches of society, but also to the indispensibility of the railway system. A Select Committee on the railways in 1840 noted that they were built 'to convey the labourer cheaply and rapidly to that spot where his labour might be most highly remunerated'. While this wishful thinking was more than amply fulfilled, the impact on leisure, if unforeseen, was nonetheless similarly impressive.

The railways clearly made possible new forms of leisure interests, more especially for those who, for financial reasons, had traditionally found recreation within their immediate neighbourhood. There was clearly a widening of horizons. Yet while the impact of the railways may have been most fundamental on the recreations of lower income groups, it also transformed the leisure of all social classes. Horse-racing for example had for years attracted a popular and criminal following, but it was inevitably dominated and organised by the wealthier strata of English society able to sustain the expense of horse ownership. Here too the railways transformed structure and organisation, making it possible to arrange the sport of kings as a major spectator sport on a national basis. In the past, distance had rarely prevented the poor race-goer or boxing fan from travelling (often by foot) to a major race or event, but the railways made it easier and cheaper. As a result many more people began to attend. It had earlier been common for spectators to walk eighteen miles from Sheffield to Doncaster to watch the St Leger, and to walk back the following day. The arrival of the trains created a wider constituency for any sporting meeting. The élitist racing fraternity did not always welcome this railway inspired 'democratisation' of the races. Jockey Club stewards, for instance, countered the excursion trains to Newmarket by staging different races miles apart so that only those on horseback could witness the race. When in 1847 that same Jockey Club finally supported a railway line to Newmarket, they did so because it had become clear that the railways offered an unparalleled advantage in the transportation of horses. By the mid-1850s racing had come to terms with the railways and depended on them for cheap and efficient transport of men and horses. Spectators too came in great numbers by train, and their admission money made possible higher prize money which, in its turn, completed the circle by generating further interest in racing.

Horse-racing was, as Wray Vamplew has shown, revolutionised by the trains. The number of race horses doubled between 1837 and 1869, and two year olds, previously too immature to travel and then race, quadrupled. Local races became national events and the numbers watching and travelling grew beyond all measure. Nor was this increase in spectators drawn purely from the gentry and aristocracy who had traditionally sponsored the sport. The main period of railway mania, from the mid-1840s, was also the era of improvements in real wages and quite apart from industrial workers, there were large groups of workers in agriculture, crafts, self-employment and casual work who could generally find free time to attend sporting events. Moreover, even industrial workers took time off to go to the races. As a result, there was a proliferation (sometimes shortlived) of race meetings up and down the country, all made possible by the railway revolution and the availability of free time and spare cash. There was, then as now, the traditional carnival-like lure of a day at the races, with the remote chance of winning a fortune.

Railway companies were swift to appreciate the commercial opportunities of carrying the eager race-goer, particularly to the myriad of meetings around the capital. It was claimed that 'on the slightest provocation railway companies placarded half London with lists of cheap trains to any country place where races were held, and in every sporting paper at least half a column is dedicated to excursionists who want to go racewards'. It was only a matter of time before the pressure of numbers and the obvious commercial market they represented led to the establishment of enclosed race courses and the emergence of the paying spectator, a pattern which was to be followed both by cricket and, later, by football.

Many Victorian Englishmen, particularly those who felt that the new means of transportation might undermine the nation's reliance on the horse both for work and for transport, regarded the railways with horror. That most characteristic sport of the English gentry, fox-hunting, seemed to be particularly vulnerable to the impact of the train. It was felt that the railway lines would chop up the countryside, while the greater speed and efficiency of the trains would render horse-breeding superfluous. In their darker moments, such pessimists even thought that those people who found their pleasures, particularly in the hunt, would henceforth quit their rural retreats for the more accessible delights of London.

Some of these fears were partially realised, but in fact the impact of the railways was, in general, quite the opposite; the railways in fact reinforced the social and leisure life of the English upper classes by giving it greater variety. More people, and a wider range of luxury goods, were henceforth to be found in rural localities; rents increased when a railway line was opened into the country, and country-house hospitality was intensified by the trains. Men and horses could, as with the races, travel cheaply to distant hunts, and the London hunter could for example travel to Leicestershire with his horses and yet still return to town for dinner. It was possible, as Raymond Carr has shown, for Lord George Bentinck to hunt in Hampshire and get back to Parliament for an evening debate, 'his riding clothes concealed by a light coloured zephyr paletot'.

The trains also brought problems for the huntsmen. Squire Selby Lowndes stopped advertising his hunts in the Vale of Aylesbury 'owing to the unremunerative crowds the London trains used to let loose on him'. Such difficulties did of course exist, but on the whole the railways widened the interest and participation in fox hunting, by transforming and widening the sport's social base. There was, more particularly, a growth in 'subscription' packs rather than packs financed privately by a master, thanks largely to the expanding interest in fox hunting among prosperous men in town and country. It was now also possible to hunt in the depths of the country yet to continue to live in a major city; by 1860 Anthony Trollope regularly took the train from London simply to follow the hunt. Indeed one new feature of the railway's rolling stock were the horseboxes provided for horses and travelling grooms, and the scenes of loading horses on to trains was to become a prominent sight on many railway stations, just as the baskets of racing pigeons were to become common sights later in the century.

The railways seemed to accentuate one problem which for centuries had troubled the forces of law and order, namely, the inherent difficulty in controlling large crowds of people. This was a particular problem at sporting events which often occasioned turbulence, drunkenness and violence. Indeed it was the general problem of crowd and social control which had for centuries past persuaded national and local government and men of substance to take such a dogged stance against forms of recreation which attracted large crowds. Boxing, a cruel, bloody sport which then as now attracted armies of gamblers and the criminal fraternity, was especially disliked, and throughout the late eighteenth century magistrates prohibited boxing matches and prosecuted those involved for a breach of the peace or unlawful assembly. But it was the complex problems of crowd control, often in a quiet rural spot where a fight had been secretly convened, which caused most alarm and difficulty. Vast crowds would converge on the field and convert the rural peace into a teeming, turbulent bedlam which local authorities were powerless to control or prevent. The *Derby Mercury* of 10 August 1842 noted that 'the inhabitants never know anything of the business until they see the crowds of vagabonds upon the grounds, who forcibly take possession of some fields suitable for their purposes'.

Thousands had traditionally walked great distances to watch a prize fight; henceforth the railways eased their difficulties – and quickened their escape from the scene. When in April 1845 a prize fight was arranged between Caunt and Bendigo, it was located at Newport Pagnell, within easy reach of escape routes across three county borders. Boxers and followers alike arrived at the nearest town by train, arriving from all points of the compass, from Nottingham, Liverpool, Manchester, Sheffield and Leicester. After the fight, which ended in the ninety-third round in Bendigo's favour and which had as much violence around the ring as in it, the staff at the nearest railway station, Wolverton, faced the kind of difficult crowd scenes which we now associate with a major soccer match. Such fights, the last of the old unreformed fisticuffs, were in the 1840s prototypes of the mass-spectator events which, thanks to the trains, could attract spectators from around the country. While the ring was the first to do this, later in the century it was the major soccer matches that reached news headlines.

Boxing itself slid further and further into disrepute in the 1850s and 1860s. By 1862, when the national prize-ring championship was held at Thames Haven on the Tilbury Railway Line, the sport was in its last stages of decay. Tickets at £2, inclusive of rail faire, were sold through the railway company, who soon regretted their involvement. Passengers on the 5 a.m. special had their fight tickets stolen by gangs of criminals at the station and the ensuing chaos was so serious that railway officials called for police help. The police, wisely perhaps, refused to come. When in 1868 a major attempt was made to reform boxing a first step was to outlaw excursion trains to such fights – a sign of how important the railways had become. From the 1840s onwards, the trains had made possible the swift marshalling and dispersal of very large crowds, but in becoming the most important means of transportation for sporting events they exposed any sport to swift strangulation; stop the trains and the crowds would find it hard to attend.

Among the more bizarre contributions of the railways to the nation's leisure were excursions to public executions. Since time out of mind public executions had attracted massive crowds; carnivals collected and there was a generally festive air whenever a wretched victim died in public. Although executions at Tyburn had ended in 1783, Tyburn Fair symbolised all the popular commotion and fun to be had on execution day (though Hogarth's prints, with their variety of crimes being committed within sight of the execution form a lasting reminder that the deterrence of executions was minimal). So large were the crowds, and so hysterical their responses that on occasions many more people died in the crowd than on the gallows. On 23 February 1807, for example, 45,000 people crowded in front of Newgate; two criminals were hanged, but twenty-seven spectators died in the crush. The trains now made it possible for even bigger crowds to assemble around the gallows. When four people were hanged in Liverpool, the railway companies advertised excursion trains, 'parties of pleasure', from neighbouring industrial towns. In 1840 the Bodmin and Wadebridge railway company carried 1,100 people, half the population of Wadebridge, in three trains, to see a local murderer hanged at Bodmin. Among the 100,000 gathered to watch the execution of John Gleeson outside Kirkdale jail in Liverpool in 1849, a large number had come by excursion train. In 1856, when William Parker was due to be hanged at Stafford jail, special trains were announced in the papers 'to run to and from Stafford to enable the public to witness the last moments of an expected victim'.

By the early 1860s, however, many people had come to view

public executions both as distasteful and ineffective; some felt that the keenness of the railways to profit from an execution was even more offensive. Abolitionists and reformers urged that the prisons should follow Warwick's example and refuse to announce the day of execution in advance and thus prevent the railway companies from making plans for excursion trips. Unhappily for the railways, public executions were finally ended in 1868 (prize-fighting also declined in that same decade) thus ending a lucrative form of income, though it is true that the proliferation of other, less bloody sports and recreations provided many different opportunities for travel. But it is worth noticing that while the railways have often been seen as the agents of new forms of leisure, it is less commonly remembered that for twenty years they shored up some of the more traditional recreations; recreations which were in fact already in decline and under attack.

While the trains were the most obvious and most revolutionary form of mechanical transportation, there were also related improvements which gave an added boost and new dimensions to English leisure. Steamships (with their metal piers to provide a convenient landing stage) rapidly became a new form of transport. When in 1832 the plans were drawn up to develop New Brighton, across the river from the expanding port of Liverpool, it was proposed 'to establish a communication by Steam Packet between that place and Liverpool'. Steamships similarly opened up Birkenhead, which the *Liverpool Mercury* thought in 1828 'may at no distant period, become of considerable importance, if not as a watering place, at least as a favourite sojurn of the merchants of Liverpool'. Even more dramatic was the emergence of the Isle of Man. Tourism began there in the 1820s, but it was the Liverpool steamers from the 1830s, and the railway connections to other English cities which began to ferry people across the Irish Sea in significant numbers. Within fifty years the Isle of Man was receiving 250,000 visitors a year, overwhelmingly from the Lancashire ports; by 1890 Baedecker spoke of the island as 'practically one large playground for the operatives of Lancashire and Yorkshire'.

The conjunction of the new trains and the steamships often brought new resorts into existence. Morecambe had been a small village previously, attracting a trickle of summer visitors; after 1848, it was transformed by the new railway line designed basically to provide a new outlet for local pig iron and a new port for the Irish ferries. Rhyl similarly emerged from obscurity when in 1848 a new railway line was opened between Chester and Holyhead. But it was the resorts which had come to serve riverborne passengers from London to Ramsgate, Gravesend, Margate and Southend which benefited most directly from the new steamers which plied swiftly down the Thames. As soon as Dickens's Tuggs family (in *Sketches by Boz*) inherited a fortune they turned their minds to quitting their London shop for something more refined. Their problem was, what to choose? '"Gravesend" mildly suggested Mr Joseph Tuggs. The idea was universally scouted. Gravesend was *low*. "Margate" insinuated Mrs Tuggs. Worse and worse – nobody but tradespeople.' The family eventually opted for Ramsgate, and two months later, they were travelling down the Thames on the steamer *City of London*.

By mid-century the steamer had become a feature of English seaside and river life. Trips around the bay, down or across a river, from one port to another, even across the Channel, had become highlights of many a holiday. Many of the new resorts which were, thanks to their new railway lines, now linked to the major cities, were soon provided with those magnificent monuments to the Victorian iron age – the piers which enabled sea-going steamers to call at resorts lacking natural harbour facilities. The new technology of iron production and innovatory engineering made possible a rash of piers, led by Brighton's Chain Pier in 1823. Within two years of its opening the Chain Pier began to receive steam packets, and the concept of the pier was rapidly accepted as a bold, attractive piece of engineering and architecture, and also as an economic investment. Southend, with its long flat stretch of sand and mud at low water, and Brighton demonstrated the economic virtues of building a pier and the example rapidly spread. By mid-century no resort worth the name could afford to be without a pier. Indeed the piers soon established themselves as major attractions in their own right. Some authorities even encouraged the construction of competing piers along the same shoreline. They were very costly to build, but their commercial appeal was such that companies had little trouble raising the considerable capital needed. Blackpool's North Pier (1863) cost £13,500; Southend's even more famous pier cost a staggering £42,000; Brighton's West Pier (1866) devoured £30,000. But on the whole they proved to be lucrative investments, attracting, for a small admission fee, many thousands of trippers who were happy simply to stroll up and down the pier. Gradually entertainments, refreshments and machines began to clutter the piers, but still the visitors poured through the turnstiles. Brighton's West Pier attracted 10,000 people; many pier companies employed staff simply to keep the human throng moving at the peak of the season. By mid-century the piers were important attractions among the variety of seaside entertainments; of the dozens which came to dot the Victorian shoreline, fifty-four remain to this day, often blighted and decayed, as reminders of the Victorian iron age.

Steamships and the general improvement in port facilities in addition to rail connections, enhanced the attractions of cross-Channel travel. Although the full flood of English tourism abroad did not come until late in the century, the new links made continental visits a possibility for growing numbers of people. By the 1860s railway companies were advertising day excursions to the French ports; 7s 6d second class, 10s first class. This was too expensive for many, but not all that more expensive than day trips from London to the south coast resorts, which in 1865 cost upwards of 5s 6d. The full impact of the English in Europe, however, had to await the extension of European railway lines, particularly into the south of France, later in the century.

Trains and steamers transformed both the face and the potential of mass English leisure, and it is noticeable that England also began to benefit from the growth of international travel. The new steamships which now crossed the Atlantic took immigrants from Europe and returned with increasing numbers of American visitors. Trans-Atlantic holidays were henceforth a feasible proposition, partly because of emergent American wealth but more especially because of the new speedy voyages. The figures speak for themselves. In 1820 a mere 1,926 Americans visited Britain. Over the next forty years the figures shot up: 1820, 1,926; 1838, 6,245; 1840, 8,000; 1860, 26,000. By the 1880s, more than 50,000 Americans were visiting Britain each year. Clearly these relatively swift and efficient voyages were more significant in their economic consequences for the movement of goods, immigrants and raw materials. But the very fact that a major American tourist trade to Britain had come into being is proof of the unique importance of the new transportation systems, and reveals their complex impact upon the leisure of mid-Victorian Britain.

The full impact of the new forms of transport would remain under-utilised as long as economic forces prevented substantial numbers of people from using them. While the nation was impressed on all sides by the trains and their potential, in the last resort it was people's ability to pay and to have free time for travel, which was needed before the age of mass travel could come of age. Trains and the new vistas they opened for many thousands of people created a new interest in travel and the rapid evolution of the excursion trip, particularly to the seaside, built up a growing demand for more regular holidays and guaranteed breaks from work.

The absence of a secure holiday calendar was most acute among those people who seemed most in need of regular breaks from work, namely the new industrial labour force and the growing numbers of poor trapped in the new cities.

We have seen how many thousands of non-industrial workers, craftsmen, rural workers and casual workers, not being tied to the demands of the new mechanical systems, could in the time-honoured system create time for themselves. But what could the industrial worker do, tied as he was to the disciplines of the clock and the machine, his time counted as money by his employers? Slowly, the emergent industrial labour force was weaned from its commitment to the more traditional holiday routines and nurtured on a new system whose rationale was unrelenting work. Moreover this process was not merely a function of an impersonal march of industry: it was actually encouraged by men of positions who sought to deny leisure facilities to the labouring classes. Men of conscience were depressed to find contemporaries who sought 'to curb, restrain and almost absolutely forbid the lowly and humble from indulging in any pastimes whatsoever'. It was of little use to these first industrial workers, rooted to a penal working system, to know that the trains which passed through their towns could deposit them in delightful spots within a matter of hours; most simply could not afford the fare, or did not have the necessary free time.

Time free from work was essential for many reasons, and the campaign to reduce the working week, directed in the first instance against the worst excesses of child and female labour in the mines and textile industries, began to bear fruit in the 1840s. In many industries free Saturday afternoons were a result, not of legislation, but of the emergent union strength and corresponding concessions by management and owners. Yet so regional and local was this movement for shorter hours that in many industries, particularly in the new light industrial and commercial enterprises of the late century, a free Saturday afternoon was still being demanded in the last years of the century.

Despite such exceptions, by mid-century Saturday had been secured as a half-holiday in a wide range of industries and it soon became a day characterised by the new sports and recreations, or by the simpler but no less important demands of family life. Thomas Wright, 'the Journeyman Engineer', noted that 'it is now a stock saying with many working men that Saturday is the best day of the week'. But free time alone was not sufficient to enjoy the opportunities for recreation for increasingly the new forms of leisure, were costly. Fortunately, for many skilled workers the mid-century ushered in a noticeable rise in real wages and it appeared to outsiders that those with strong union backing were able to secure financial advantages over the unskilled and unorganised whose earnings fell behind. Consequently those groups of working people who were in the best position to take advantage of the new forms of leisure were the skilled, organised, relatively well-paid upper reaches of working-class life.

The poorer, less skilled were not as prominent in taking to the trains, unless, of course, they were subsidised by local philanthropists of organisations. There was quite clearly, a divide, indeed a number of divides, within working-class society, often along a trade, regional or age basis, but manifested in fundamentally economic terms. And while by mid-century working people were more in evidence on the trains and, for instance, at the seaside, reports from the growing armies of social investigators bear cruel testimony to legions of English poor in the cities whose access to the nation's growing leisure facilities were either non-existent or restricted to the local pub. For poor women and children, leisure patterns were most often fashioned from the self-entertainment of street life. For the more prosperous working class, however, their growing consumer power reflected in the growth of substantial savings in the Friendly Societies, works and union savings banks, the expanding scope for leisure generated by the railways formed an attractive alternative to the routines and dullness of urban, industrial life. Excursions to the coast, steam trips down the river or visits to the more expensive plebeian enjoyments in the capital and the expanding musical facilities, all drew on the more prosperous reaches of working-class life. And because of the rapid rise in population there were many more such people in evidence, joining what had since time immemorial been the preserve of their social superiors.

All social groups able to enjoy the new forms of leisure found their recreations changing. Few aspects of the new pleasures, and even fewer of the older ones, remained unscathed by the impact of the railways; the most obvious and far-reaching was the evolution of excursion travel.

Few would have quarrelled with the judgement of William Johnston in his book *Britain as It Is* (1851) that 'the most important event of the last quarter of a century in British history is the establishment of the Railroads'. Johnston did not approve wholeheartedly, however, feeling that among other things, the railways

> have done much towards changing the old deliberative and
> thoughtful habits of Englishmen. People who breakfast in York,
> and dine in London – who may be summoned from Liverpool to
> the Metropolis in three or four minutes by the electric telegraph,
> and answer the summons in person within six or seven hours by
> the express train – acquire a habit of pressure and velocity in all
> they do.

This 'pressure and velocity' was to be seen not simply in the nation's business but also in the nation's pleasures. Indeed the trains soon ensured that leisure itself became part of the nation's business, for the first excursion trains were an early sign of the new industrially inspired commercialisation of English leisure.

3 Sinful recreations

In 1844 Frederick Engels complained that 'next to intemperance in the enjoyment of intoxicating liquors, one of the principal faults of English working men is sexual licence'. While many Victorians seemed obsessed with these two problems, or rather with their prevalence among the poor, it would be absurd to claim that either or both were new or peculiar to the nineteenth century. What did appear unique was the sheer size and scale of the problems. Clearly, sexual licence and drunkenness were not restricted to any one social class, but they seemed most acute among the poor because of their lack of realistic alternatives. Reformers throughout the nineteenth century therefore set out both to curb the worst features of these pitfalls and to provide those who seemed to fall victim to them with alternative 'better' recreations. Organised drink and prostitution were major Victorian industries and it was no accident that two of the most powerful contemporary pressure groups directed their efforts against them – an indication of the strength of the problems they set out to remove. In both cases the central difficulty was not so much prostitution or drunkenness itself, but the complexity of social and economic forces on which they thrived. Men and women turned to drink or prostitution for a wide variety of reasons – for enjoyment, comfort, relief or escape – and in many respects these 'sinful pleasures' belong not solely to the world of Victorian leisure. Nonetheless both were enormous industries catering for the leisure needs of millions of people; they were among the first of the new mass commercialised leisure occupations of the new urban age, providing pleasure on an unprecedented scale.

It is difficult today to envisage the importance of alcohol in pre-industrial society. Alcoholic drinks were important not solely as beverages but also as stimulant, sustenance and reviver for whole sections of the labouring population. Men tended to drink (spirits, but primarily beer) simply to enable them to endure their working conditions. Alcohol was to a large degree the lubricant of the pre-industrial economy, to be replaced as the nineteenth century advanced by the more sober demands of the new machine age, aided by a new sobriety of the industrial work ethic. Alternative drinks were both rare and dangerous. Water for instance was unsafe to drink and in urban areas often remote and limited in supply. Milk was often unpleasant, expensive and extremely dangerous, and by late century it was discovered to be the carrier of TB, the 'white man's disease' of Victorian England. It is true that the early years of the century saw a rise in coffee consumption and confirmation of tea as the distinctively English drink, in addition to the introduction of new non-alcoholic beverages such as ginger beer and soda water, but intoxicants remained the most important of all English drinks. Their importance seemed guaranteed by workmen's traditional dependence on them, by the variety of social roles which drinks fulfilled and by the importance of the drinking place.

Alcohol supplied much of the energy put into arduous physical tasks, but drinking at work was equally common among artisans and craftsmen. New industrial processes, however, made inroads into the consumption of alcohol at work, even allowing for the survival well into the century of pre-industrial work patterns, of 'St Monday' replete with excessive drunkenness. Furthermore, the development of an increasingly industrial society brought more and more working people under cover and less in need of alcohol as a reviver and provider of resistance against the elements. The corollary was also true, and it is noticeable that the old traditional relationship between drink and work continued, in its less abated form, in the 'older' jobs which were still exposed to the elements, on the streets, the docks or the land.

The widespread and complex role of alcohol in early Victorian England has been superbly described by Brian Harrison. It was a painkiller, a morale-booster, a sleeping draught and a medicine; it provided 'Dutch courage' and offered an escape to those who – in growing numbers – found the reality around them too harsh to bear. Drink was essential for festivities, both religous and lay. It was, in sum, an essential ingredient in English social and economic life; without it, life would not merely become intolerable but, in many respects, impossible. Alcohol was, in the words of Brian Harrison, 'the thirst quencher, the reliever of physical and psychological strain, the symbol of human interdependence'.

From such a welter of roles it is difficult to distinguish the place of alcohol as the provider of pleasure. Even if we examine the drinking place (of five major kinds – inn, tavern, alehouse, ginshop and, after 1850, beershop) it is not always possible to distinguish drinking for pleasure from its other social roles, for the place of drink had long occupied a key position in society. To this day, many pubs offer food and accommodation and are used as auction rooms for houses, furniture and cattle sales. In the early years of Victorian England, drinking places had an even more varied position. They were, in the first place, centres of transportation for the coaching system, though this was later undermined by the railways. They provided food in a society generally without alternative eating places. Equally important in the political history of the century, the drinking place offered a meeting place, as they still do. From the early radical societies of the 1790s to the presentday Labour Party, political meetings have been convened in pubs and taverns. The London Corresponding Society was developed, organised and based on taverns in London, their constituent divisions being best known not by their number but by the name of their tavern meeting place. Doctors held their surgeries and inquests in taverns; food, goods and services could be bought through the place of drink, which also catered for political or union meetings, and savings or burial clubs. Indeed there were few areas of nineteenth-century working-class life which remained untouched by the pub. And for those in search of warmth, light, liquid refreshment or convivial company, or simply looking for an escape from dark, cold and over-crowded homes, the place of drink was always on hand, and almost always open. In many places the drinking place was the most natural and obvious local focal point, often more so than the local church.

As the century advanced there were many more places of drink, their density greatest in working-class areas (inevitably, since the classes above began to desert the public drinking place for the greater comforts of drinking at home). It was no accident that the breweries were so often built in working-class quarters. It was equally under-standable that the temperance movement should see a causal con-nection between the place of drink and poverty; the breweries and pubs seemed directly responsible for the depths of misery and despair around them. There were many instances where this was indeed the case, but on the whole the social formula tended to work in the opposite direction. Men and women drank to excess because they were poor; fewer were poor because they drank. Nonetheless the temperance movement was right in suggesting the importance both of the drinking place and of drink itself in working-class Victorian society. What that movement could never achieve was the replacement of alcohol by other drinks, and the pub by alternative institutions. Drink was the cement of social fabric at the lower reaches of society; to take a man away from his beer and out of his pub was to isolate him, to maroon him from friends and from the familiar and often vital cultural forms. In the harsh circumstances which dominated working-class life such enforced isolation, involving being thrown back on the even bleaker environment of domestic life, was more than most men could tolerate.

Victorian working men went to the pub to enjoy themselves. Apart from the pleasures of drink there was a range of recreations and pleasures originating in and organised through the pub. Again modern examples, from football clubs to seaside trips, are striking. Many early Victorian sports were arranged by the drinking fraternity, particularly those sports which were either illegal or attracted a strong criminal element. Boxing was perhaps the best example. Boxers, like presentday footballers, often took over a pub on retirement but, more importantly, the services and clientele of local pubs were often used to organise and stage a prize fight. Pubs tended to become the head-quarters for both sides in a prize fight and had the additional benefits of being able to provide the valuable services of gambling and prostitution. A number of London pubs offered sparring matches on a regular basis, with a resident boxer ready to challenge anyone keen enough to hire the pub's gloves. The Queen's Head, off Windmill Street, was famous for such matches, and in the Black Lion, off Drury Lane, in mid-century matches were arranged by Sambo Dutton, a black boxer who 'enlivened things by dancing a hornpipe upside down, his feet beating on a board hung from the ceiling'.

Pubs were sometimes the venue, or the means of organising, sports of an even more grotesque variety. Although blood sports had, as we have seen, been under attack for some time, there was an undoubted popular demand for them, a demand more than satisfied by many London pubs. In the mid-century ratting enjoyed a marked revival under the aegus of publicans who organised 'fights' on their premises, attracted doubtless by the extra income from sales, admission charges and gambling. Henry Mayhew reported that Jimmy Shaw, a London prize fighter and publican bought upwards of 700 rats weekly, with sometimes as many as 2,600 on his premises at any one time. Superbly described by Mayhew, the crowded, drunken ratting scenes in London taverns seemed more in keeping with Hogarth's London. Yet these were the years of the railways and the Great Exhibition – a reminder of the strong survival of pre-industrial recreations in a rapidly modernising society.

More commonplace was the long-established relationship between the pub and prostitution. There were of course many pubs which were more famous for their array of prostitutes than for their drink, and while London was particularly well served by its legions of prostitutes who plied their trade in droves throughout the streets, there were also innumerable drinking places renowned for their brothel services. Not surprisingly nineteenth-century reformers associated the publican with the prostitute. Indeed, wherever a social problem could be isolated it seemed to find sustenance and shape under a publican's roof. In the eyes of hostile witnesses the publican personified the gamut of social ills; he took money from the poor and gave them drunkenness in return, he harboured the prostitute and the criminal, organised the last of the small-scale blood sports, encouraged gambling and shored up the collapsing world of prize fighting. Those middle- and upper-class Victorians who found themselves progressively alienated from the public drinking place (in sharp contrast to the eighteenth-century pattern) came to feel that the drinking place was the cause of the nation's, but more especially the capital's, deepest social ills. In fact the public house was, by and large, merely the occasion, the venue, for these ills. It was however indisputably the immediate cause of a great deal of drunkenness. And despite the array of pleasures and recreations provided in and by the place of drink, it was drinking itself which survived as 'perhaps the most popular of all recreations. It displayed most of the characteristics of "play"; it was voluntary activity, pursued in free time, in a special location, and in the secrecy bestowed by frosted glass and the "snug".'

The drink industry was a major enterprise which worked in close alliance with strong agricultural interests and had important links with finance and retailing outlets. It was also a major employer of labour; sellers of drink were as numerous, for example, as sellers of food; 11,000 out of 140,000 people in Birmingham in 1836. Moreover, with local exceptions, the place of drink was open throughout the week. Not surprisingly the owners and brewers were wealthy; the publican was often a source of great local working-class envy and ambition. But by the 1830s, despite the squeals of a vociferous though varied opposition, the scale of drunkenness in England diminished. There was a deceptive appearance that population growth and the rapid expansion of the new industrial cities had led to an increase in drunkenness, but the worst excesses, particularly through spirits (so common in the previous century), had ended. In part this was because of the efforts of social evangelists, particularly the nonconformists, and partly because of the spread of tea drinking. By 1830 tea was regarded as a necessity in working-class circles and, as E. P. Thompson has shown, 'families that were too poor to buy it begged once-used tea-leaves from neighbours, or even simulated its colour by pouring boiling water over a burnt crust'.

Drunkenness however continued to be a major social problem. Inevitably, the statistics present a number of difficult problems; they might show an increase for example simply because of the arrival of a new Chief Constable determined to act against local drunks. In the 1860s arrests for drunkenness never fell below 17,000 a year; in the next decade they stood at 30,000. Throughout England and Wales the number of people charged with drunken offences increased from 75,859 in 1857 to 205,567 in 1876. But such figures hide regional and local peculiarities and mask completely one of the central determinants of prosecutions for drunkenness, namely the official determination to act against it. Ironically it is the non-statistical evidence which has, in the skilful hands of Brian Harrison, revealed the true decline, rather than increase, in the scale of the problem. It need not surprise us however that perhaps *the* outstanding feature of Victorian drunkenness statistics is that the great majority of those arrested were working men. Drunkenness, like disease and poverty, afflicted society unevenly: it was, as sharp-eyed critics had claimed for years, a result of circumstances rather than personal failings, and it could be argued that drunkenness was just another 'crime' enacted and punished by one class against another. The jails were filled overwhelmingly by the poor who had transgressed against the propertied sensibilities of the system which denied them a number of rights while offering them none of the tolerance normally allowed to their superiors.

Working people were clearly not alone in finding pleasure and comfort in drink, for both the middle- and upper-class male was, if anything, even more committed to the pursuit of alcoholic pleasures. It would be absurd to claim that upper-class drunkenness did not exist, yet it failed to make any but the slightest impression on the statistics; again, this is scarcely surprising for such drinking normally took place in the home or in private clubs. A drunken gentleman bundled into a cab was unlikely to be arrested; his poorer contemporary, staggering home on foot was a more obvious target, and more obviously a 'nuisance'. There were in addition the more complicated factors of police deference towards the transgressions of social superiors and the different policing of different social areas. Of 515 drunks arrested in Sheffield in 1863–64 only one was described as a gentleman.

There was nothing new in the excessive drinking of the upper classes. William Pitt the Younger had been renowned as a 'two-bottle' man, but the more extravagant displays of upper-class drinking which were common in Regency England had come to an end. The days when gay aristocratic blades would parade their prowess in the lowest of dives slowly died out, though the Prince of Wales and his indulgent cronies revised the practice on a smaller scale towards the end of the century. It is a significant insight into the growing awareness and strength of Victorian class divisions that the English working class was left to drink by itself. By the 1850s according to Harrison 'no respectable urban Englishman entered an ordinary public house'. In part this was due to the amazingly rapid emergence after 1830 (when the tax on beer was removed) of the beer house with the starkly functional purpose of serving nothing but beer, and partly to the evangelical efforts to curb the worst excesses of drink. But in large measure it was also a result of the growing social divides and physical separation of Victorian society.

Working men turned to the pub for warmth, light and fellowship which they could never hope to find at home. The temperance movement slowly came to appreciate that the cultivation of domesticity among drinkers whose social life focused on the drinking place was the most persuasive force in driving men away from the pub: there was a good example to hand, for among the emergent middle class the cult of domesticity seduced more and more men from public drinking places.

For the luckier sections of society home was large, warm, well lit and well provided for, and it became the place for the kind of lavish entertainment which was so minutely documented by the new *genre* of cookery books, exemplified by Mrs Beeton's *Household Management*. The Victorian middle and upper classes gorged themselves through a range of meals the complexity and size of which today would only be found at state occasions. And the multiple courses were washed down by a vast amount of alcohol. Mid-Victorians took up the idea of a drink before dinner, a *coupe d'avant*, before eating to the accompaniment of sherry, madeira, champagne, claret and burgundy – and all this before the gentlemen adjourned to their own bottles. The male after-dinner drinking which frequently ended with servants bundling the drunks into bed or into a cab was frowned upon by the Queen, who insisted that the men should remain with the women after the meal. This royal example was remarkably influential, but the pull of cigars and yet more drink continued to draw many men away from the women.

Mrs Beeton's famous recipes and culinary guides of the 1860s are an important guide to the social habits of the classes she was writing for. She died in childbirth at the age of twenty-nine. Her menus, a delight to any modern *bon-viveur*, were regarded in mid-century as a welcome move towards greater simplicity in dining. Not surprisingly there was a corresponding upsurge in patent medicines and home-made recipes to deal with the attendant indigestion and drunkenness. Coffee was used to counterbalance the alcohol; when that failed the hangover victim took a mixture of Rochelle salt, senna, tincture of cardomom, taken with a glass of ratafia or *Eau de Cologne*. But there was no escape from the ravages of excessive food and drink on the shape and size of prosperous Victorians, both male and female. An American visitor noted in 1855, 'there is hardly a less beautiful object than the elderly John Bull, with his large body, protruding paunch, short legs and mottled, doubled chinned, irregular-fashioned features.' The women seemed no less sturdy for they 'become perfectly grotesque after middle age; so massive and not seemingly with pure fat, but with solid beef'. Given this picture of over-indulgence among the better-off it was difficult for reformers, particularly the temperance movement, to advocate the healthy virtues of restraint, moderation and smaller physical size. The well-to-do were large; they ate a lot and often drank to excess in their regular round of pleasure (though the picture changes at the lower reaches of middle-class life). Criticisms of working-class over-indulgence, particularly in drink, had the hollow ring of hypocrisy in the ears of the lower orders.

Wining and dining was both a major source of non-working-class Victorian entertainment and a carefully presented display of personal wealth. It had the hidden virtue of providing work for many thousands of domestics from whom the stories about life 'above stairs' rapidly passed into the gossip of working-class life. The customs of eating and drinking among the rich and the poor were starkly different. The one represented a display of prosperity and recreation; the other a more familiar and traditional struggle to stay alive. Such contrasts were of course age-old, but in Victorian England they had become so commonplace, so sharp and so flaunted as to compound their offensiveness.

Although at first sight it seems unusual to equate the upper-class home with the working-class pub both nonetheless fulfilled similar functions for their respective users. Both provided food and drink; both offered company, music and games. Their differences were even starker, but in functional terms they were related. The music of the *soirée* was paralleled by the variety of pub music, which in its more organised form emerged into the music hall; the charades, cards and make-believe gambling games of the upper class gathering had pale though more boisterous reflections in pubs throughout the country. Even at the less-crowded family evenings, the middle and working classes found similar entertainments in vastly different circumstances; the Victorian middle-class father reading aloud to his children and family or the reading of newspapers and political broadsheets in the public house. For the working man to deny himself access to a pub would have been as serious a loss of recreational facilities and social life as the more prosperous citizen who resolved never again to enjoy the domestic hospitality of his peers.

The pub was the pre-eminent working-class institution even after the emergence of the off-licence in the 1860s and the development of bottled beer which encouraged the taste for drinking at home, particularly among women. But off-licences were hardly likely to attract the higher reaches of upper-class society, who tended in any case to order their drinks in bulk from suppliers. Any shift away from the pub did not effectively take place until economic circumstances began dramatically to alter the quality of working-class domestic life. Improvements in working-class domesticity, noticeable on a major scale in the upper reaches of working-class life in the last twenty years of the century, were a result of improving material conditions, and no amount of pressure on the individual to alter his ways could persuade a man that an austere, dark and overcrowded home was a valid alternative to the enjoyments of the pubs.

Wives however had little choice in the matter for, tied as they were by gaggles of children, they were unable to enjoy the public recreations available to their menfolk. Indeed it was this blatant masculinity of pub life which so offended generations of critics. While men enjoyed their pubs, their beer, games, music and warmth, their wives were forced to endure the harsh domestic circumstances from which the men had fled. Middle- and upper-class women, though by no means liberated in any modern sense, were at least incorporated into a recreational world which was bisexual in its domesticity. When working-class women drank, they did so more often than not from the jug or the bottle, at home. It would be hard to deny that the male-dominated pub provided working men with a greater variety of recreations and, ultimately, a superior quality of life to that of their women. It was a common sight well into the twentieth century to see wives and children intercepting husbands and fathers on pay day *en route* to the pub. Those knots of women and children gathered at factory gate and pit head knew that their menfolk's wages were destined (unless stopped) to find their way into the publican's pocket.

In working-class life therefore, the pub came to shape a number of powerful, contradictory responses. To men it was their own world, replete with friendship and enjoyment, but women tended to see it more through the eyes of the teetotaller, even when they themselves drank, as the cause and occasion of their family's misfortunes.

The importance of the pub in working-class life can be seen in its historical geography. Pubs tended to be bunched in their greatest numbers in working-class communities, though this pattern had a great range of local variations. The better the social tone of a district, or even a street, the less likely you were to find a pub. To a large degree these omnipresent institutions, as characteristic of working-class communities as the armies of ragged children playing in the streets and yards, formed a recreational network for working men. It is true that the rise of Dissent, particularly in the north, began to offer other, less spectacular diversions based on the chapel and Sunday school, but any 'improving' force in Victorian society, which aimed itself at working-class life was forced to challenge the dual importance of the pub and of drink. When, late in the century, new forms of leisure began to emerge from this missionary effort, their success lay in the fact that they were launched from new and increasingly powerful social bases within working-class life: the church, Sunday school, union or place of work. It is important to remember that when the new working-class football teams proliferated in the north and Midlands they did so, not on the whole from pubs, but from those working class institutions which were of relatively recent vintage. Nonetheless even these institutions were, like the pubs, primarily male concerns. But in many respects they formed a recreational challenge to the dominance of the pub in working-class culture in that they offered, within certain geographical boundaries and within the limits of a man's finance and free time, a range of leisure which for so long had been monopolised by the place of drink.

The problem created by Victorian drunkenness could be seen by any casual visitor to an English city. So too could the related problem of prostitution, much of which, as we have seen, was based on the place of drink. Again, there was nothing new in the connection between drink and prostitution for it seems to have been a common association in any number of more ancient societies. But, as with drink, it is difficult to define prostitution merely as a variant of leisure, for though hired women clearly gave a variety of pleasures to thousands of men, it seems to have been less enjoyable for the women themselves who, on the whole, were drawn into a life of prostitution by force of economic circumstances. Ironically it was this use of leisure which brought together Victorians of different social classes. The pursuit of commercial sex involved a social levelling difficult to find in other areas of society, though one could trace a similar pattern in the traditional pattern of upper-class seductions of domestics and serving girls. Any definition of prostitution, however, must ultimately depend on the vantage point we adopt, although it is indisputable that prostitution constituted a major commercial enterprise which in its size, financial implications and social ramifications closely paralleled the recreational dominance of drink.

The source of prostitutes was apparently endless and, like the origins of drunkenness, was to be found in the harsh social conditions of Victorian plebeian life. Generations of nineteenth-century English-men were able to enjoy the sexual favours of their hired companions largely because prostitution offered poor women, not leisure (and pleasure even less) but the sole escape from hardship. Poverty had traditionally been the recruiting agent for prostitution throughout the ages: what made Victorian commercial sex so distinctive was the large numbers involved. Visitors and residents in the cities found it as hard to escape from prostitutes as from drunks, in daytime or night-time, and nowhere more so than in the West End of London. Theatres, bars, shopping arcades and street corners – all teemed with women plying their trade within easy reach of a range of brothels and rooming houses where business was transacted. The variety of sexual offerings was staggering; child prostitutes, a thriving market in virgins (and an equally thriving trade in recreating lost virginity) women of theatrical talents and considerable wealth, with a talent to amuse at the dining table as well as in bed – all these, through to the diseased crones offering themselves to men of their own wretched condition. At its upper reaches however, prostitution sometimes attained a level of respectability (often thanks to close connections with the theatre) which is hard to envisage today. Noel Coward's Mrs Worthington was well advised to keep her daughter off the stage even at a later date. Whatever the economic fortunes involved, contemporary evidence is overwhelming in attributing the source of prostitution to the harsh-ness of life, the scarcity of work and poor wages for women.

Henry Mayhew is one of the best remembered investigators whose evidence confirmed that this enormous leisure industry was rooted in poverty. Unmarried mothers, widows with children, badly paid girls and women in the grossly exploitive sweated trades, unemployed domestics, underemployed street hawkers or women who simply refused to split up their families to go into the hated work-house: these and many more turned to prostitution simply to stay alive. Above all else the story of Victorian prostitution must surely provide the starkest and cruellest evidence of contemporary female exploitation. Moreover these women were the victims of a rapacious double standard: for though they catered for the sexual delights of many men whose sexual frustrations were in large measure a product of prevailing taboos about marital sex, those same men were largely responsible for the belief in the worthlessness of a woman once she had been guilty of intercourse. An unmarried mother was denounced as a harlot, and it was often inevitable that such would be her fate. Innocent girls, from town and country, were the natural targets of predatory males who sought to break out of their own suffocating domestic morality by enjoying the freedom which, publicly, they so denounced. Understandably, it was the prostitutes who spoke so tellingly about Victorian hypocrisy, for they were often the playthings of men who espoused a contrary morality. A woman who wrote to *The Times* in February 1858 had been introduced to her trade at the age of fifteen by 'one of our be-ribbaned visitors'.

It was impossible to count all the prostitutes, partly because they were so widespread, but also because many of them were part-timers who sought merely to supplement their inadequate earnings: it was as if there were a spectrum of prostitutes from part-timers and the most wretched at one end, to those who moved freely, often via marriage, into the upper reaches of society. Dr Aston thought that the police statistics, of 6,515 women working in 2,119 establishments in London, 'give but a faint idea of the grand total of prostitutes by which we are oppressed'. In 1857 for example *Lancet* thought that one in six of the capital's houses were brothels. It was, as Victorians admitted, 'the Great Social Evil', its numbers varying from one commentator to another. *The Westminster Review* of 1850 thought there were 8,000 in London, 50,000 in England and Scotland. But the fourth volume of Mayhew's *London Labour and the London Poor* put the figure at 80,000 for the capital alone. Whatever the disagreement about figures, Victorians were agreed that they were ubiquitous, one for every eighty-one men in London and Edinburgh, according to Dr Aston. It was calculated that some £8 million was spent each year on prostitutes, a figure which, if accurate, would propel the trade towards the top of the league table of commercial recreations.

Prostitutes were clearly linked to that brittle, taut morality of the middle-class family which allowed no sexual licence to the women-folk, while encouraging their men to find satisfaction outside the family. Indeed, Professor J. F. C. Harrison has argued convincingly that 'behind the early Victorian family, and essential for the main-tainance of the façade, was the great underworld of prostitution. A relationship of mutual interdependence linked these two institutions together; they were in fact the obverse and the reverse of the same coin.' The self-denial of sexual pleasure within marriage meant that thousands of men turned for pleasure to the ladies of the streets. How much pleasure they gave in return is hard to define.

There seems to have been a connection, however distant and tenuous, between the advance of an inhibited sexual morality, which stood in stark contrast to the less restrained moral code of the previous century, and the rise of urban prostitution. At its simplest it may merely reflect the growing number of women who turned to prosti-tution for economic reasons. But it was more likely to be a function of a complexity of forces, one of which was the dissolving of an old moral code in the crucible of the new urban areas. But where, in the economic plight of the women involved, was the pleasure and enjoyment?

Max Weber has claimed that 'prostitution is a cultural phenomenon just as religion or money', and it seems clear that the Victorian variety was a reflection of a deeply divided society where, by and large, poor women were propelled into vice by circumstances they could not control and yet often found themselves catering for men of a superior social station who deplored, yet needed, their 'immoral' world. Not all prostitutes, of course, catered for their social betters, for there was a thriving trade in working-class communities where middle- and upper-class gentlemen did not venture. This was particularly noticeable in dockside communities where the itinerant seafaring men had need of prostitutes. Some women specialised in catering for particular racial groups; others provided a sexual service for specific men only, in a relationship which looked remarkably like marriage. With the obvious exception of sailors and men in the armed forces, it is difficult to suggest the degree to which working men resorted to prostitutes. The frustrations which so haunted the formally prudish world of middle- and upper-class marriage seems to have been absent in poorer, more overcrowded circumstances of working-class life. Indeed time and again, outsiders commented on and were shocked by the sexual licence in working-class homes, though this was often brought about by overcrowding and whole families living in one bed.

There was increasing evidence of widespread premarital sex among the lower orders, a trend recorded time and again in official papers, reports and buried in the growing statistics of the census returns. Moreover, this evidence came to hand from many different parts of the country. One man reported in 1870 that 'the laxity of morals among the female peasantry of Wales is unhappily notorious. The inveterate custom of nightly courting has destroyed all delicacy of character'. The story was much the same from north of the border in that same year. 'Taking the Annual Reports of the Registrar General and the investigation of Dr Strachan as a basis, we are brought to the inevitable conclusion that amongst the Lowland Scotch of the labouring class, a very small proportion of the women preserve their chastity up to the date of their marriage.' Promiscuity was often claimed to be a feature of lower-class life, but of course such observations had been a traditional descant from the better-off towards their inferiors.

Middle-class Victorians, and their medical and social spokesmen, regularly denied that sexual activity could be in the least bit pleasurable for women. Time and again opinion asserted the basic non-sexuality of women; their sexual role was simply to cater for the needs and desires of their menfolk – or their customers. Kraft-Ebbing, writing in 1886 thought that 'Woman, however, if physically and mentally normal, and properly educated, has but little sensual desire. If they were not otherwise, marriage and family life would be empty words'. Even William Aston, whose sympathetic observations on

Victorian prostitutes were among the most objective of the age, felt that sexual activity was bad and dangerous, and that life itself was a constant struggle against carnal temptations. The central difficulty facing the historian however is to get behind the evidence on sexuality, most of which was compiled by men of a particular social class, and reconstruct the feelings of the women involved, on a subject which people are notoriously reluctant to discuss.

Ironically one excellent source about Victorian sexuality is contemporary pornography. There was an abundance of magazines and books catering for pornographic tastes, and the attitudes they reveal is quite the reverse of prudery. They were of course written primarily for men and by men (and of a class able to afford these generally expensive publications), but in this world of sexual fantasy, women were allowed sexual pleasures and feelings which were normally absent from the more formal medical or social treatise on sexuality. Even the Victorian novelist was obliged (so as not to offend his readers' sensibilities) to conform to a strict moral code which expected (and got) a particular form of behaviour among women. Pornographers on the other hand, exemplified by the notorious 'Walter' in his massive book *My Secret Life*, had no such restraints and could portray their female characters as fully liberated sexual creatures, able and willing to enjoy a variety of sexual experiences. Indeed it is characteristic of *My Secret Life* (secret no more thanks to a cheap paperback edition) that the author put much of his considerable efforts into trying to make his various partners sexually happy. But it is also significant that the great majority of his partners were working-class and poor; when money failed to buy them, Walter's social dominance generally played successfully on his victim's sense of deference. It is clear that the great bulk of Victorian pornography, itself a growing industry, ran counter to prevailing sexual beliefs and as such it offers an unusually rich insight into a usually opaque area of behaviour. Arguably, the main point to emerge is that many Victorians, despite contrary contemporary evidence and popular attitudes inherited to this day, regarded sex as an enjoyable social and private pleasure. This may seem a truism (in the sense that biologically Victorians were little different from mankind today). But it is possible to come away from contemporary literature on Victorian sexuality without the slightest impression that contemporaries regarded sex as pleasurable, and it remains impossible to assess how much pleasure was involved for those tens of thousands of prostitutes who, in their turn, did indeed give pleasure to the nineteenth-century Englishman.

There was often a price to pay for sexual activity, for the incidence of venereal disease, in a society without adequate detection or medical remedies, was alarming. In fact the incidence of VD accounts in large measure for the strong preference for virgins. There was no doubt that by mid-century VD had become a major threat to public health, a fact which prompted Acts in 1864 and 1869. Unhappily these Acts, enabling the police to inspect diseased prostitutes, were directed only against the prostitutes and not against their customers who might also be suffering. Moreover the legislation allowed the police a degree of personal control over prostitutes which, at its worst, merely put the women at the policemen's mercy. The campaign against these Acts, led by the irrepressible Josephine Butler, succeeded in suspension of the Acts in 1883, but the campaign had a wide base and a powerful dynamic which eventually produced legal control of the worst excesses of prostitution in 1885; thereafter it was so circumscribed that it had to operate in the unhappy world of illegality. Predictably, this did not destroy prostitution itself.

The slow improvements in prostitution came about, like that in drink, not so much through the efforts of the reformers, but because of economic amelioration. It is hard, as ever, to trace the changing statistics of prostitution with any accuracy; harder still to relate them to the wider changes in society at large. And while it is true that both prostitution and drink continued to be major social problems into the twentieth century, they were, at the same time, industries catering for the leisure needs of millions of people. It would be hard to deny that in both cases, most of the leisure was reserved for men. Women clearly drank and enjoyed sexual activity, and some prostitutes enjoyed the services they provided. But both drink and commercial sex catered primarily for the pleasures of men. Those Victorians, even among the working class, who were given free time, money and opportunities to indulge in their interests were, on the whole male. Women had, in general, to create a recreational world from within the limitations of family life. Not until the emergence in the second half of the century of new, mass leisure pursuits fed by commercial interests, was the dominance of drink and prostitution to be undermined as the major and most obvious forms of urban recreation. And the new activities were, in general, to be untouched by that complexity of moral problems which inevitably clung to the issues of commercial drink and sex.

4 Useful pleasures

No history of Victorian England would be complete without an acknowledgement of the importance of religion. Most historians however have treated nineteenth-century religious history either as a theme in the wider history of religion, or as a theological matter. Rarely has Victorian religion been seen in the way millions of contemporaries regarded it, namely as one of the major leisure pursuits of the English people. And yet the churches, Catholic and Protestant, orthodox and dissenting, were among the major social institutions in both town and country and, increasingly as the century advanced, they spawned a wide range of ancillary organisations, clubs and societies. From church activities were to flow many of the men and organisations which, in the second half of the century were to prove seminal in the redefining of English leisure. But even in the first half of the century, when conditions for many of the nation's increasingly urban population were undoubtedly harsh, churches and religious organisations played a significant role in catering for leisure. At its simplest, many Englishmen (though to contemporaries, not enough of them) chose to spend their leisure time, on their sole day of rest, in church or Sunday school.

In a society dominated by massive and rapid change it was predictable that many of those changes would be reflected in the churches which, in many respects can be seen as barometers of social change. To the chagrin of the Old Order it was apparent that the former hegemony of the established Church of England was rapidly being undermined by demographic change, which threw up large pockets of population beyond the organisational framework of the Church itself, a process made worse by the inroads made by the new dissenting sects. Many early Victorians who bemoaned the advent of the new industrial England, frequently regretted both the decline of the Church of England as the church of the common people, and similarly deeply distrusted the emergence of widespread dissenting organisation's, whose deep-seated support and articulate popular voice seemed to conflict with the tone and attitudes of the Church of England. More alarming still to many people was the decline in religious belief and attendance at church. Early nineteenth-century

England appeared a nation whose religion was not so much changing as disappearing. Most of the evidence for this pessimistic view, trumpeted aloud in local and national newspapers, was impressionistic. But in the 1851 religious census it was given substance.

The census showed that church-going in England had become a minority occupation; from the population of 17,927,609 only 7,261,032 attended church or chapel on the day of the sample. (It ought to be noted however that a similar proportion today would be greeted as a major manifestation of religious commitment.) Yet modern eyes find equally striking the fact that some 7¼ million people spent part of their major day of rest at church. However varied and complex their motives it would nonetheless be hard to deny that religion occupied a central position in the non-working lives of millions of Victorians. The paradox is that the obverse is also true; spiritual apathy and indifference were dominant features of the Sabbath throughout wide areas of urban society. But this bleak image, real in itself, has, from that period onwards, coloured our overall conception of Victorian life and has led contemporaries and historians to overlook or minimise the social importance of religion in the life of the nation.

Statistics from the 1851 census gave added strength to the long-held belief that the Church was failing the English people, more particularly among the lower orders where the growth of unbelief and non-attendance was most acute. In 1845 Engels noted: 'All the writers of the bourgeoisie are unanimous on this point, that the workers are not religious, and do not attend church.' Even the less partial official report of 1851 made much the same point, that most of the non-attenders belonged to 'the masses of our working population'. These judgements and the data on which they rested represented but one aspect of a complicated phenomenon. There were after all at least 7¼ million active church goers. And for these millions the churches and their ancillary organisations provided much more than a simple meeting place for worship. Indeed it could be argued that those people who attended their local churches and chapels were disproportionately influential within their own communities, even when that community was, in the wider sense, indifferent to church and chapel. There are few better examples than Samual Bamford, the northern working-class radical who recalled his own childhood memories spent in the local Sunday school on the Sabbath: 'My readers will expect hearing that the school was well attended and it was so, not only by children and youths from the immediate neighbourhood, but by young men and women from distant localities.'

In the first half of the century, for Bamford and others similar working-class people, the Sunday schools more than the churches occupied a central role in their social lives. In fact the most recent historian of the Sunday schools has suggested that 'by the 1820s, outside the Metropolis, nearly every working-class child must at some time have attended one. They were instructed, largely by teachers from their own class, in reading, writing, religion and occasionally other subjects for periods of four to six hours each Sunday over a period of on average, four years.' The English Sunday school of the early nineteenth century, more particularly in working-class communities, was a major institution both in the provision of leisure facilities and, perhaps more crucially, in generating popular literacy and encouraging a growing emphasis on the printed word. Popular literacy, which lay at the heart of so many new forms of Victorian culture and politics, was clearly not created by the Sunday schools, but they undoubtedly spread it more widely, particularly among working people.

Beginning in the 1780s as an offshoot of the Evangelical revival, the Sunday school movement rapidly established itself in lower class communities, providing education for the nation's children. The ideological and theological motives behind the movement were varied and sometimes contradictory, but the end result was a major drive to establish literacy among those children generally denied access to education. By the early nineteenth century, the Sunday schools had taken on a distinctly plebeian tone and style, with working-class teachers ministering to working-class children through an educational structure which was unusually democratic. Moreover it was a voluntary and yet time-consuming business for teachers and pupils, and the fact that millions passed through the system speaks both for its appeal and importance. Children spent upwards of five hours each week, for up to four years, learning the rudiments of literacy in what amounted to an important step in the evolution of a mass literate population, as the *Morning Chronicle* stressed in 1849:

> Long before educational committees of the Privy Council and the British and Foreign Societies were heard of, long previous to the era of Institutes, and Athenaeums, the Sunday schools were sedulously at work, impregnating the people with the rudiments of an education which, though always rude and often narrow and factional in its teachings, was yet preserving a glow of moral and religious sentiment, and keeping alive a degree of popular intelligence which otherwise would assuredly have perished in the rush and clatter with which a vast manufacturing population came surging up upon the land.

Even in the drabbest of poor communities, the weekly visit to the Sunday school was an event of major importance, savoured for days before and pondered over for days afterwards. In this sense (and like the other infrequent holidays) the Sunday schools had an importance over and above the spending of free time; while they dominated the sabbath for millions, they also cast an important shadow across the rest of the week. Sunday itself involved a ceremony of cleanliness, spruceness, punctuality and orderliness which often stood in sharp contrast to the other days of the week. 'My sister and I went to bed early on Saturday nights so that my mother might be able to wash and mend our clothes and we have them tidy for Sunday,' wrote George Edwards. In a similar vein a Primitive Methodist minister preacher recalled: 'I got a washing that morning [Sunday] such as I had not time to get on other mornings. I had poor enough clothing to put on, but my eldest sister always helped me in my toilet on Sunday mornings.' Spurred on by such routines and the sense of occasion, there were some 1,400,000 children attending Sunday schools in 1833; 2,100,000 in 1851.

The early nineteenth-century Sunday school provided a respite for harassed parents in addition to providing a range of social services within the local community: clothes for the needy, savings clubs for sickness and death, and even opportunities of employment. Equally they created a number of leisure activities; even in their more formal educational role the Sunday schools were dispensing leisure and recreation. Even when sitting in rows or groups listening to the scriptures or learning the alphabet, children were provided with an indoor meeting place and a deliberately useful and structured use of their free time. Teachers often gave all their leisure to the demands of the Sunday schools. For the young however, until the rapid proliferation of informal education from the mid-century onwards, the Sunday schools frequently offered the only institution in a locality which catered for their free time. School anniversaries and prize-givings, choral concerts, public parades on festive days and even the more exceptional (though with the passage of time, the increasingly common) excursions and trips, punctuated the weekly routines of Sunday school life, bringing a degree of mass organised leisure where in general none existed. Historians have stressed the importance of the banners in the pageantry and iconography of working-class movements, but it is worth remembering that such colourful and public displays similarly characterised the marches and celebrations of Sunday school children. Feasts and banners, marches and bands, music and orderly and well-regimented public displays of collective endeavour and pride, these, throughout the early years of the century, were among the hallmarks of the English Sunday school.

To see these schools merely, or even largely, as agents of an interested ideology anxious to secure a disciplined future labour force is both to misunderstand and to misinterpret their culture and importance. The Sunday schools rapidly became a feature of working-class urban life. It is symptomatic that many of the early pioneering excursion trains were filled in the 1840s by Sunday schools heading for the coast, their journey marked by communal hymn singing and rejoicing. Three thousand children travelled from Birmingham to Cheltenham in 1846; a similar number in that year journeyed from Macclesfield to Stockport. No fewer than 6,125 parents, children and teachers were taken by train from Norwich to Yarmouth in 1846. There was, moreover little doubt that in all these massive groups –

spectacular even by modern standards – there were many children who simply would never have enjoyed such treats without the efforts of the Sunday schools.

The early nineteenth century Sunday school offered a multitude of services at all levels: spiritual, recreational, educational and, in some cases political. More often than not this activity catered for a majority of the nation's children and in working-class communities the schools' appeal tended to be most effective among the upper 'respectable' reaches of working-class life. Their contribution to the evolution of popular culture, more especially that literate culture which found its strongest expression in the printed word, self-education, self-improvement and the search for respectability, was incalculable. From those strata of working-class life there emerged many seminal features in the nation's political and cultural life, particularly in the years of material improvement later in the century.

The Sunday schools seemed to provide an ideal antidote to the much-discussed complaint that the English people needed more formal leisure facilities on their day of rest, provision severely limited by the success of the sabbatarian lobby. Sunday schools were an orderly, structured and 'useful' alternative to the boisterous, time-wasting and unproductive hours of freedom which seemed to dominate the lower-class sabbath across the country. Teachers, ministers and spokesmen for early Victorian schools were among the loudest critics of the old recreations, and proponents of the movement to purge the nation of its addiction to old recreational forms. Inevitably some of the bitterest complaints against Sunday football among local boys came from ministers and Sunday school teachers who wanted to bring the children into their churches and class rooms. Children at the Haslingden Sunday school in the early nineteenth century were later described as 'semi-barbarous youths who were collected from the moors and vales' and who 'previous to attending the schools spent sabbath days in wrestling, fighting, bull-baiting, cock-fighting, and football playing'. Time and again the Sunday schools were at the forefront of the campaign to drive children's games from the sabbath. Patrols were even dispatched to break up such games and to haul 'offending' children into the schools.

Much of the initial inspiration behind the creation of the Sunday schools was not so much a distaste for popular recreation as a positive fear of plebeian idleness. The Lord's Day gave the common people free time which, many thought, merely encouraged the vices of sloth; such sloth was inimical to good social order and even to the safe preservation of private property. To the jaundiced eye the rapid growth of the population, often beyond the pale of law and order, seemed to offer daily confirmation of these fears. There was after all a great deal of antisocial behaviour on Sundays, and not only in the cities. Farmers were sometimes reluctant to attend divine service for fear of damage to their property by idle youths. In Gloucestershire at least, the impact of the Sunday schools was thought to be largely responsible for removing such threats and putting 'idle' hands to some useful purpose. Yet though the desire to control this plebeian antisocial behaviour was one inspiration behind the Sunday schools, this in no way explains why generations of pupils volunteered to attend the schools. Coercion, both social and parental, was obviously one element, but the evidence suggests that most people went to Sunday school because they wanted to, that they enjoyed themselves and benefited by attending. In time the Sunday schools came to be seen as a natural fact of life.

To hostile eyes, the place of drink represented the worst side of early nineteenth century leisure, but the world of the Sunday school offered a totally contradictory and resistant picture where leisure time was consumed by the pursuit of social improvement. Much of the schools' success may have lain in the fact that they offered much more than religion (just as the pubs offered much more than beer). They contributed powerfully to the refinement of recreations, particularly among the young, and, while it would be an exaggeration to suggest that the schools were formative in curbing the pre-industrial recreations, by mid-century it was universally accepted that they had helped in stabilising society. In large measure this was because they had successfully cultivated social and recreational links between different social classes. Following a visit to the seaside by 5,000 working-class children and 3,000 spectators, the *Norwich News* of 1846 commented,

> We are glad, too, to perceive in this and similar instances,
> evidence of the growing tendency in religion to associate itself
> with the innocent amusements and social enjoyment of the poor,
> and thus to promote a genial intercourse between all classes . . .
> more has been done by modern evangelical religion to raise the
> scale of social recreation; and by breaking down rigid barriers of
> caste, to bring high and low into happy harmony, than by all
> the well meant but quixotic antics of Young England. . . .
> Sunday School outings are better adapted to regenerate society,
> than the revival of the maypole and the antiquated rubbish of
> the Book of Sports.

One of the most useful contributions of the Sunday schools was their emphasis on education and the encouragment of literacy among their people, though they shared this attribute with (and to a degree passed it on to) the temperance clubs, mechanics institutes, cooperatives and other political organisations. It is a truism to state that working class political and industrial life was conducted largely through the printed word, in newspapers, broadsheets and magazines. Yet the ability of working people to read and write was developed in their leisure hours. Popular literacy was the result of the 'useful' enjoyment of leisure, and having, in its turn, major ramifications on the shape and direction of nineteenth-century political history. Moreover, the fact that literacy was thought worth acquiring in precious free time offers another insight into the complex attitudes of ordinary people towards their leisure; many thousands learned to read and write not because their betters thought it good for them (which they did), but because they themselves wanted to become literate. It was a complex phenomenon which no single 'opiate' theory of society can adequately explain.

The evidence for literacy before mid-century is confused and sometimes conflicting, but by the late 1840s the figures suggest that some 40 per cent of the nation was literate, though with sharp regional variations; literacy tending to be higher where the population was densest. It was significant that, in the words of *Chambers' Journal* in 1840, that journal was read by 'the élite of the labouring community; those who think, conduct themselves respectably, and are anxious to improve their circumstances by judicious means. But below this worthy order of men, our work, except in a few particular cases, does not go.' It was precisely among these men that the Sunday schools had made their major inroads. Yet despite these comments, there is contradictory evidence to suggest that literacy percolated much further down the social scale, though this begs the question of whether only the literate could comprehend political and social questions. Even so, it was the literate, self-educated minority, nurtured on the Sunday school tradition of self-improvement and the quest for respectability, who became the prominent leaders of early working-class movements. While remembering that working-class culture did not depend on a literate tradition, and was rich and diverse nonetheless, it was inescapable that one of the major transformations of nineteenth-century England was the evolution of a largely literate society. As the century advanced and society became increasingly complex, literacy was seen to be vital not merely in political terms, but also at work and even at play. Radical agitation depended on the printed word, so too did the railway companies, the popular press and a whole range of recreations. Literacy became an important, though clearly not vital, asset. And before the coming of compulsory education in the last quarter of the century, the pursuit of literacy and of knowledge was an important feature of the leisure time of ordinary people.

As the century advanced, the printed word became increasingly important; newspapers, tracts, magazines, programmes, cheap books and a variety of other printed materials began to shape the wider social world of the English people. The political face of England was changed, to a large extent by the impact of the printed word. But the evolution of reading as a leisure pursuit in its own right was slower in gaining ground. When cheap popular literature emerged as a major feature towards the end of the century, it was sorely to disappoint those men who had for years regarded literacy as the key to national enlightenment. To a degree this was primarily because, from the 1790s onwards, men keen to promote literacy did so for overtly political ends; if working men could master the ability to read and write, it would be seen as a fundamental step towards political emancipation. Increasingly, however, cheap literature was directed, not towards political agitation, but towards the enjoyment of a new kind of cheap and ephemeral popular material. On the other hand there was a powerful literate tradition among working people that found its strength in 'serious' literature, led by the Bible and other inspirational works, but adherents to this cause frowned on the growing body of less serious literature. It was soon clear that the new reading public was not going to reserve its leisure reading either for political agitation or self-improvement. One observer on the mines told a Parliamentary investigation in 1850 that many Scottish miners 'read such books as Adam Smith's *Wealth of Nations* and are fond of discussing the subjects he treats of. They also read the lives of statesmen, and books of history; also works on logic, and sometimes mathematics.' But it seems unlikely that such men and their literature were typical or commonplace. More frequent were those who found their enjoyment in the new 'penny dreadfuls' which, thanks to new production techniques and entrepreneurial guile, began to flood the market in the 1830s and 1840s.

Popular literature was not of course an invention of the century, but traced its immediate roots to a range of publications, from romantic novels to lurid woodcuts, cartoons and ribald and bloodcurdling handbills of previous centuries. Though this tradition continued, it was rapidly supplanted by the new 'comics' published in weekly parts. Pioneered by Howard Lloyd these weeklies were 'Gothic shockers' aimed at creating morbid curiosity and widespread sales. From the first, they aimed at the lower reaches of society, as Lloyd's manager confessed:

> Our publications circulate among a class so different in education and social position from the readers of the three volume novels that we sometimes distrust our own judgement and place a manuscript in the hands of an illiterate person - a servant or a machine boy for instance. If they pronounce favourably upon it, we think it will do.

Employing a small group of writers who were highly imaginative and skilled at pitching the publication at the lowest common denominator Lloyd built up an enormously successful empire, simply by selling cheap weekly publications. His success pointed to the future of entrepreneurial encroachments into popular leisure and culture, for he proved that it was possible to establish a major economic concern and create new, nationwide tastes, by appealing commercially to those sections of the community which appeared at first sight to be least able to afford spare cash for leisure. The penny dreadfuls were an object lesson, well learned by other major entrepreneurs later in the century, that while working people might individually have only a handful of coppers to spend, cumulatively this added up to a major economic reserve. And it was, quite clearly, ripe for exploitation.

To a certain extent Lloyd's penny dreadfuls capitalised on the enormous commercial success of Charles Dickens whose works were shamelessly plagiarised, thanks to the laxity of contemporary copyright laws. *Oliver Twiss* and *Martin Guzzlewit* were among Lloyd's publications, but it was more lurid titles and heroes which established themselves as national names. Sweeney Todd appeared in 1840 in a Lloyd publication entitled *The String of Pearls (A Romance)*, remaining a national name until the presentday. Lloyd's staff writers, their industry matched only by their imagination, churned out series of such Gothic horrors: *The Black Monk, The Castle Fiend, Varney the Vampire*, and many more to satisfy the morbid curiosity of their growing readership. Up to mid-century these publications were aimed at a male readership of all ages, but public alarm was growing that armies of literate youths were reading only the more gory publications. This concern led, after 1855, to the publication of a new type of magazine designed for boys (or girls) only and, it was claimed, 'healthier' and less degrading. Thereafter, though it was clear that there was a new market for such magazines (familiar to modern eyes as the forerunners of presentday comics) they tended to supplement rather than replace the penny dreadfuls.

Then as now there were conflicting worlds of publishing inspired by different aims and ideologies which, from the 1830s onwards, competed for the attention and custom of the literate masses. Those men, personified by Samuel Smiles, who sought to inculcate the virtues of self-help among ordinary people, published magazines and booklets aimed at bringing enlightenment to the literate poor. *The Penny Magazine, Chambers' Edinburgh Journal,* and manuals like George L. Craik's *The Pursuit of Knowledge under Difficulties* (1830), *Family Economist* and *Family Friend*, all sought to encourage the virtues of hard work and self-improvement. While it would be wrong to ignore their appeal to the literate poor, it would be equally misleading to suggest that such books held pride of place in the reading habits of working people. Arguably, more commonplace was the man or youth, perhaps in need of 'self-improvement', his head buried deep in the weekly pages of a horror-soaked Lloyd publication. It seems unlikely that these two schools of literature appealed to the same market, though ultimately both depended for their existence on the willingness and ability of low income groups to spend their money on literature. There can be no doubt however that the early optimism which had in large measure inspired the early radical idealism and commitment to popular literacy, took a severe battering from the rise of the lurid world of weekly, popular literature. Violence and death were more appealing literary qualities than economic or political argument. By mid-century the printed word had opened up vast new markets, but the offerings were characterised more by cheap thrills than self-education. When, later in the century, material conditions began to improve and wider sections of the population were able to partake more fully in leisure activities, reading was to become even more prominent. The proliferation of libraries, for instance, offered space for more contemplative reading and self-improvement, but by then they were competing with an expanding range of alternative forms of leisure.

There was another world of literary interest which, though its style and durability were worlds removed from the 'penny-dreadfuls', was often cannibalised and rendered down into popular form by the hacks of the cheap weeklies. For those Victorians with free time and spare money, people whose employment was not totally demanding and whose domestic obligations tended to be shouldered by their servants, reading for leisure was widespread. Publishers catered specifically for the reading needs of all sectional groups within the middle and upper classes; young and old, boys and girls, the religious, intellectual, fashionable, the housebound or the sporting, these and many other groups found ample literary output to satisfy their tastes. Some prominent Victorian authors were able to appeal to most groups, and the more famous novelists were among the best paid and the most lionised figures in society. Viewed overall, however, what is striking is the sheer *volume* of Victorian fictional reading – both low and high – helping to confirm the view that reading had become a major leisure pursuit. Quite clearly it was commonest in those circles where time had to be killed as pleasantly as possible rather than be consumed by work or family duties, and where literacy, thanks to the expensive facilities of private schools and tutors, was more commonplace. Publications spilled from the presses in growing numbers and variety; gentle romances for the ladies, reprinted sermons (hard to imagine today) for those in search of inspiration, novels, adventures, travel and educational books, all jostled for the readers' attention and purchasing power. Victorian England was a society where a great part of leisure time was dominated by the printed word. The weighty array of nineteenth-century literature extant to this day provides the modern historian with much invaluable evidence.

The world of publishing was a manifest result of the new technical age which made possible cheap, mass-produced literature which was available throughout the country through an efficient marketing and retailing book and newspaper system. It was also the symbol of a cultural climate which according to Professor Altick 'stressed the value of education and ideas and exalted books as the noblest product and symbol of civilisation. To Victorians, the printing press, driven by a steam engine was, indeed, the most pregnant emblem of their achievement and aspirations.' Literature came to be regarded as the hallmark of civilisation, and it is revealing that Victorians were dismissive of those pre-literate civilisations which succumbed to British imperial control in the course of the century. This emphasis on literature seems to modern eyes to be both familiar and obvious. Yet in the early years of Victoria's reign it was a new phenomenon, and forms a qualitative shift towards presentday society.

To claim that Victorians were increasingly dominated by the printed word is not to say that literature was equally influential throughout society; its importance varied from one class to another. But there is no escaping the importance of the printed word, through which society was increasingly shaped, regulated and entertained. The wider economic industrial needs of the nation were determined by the printed word: inevitably this came to be the case with leisure. Again, this is far from claiming that literacy was a prerequisite for the enjoyment of leisure. But it is to suggest that, as the century advanced, new leisure activities were shaped, directed and elevated to the level of mass consumption by the deployment of the printed word. Excursions to seaside towns were advertised on billboards and hoardings, football matches announced and reported on in local newspapers; travelling circuses and the developing music hall depended for their growing custom both on word of mouth and on handbills, advertisements and press reports. Literature itself was dependent on heavy commercial advertisements. Thus, from the mid-century onwards, the mass leisure facilities jostled for space in newspapers and on walls along with millions of other goods and services anxious to catch the public eye and purse. But it is indicative that the leisure industries aimed themselves at a literate market. Literature and literacy were thus both functions and cause of a growing preoccupation with the pleasurable (and sometimes useful) use of free time.

Part Two

Leisure for all?
1870-1914

5 Leisure and material improvement 1870-1914

The most obvious and severe restraint on popular leisure in the early years of the nineteenth century was, as we have seen, economic circumstances. Nonetheless, there had been revealed a market for more varied and more organised recreations among the nation's urban dwellers. But until people found themselves with more spare cash to spend on their leisure interests, and with more time to enjoy them, the full potential for mass leisure would remain untapped.

The movement to secure more free time and better pay was perceptible from the early days of industrialisation, and the very harshness of industrial life triggered off demands, most strident in the textile industries, for amelioration. The consequent Factory Acts began a long and painfully slow process which gradually reduced the working week in industry. However, it took an uneven course and certain areas of economic activity (notably the non-industrial sectors) remained curiously immune. But by mid-century the idea was established that Saturday afternoon should normally be free from work. Legislation alone was not responsible, for trade unions were able, after protracted struggles, to secure voluntary agreements within their own industries. The overall result was that the emergence of the shorter working week and Saturday free from work was slow, fragmentary and uneven and did not reach the unskilled until the late years of the century. But it is revealing that when in 1897 the Webbs debated working hours in their book *Industrial Democracy*, they accepted eight hours as 'the Natural Day'.

The demographic context of these changes was crucial. The population was expanding rapidly and after 1851 a majority of the nation lived in urban areas. Indeed population growth was, in the words of Peter Mathias, 'the elemental fact which conditioned so much of English history in the nineteenth century'. A larger and growing labour force found itself with increasing amounts of spare time. With obvious exceptions – abundant and shocking in themselves – more and more working people found their free time no longer restricted to Sundays and the occasional local holiday. And it was the evolution of this leisure time which ultimately corroded the strength of the sabbatarian lobby and the religious resistance of influential people. By the third quarter of the century Saturday, not Sunday, was well on its way to becoming the natural and national day for leisure.

Free time in itself was not sufficient for enjoyment of many of the new leisure facilities, which were commercial and therefore costly. The mid-Victorians in search of recreations also needed money, and the conjunction of these two factors (both a consequence of major changes in the national economy) began to transform the face of English leisure. Many of those groups able to secure free time for themselves also improved their financial position. Skilled workers in particular, with powerful union backing, enhanced their earnings while maintaining their economic advantages over the unskilled. The overall picture however is confusing for although there was undoubted general material improvement for large groups of working people, England was renowned for the extent and depths of its urban degradation and poverty. This 'other England' notwithstanding, there was from the 1850s onwards marked improvement in the economic lot of substantial numbers of English people. Even some unskilled groups and rural workers were able to find better-paid work. There was, in general, according to Hobsbawm,

> a remarkable improvement in employment all round, and a large scale transfer of labour from worse- to better-paid jobs. This accounts largely for the general sense of improvement in living-standards and the lowering of social tensions during the golden years of the mid-Victorians, for the actual wage-rates of many classes of workers did not rise significantly.

One major indicator of the new economic potential was the rise in savings. At mid-century some 1½ million depositors saved through the Friendly Societies; by 1873 a similar number were active depositors in the Savings Bank and 1½ million in the new Post Office Bank; in both of these the majority of savers were working-class. Thus, by the mid-1870s the ability to save money had become a feature of working-class life; the virtues of thrift which had in the harsher times of the 1830s and 1840s been vital for survival were now, in changed economic circumstances, turned to more profitable ends. Spare money was no longer the monopoly of the upper classes (though obviously the scale was quite different) and this was a fact of major significance in the evolution of new recreations. 'Even in their pleasures [wrote Thomas Wright] those of the working classes who would enjoy them thoroughly must be provident, must "save up" for them – provide for their sunny as well as their rainy days.'

There were undeniably many millions of people who could only envy their better-off compatriots, and for whom a small deposit in the Post Office was as distant as ever. That long line of social investigators, from Henry Mayhew through to the First World War and beyond, present a picture of widespread and apparently immovable poverty in both town and country. Victorian cities clearly provided the most damning dossier of residual poverty, but the countryside too was a harsh habitat for an oppressed and generally silent labouring force whose routines in many respects remained unflinchingly severe. Similarly there were, in town and country, growing numbers of working people who lacked the benefits of union membership and who consistently missed the material improvements of other groups. Among the new clerical, office and shop workers, and women in the sweated trades low pay and excessive hours of work were commonplace. Even allowing for these facts, it is well to remember the words of Peter Mathias that 'an important feature of the half century before the outbreak of war in 1914 was the rise in the standards of material well-being enjoyed by the nation as a whole'.

The central feature of the transformation of English recreations in the last quarter of the century is that the new forms depended essentially on forms of consumer goods and services which in purely economic terms were functions of an expanding economy. The new leisure industries – sports, seaside towns, music halls, musical industries and travel – were both functions of material conditions and creators of employment. Increasingly heavily capitalised recreations, like other consumer industries, began to compete for income in the competitive world of advertising, for, like the new clothing, foodstuffs and chemical products, they were utterly dependent on the ability of the English people to pay for their pleasures. To a degree this had traditionally been true, though on a much smaller scale; the itinerant musician, juggler or beach performer was equally dependent on his audience for a livelihood. What began to change from mid-century onwards was that popular recreations bcame major industries.

Ironically, many of these major economic changes of which the emergence of leisure was but one, made themselves felt in an era frequently characterised by historians as 'the Great Depression'. For more than twenty years, from 1873 to 1896, the nation, in common with other advanced societies, seemed to wallow in a trough of business gloom and depression which, if nothing like the 1830s or 1840s, nonetheless severely hurt wide sections of the population. Within this depression however there were distinct areas of economic growth; local, regional or individual buoyancy is frequently present despite contradictory national trends. Though the heavy industries faltered, the new distributive businesses thrived; the 1,500 multiple stores of 1880 had grown to 11,645 by 1900 while the 217,000 people in commercial occupations in 1871 had expanded to 896,000 in 1911. There was a massive increase in consumer demand if only because of the expansion of population which in a quarter of a century added ten million people to the number of consumers of clothes, foods and services. In those same years there was a rise in the demand for better material conditions of life. It was a circular phenomenon, for the producers and distributors were busy disseminating the belief that their goods and services were indispensable to a better life. In some respects they were, but on the whole what was happening was a major commercial revolution, familiar to modern eyes. Manufacturers and businessmen encouraged (largely through advertisements) an addiction to goods and services previously unknown, convincing people that material goods once preserved for the rich were now within the reach of ordinary people. Many formerly rare and expensive items became commonplace, and foremost among them were the products of the leisure industries.

A rise in real wages in the last quarter of the century was the prime cause in the explosion in consumer spending and the related growth of consumer industries. But the consequences of this revolution went far beyond the field of economics; they were for example responsible for major changes in contemporary attitudes. People developed aspirations towards the new material benefits around them. By the turn of the century even the poor came to assume that they had a right to leisure and to enjoy in the varied delights of the new leisure industries; unfortunately many of these new amenities, though not expensive, were dependent on spare cash. The inability to afford such pleasures did not prevent the poor from believing that they had a right to enjoy them; leisure as a natural aspiration of life became a major feature of English society, as turn-of-the-century social investigators were surprised to discover. Booth's final survey of the London poor for example registered this major change in the attitudes. Among other things, it was noted that poorer people in the capital began to ask a new question of life. 'To "what shall we eat, what drink and wherewithall shall we be clothed?" must now be added the question, "How shall we be amused?"'

The aspiration towards pleasure was commonplace and ubiquitous but inevitably it was thwarted for many people by harsh economic realities. The other, darker side of urban England contrasted starkly with the proliferation of pleasurable activities elsewhere. General Booth of the Salvation Army told his readers that 'notwithstanding the cheapest rates and frequent excursions, there are multitudes of the poor who, year in and out, never get beyond the crowded city'. Nonetheless it is significant that one of his solutions to the problem was to suggest the establishment of 'Whitechapel-by-the-Sea' for the urban poor. Whenever money allowed, a trip to the seaside was an indispensable treat in the English summer. In York at the turn of the century, Rowntree had discovered that even among the local poor (his group D), a trip to the coast was common: 'During the August Bank Holiday week, working men from York crowd into Scarborough and many of those who do not take such an extended holiday avail themselves of cheap day and half-day excursions run by the North East Company.' Seaside trips of this kind were no longer exceptional, though easier and cheaper for working people in a railway town such as York. Contemporaries told Charles Booth in London that 'holiday making is spoken of as "one of the most remarkable changes in habit in the last ten years" and the statement is applicable to all classes.' Of course, economics alone are not a sufficient explanation for this phenomenon. It was a simple piece of legislation, the Bank Holiday Act of 1870 which was, unexpectedly, responsible for encouraging the growing national urge to rush to the seaside.

It is ironic that the legislation which established the now typical English holiday was intended for a specific group of working people. Its architect and proponent, Sir John Lubbock, had, on being elected to Parliament, declared his intention 'to secure some holidays and some shortening of hours for the most hardly worked classes of the community'. Lubbock had in mind, not the working classes, but those immediately above for, in his words, 'artisans do not need another holiday so much as others less fortunately situated. They have secured for themselves short (I do not say too short) hours and a weekly half-holiday. The so-called working man, in fact works less than almost any other class of the community.' Nowhere was this problem more acute than in the banks, one of the late century areas of expansion, whose employees were granted only Christmas Day and Good Friday free from work. It was primarily to secure an extra holiday for these people and others, to guarantee 'that no person shall be compelled to do anything on a Bank Holiday which he could not be compelled to do on Christmas Day or Good Friday', that Lubbock steered the Bank Holiday Act through Parliament, its passage eased by the deceptive title. Lubbock later admitted that 'if we had called our Bill the "General Holiday Bill" or the "National Holiday Bill", I doubt not that it would have been opposed.' Its success was immediate and profound, and its greatest breakthrough was to secure for the armies of clerks, shop and office workers a day at the height of the summer when they could enjoy a break from the work.

The collapse of the pre-industrial holiday calendar was particularly acute for those tens of thousands of commercially based workers who, lacking the union strength of workers in heavy industries, found themselves in the years before Lubbock's Act, denied any substantial holidays from work. Yet historians of the nineteenth century, so often concentrating on the struggles of organised labour, particularly in the heavy industries, have frequently distorted the picture of life and labour in Victorian England by overlooking the travails of other working people, no less distressed for having upward aspirations, whose lack of formal organisations has made them less conspicuous in the documentation. It is worth remembering that the struggle for the half-day holiday for shopworkers continued up to the First World War. Clearly the struggle for leisure time cannot be measured solely in terms of legislation or in the victories of organised labour. For many of the unorganised labour force, the bank holiday was to prove a godsend.

The timing of Lubbock's Act was fortuitous for working people drawn into the new commercial enterprises. For those women who did not enter into service (an occupation which in many respects entailed the most exploitive of working conditions) there were now a number of attractive alternatives. To a degree the decline in both domestic service and (for men) agricultural work, was partly a function of the proliferation of other forms of employment. It was noted in 1902 that 'the young girl of today prefers to become a Board School Mistress, a post-office clerk, a type-writer, a shop-girl or a worker in a factory – anything rather than enter into domestic service.' Such openings proliferated.

'Specialised multiple grocers like Liptons or Home and Colonial, shops like Freeman Hardy and Willis, chemists like Boots (with 150 shops by 1900), tailors like Hepworths, newspaper and book shops like W. H. Smith and scores of others transformed the retail trade.' This retail revolution created vast numbers of jobs and, equally important, often provided a different style of work. In many cases such jobs required skills and qualities which (excepting service) had rarely been demanded of working people; neat appearance, clean clothes, 'civility' in manners, and frequently an ability to read and write. It was a sign of the times that these qualities were to be found in abundance, as more and more people were able to secure for their children 'respectable' jobs which they themselves could never have hoped for. To suggest that in adopting the style and attributes necessary for those posts working people were somehow conceding to bourgeois values is both to ignore and to insult the individual and collective virtues which were common in working-class life throughout the century. The suggestion that the working-class striving for domestic and occupational respectability was an attempt to ape the virtues of their betters, remains one of the most durable of historical condescensions bequeathed by historians to people they fail to comprehend.

Aspirations towards a better and more varied life, for one's children if not for oneself, became a notable feature of English social life in the late years of the century. To a large extent such aspirations were self-generating for, as opportunities for fun or work increased so people came to expect more of the world around them. Ultimately, however, much depended on purchasing power and it is at this point that we return to the problem of wages. Eric Hobsbawm has shown that average real wages rose by about 40 per cent between 1860 and 1875. Thereafter, with the exception of a few years in the late 1870s, they climbed until by 1900 they were one-third above the 1875 level. 'Probably the most rapid general improvement in the condition of the 19th century worker took place in the years 1880–95', largely because of the fall in basic living costs (which benefited poor as well as better-off). New goods, led by foreign meats and fruits, began to transform the diet of the English lower orders, just as the range of consumer goods, of which the new foodstuffs were part, transformed social life. There was an unmistakable rise in the expectations of daily life, expectations which no longer stopped short at mere self-sufficiency but which insisted upon new qualities of range and variety. And it was into this world of rising expectations that the new forms of mass leisure were able to intrude and bring a variety and degree of collective enjoyment which had, until recently, been the unquestioned preserve of the upper classes.

This picture of rising expectations and standards in the last quarter of the century seems utterly inconsistent with the image – and reality – of the other England: the poverty-stricken layers of upwards of one-third of the population, entombed at the bottom of the social hierarchy, to whom the improvements around them must have seemed all the more offensive in lying beyond their reach. Even among working people who enjoyed material improvements, the unavoidable pitfalls of old age, sickness, under-employment and total unemployment and large families could wipe out their material gains, sometimes literally overnight. Charles Booth, more aware than most of the precariousness of material security, wrote in 1894: 'On the whole people are poor because they are old.' And among the irredeemably poor, the wretchedness of daily life was both a stark and a mocking contrast to the improvements they could see around them. The diet, housing, health and in consequence the physical features of the English poor seemed to be resistant to the wider forces of amelioration. For these people, the rise of the new consumer industries must have merely compounded their sense of frustration, for their deprivation increased relative to their contemporaries' improvements.

On rare occasions when material benefits came the way of the poor, they did so, as they had throughout the century, by the charitable efforts of local churches, Sunday schools and philanthropists. In this way many poor children first saw the sea or were led into the countryside. Robert Roberts, recalling his own Salford childhood, remembered that 'one scrimped and saved to get a new piece of oil-cloth, a rag rug, a day at Southport, a pair of framed pictures'. Even then it tended to be 'our top people [who] paid annual visits to Blackpool, New Brighton and Southport'. The picture we are left with seems strange and contradictory, yet the contradictions can be resolved by remembering that urban poverty and rising expectations of life and leisure were not incompatible, but in fact existed side by side in uncomfortable and ill-fitting partnership.

No particular form of mass leisure activity was typically a function of the changing nature of late century consumer power, but one above all others came to exemplify the growing national insistence on having a good time. The excursion trip, best of all to the seaside and particularly on a bank holiday, was, from the 1870s, seen to be the indicator of the national urge for leisure. Lubbock's Act tapped the enormous and growing potential for mass leisure which, until then had remained largely dormant. On that first August bank holiday the English people set out to enjoy themselves on a collective scale, and to a degree which not even the startled supporters of Lubbock's Act had foreseen. The national scenes of mass migrations of people by train, steamer and on foot were unprecedented, and while they would be familiar to a modern observer, they took contemporaries completely by surprise. *The Times* reported that

> . . . cyclists of both sexes covered the roads. River steamers and pleasure boats carried their thousands to Kew and the upper reaches of the Thames. The London parks were crowded. The Botanic Gardens and Zoological Gardens formed great attractions, and the flowers of Battersea Park drew large crowds all day. The India and Ceylon Exhibition was visited by an enormous crowd.

But it was the railways which took the full weight of the holiday-makers, to the concern and amazement of the generally unprepared railway officials. 'From 8 a.m. the cry at every railway station was "Still they come".' Despite rushed extra trains, from many stations 'it was simply impossible to get to the seaside'. Nor was this first bank holiday a fluke, a temporary bolt for the fresh air; as the years passed the numbers involved increased, partly because the population increased, but also because more people could afford to travel by train on their bank holiday break. In succeeding years the railway companies, and the public gardens, parks, zoos, rivers and seaside resorts braced themselves for the expected hordes. Within twenty years of its inauguration the August bank holiday saw 500,000 people leave London for the coast and country, while some 360,000 visited the capitals and parks. A clergyman at Hackney reported to Booth that 'the district is almost deserted on Bank Holiday. The women go off as well as the men.' Moreover there was a natural tendency for work-people to extend the Bank Holiday simply by staying away from work. 'It is useless [moaned one employer] to open the works on the day after Bank Holiday, for two days.'

The three decades following the introduction of bank holidays saw the establishment of many major forms of mass organised leisure which were to last well into the twentieth century. The very concept of the bank holiday itself was a significant step forward in the provision of a national and legally determined leisure time for all. This was not the only provision for leisure time (most of which was secured by industrial agitation and local custom), but the importance of the Bank Holiday Act was that it secured free time even for those without the collective and industrial muscle to insist on it. It was of great importance that Parliament had intervened to safeguard free time for the people as a whole and, while it could be argued that the Act offered only the briefest of respites from work, it was nonetheless a major innovation in establishing the principle that the state had a role to play in safeguarding free time. Again, such a fact seems unexceptional today. A century ago however it constituted a major step forward for a society which had, since the onset of industrialisation, been more concerned to exact rigorous working conditions than it had to safeguard leisure time.

The significance of the Bank Holiday Act was further enhanced by the changing economic fortunes of the nation's growing population. As urbanisation progressed (by 1911 some 80 per cent of the 40 million people lived in towns) and the cities themselves became increasingly complex, it became apparent to growing numbers of people, in national and local government, in positions of industrial authority and of course among those forced to live in the Victorian city, that more provision would have to be made for leisure. There was no doubt of the national potential (and desire) for leisure, best evidenced by the annual bank holiday rush to the coast and country. Apparently there was no longer a problem about the nation's ability to pay for its pleasures. At times it must have seemed that any capital investment in leisure facilities would reap a rich return, as financiers and entrepreneurs, often local men but also drawn from metropolitan circles of finance, stumbled over each other to give the public what they wanted. Public tastes inevitably varied, ranging from the isolationism of the English aristocracy who, always anxious to copy their monarch, constructed Gothic retreats (preferably in the Highlands), to the more crowded delights of seaside places at Blackpool or Scarborough. However different in kind and cost, these pleasures belonged to the same overall pattern which saw the English people with growing amounts of money to spend on more than the mere essentials of life. Individually working people had very little to spend, but collectively their funds added up to capital sums of major significance. This plebeian consumer power was reflected in the sums deposited in late nineteenth-century working-class banks and in the fortunes made in providing for working-class pleasures. Of all those pleasures few were so striking or so characteristically English as the summertime rush to the sea.

6 Down to the sea in droves

The English seaside resorts reached the peak of their popularity in the years 1870–1914, though they traced their roots back to the much more traditional cult of 'taking the waters'. Drinking and immersing oneself in natural spring waters had, since antiquity been common throughout Europe at sites wherever geography yielded unusual water supplies. In the sixteenth and seventeenth centuries the spas were given an added boost by the suggestions of contemporary science that mineral waters possessed a range of medicinal virtues. The consequent growth of the spa towns was encouraged by fashionable and medical usage, but more especially by royal and aristocratic patronage. And by the mid-seventeenth century it was impossible to distinguish the sick from the merely fashionable visitor. 'We pass our time awaye [wrote Sir Edmund Verney in Bath in 1635] as merrily as paine will give us leave.' Bath above all others exemplified the elegance and style of a fashionable spa town, yet even at the height of its fame a publication by Dr Richard Russell was to lay the foundations of a revolutionary change in the custom of taking the waters. Russell's tract *De tabe Glandulari* suggested that sea water possessed the clinical virtues traditionally associated with spa waters and though it is true that others had advocated the benefits of cold water bathing, it was Russell's move to practise his theories in the small Sussex village of Brighthelmstone (Brighton), which pointed the way to the shift to the coast.

Wealthy patrons of the spas began to switch their fashionable allegiance from the inland spas to the embryonic spas-by-the-sea on the south coast and along the Thames estuary, a process which hastened both the urban development of the towns involved and of communications from London. In Scarborough a fully-developed spa on the edge of the sea was already in existence, for in the seventeenth century a natural spring had been discovered there. Scarborough catered largely for fashionable society of the north, but was in essence a seaside resort catering for the whims and recreations of its wealthy patrons with bathing, horse-racing on the sands, gaming rooms, theatres, balls, masques, circulating library and assembly rooms. But it was noticeable that by the late eighteenth century, when weather permitted, it was the beach and the water's edge which had become the focus for visiting society.

In the south, the evolution of the new seaside towns – Weymouth, Hastings, Folkestone, Southend, Margate, Lyme Regis and Brighton – was greatly helped by royal patronage, particularly in the case of Brighton where the Prince of Wales, later George IV, set his personal style both on local society and, more lastingly, on the architectural face of the town. All the new towns were similarly influenced by the legacy of the spa towns in the architectural style and recreational facilities they offered. Indeed the seaside towns soon became replicas of the spas, offering familiar facilities in a different, seaside setting, and with a changed medical inspiration. Among the new social fads was the rapid development of sea bathing, regulated by medical advice and fashionable dictates, which generally took place from the steps of bathing machines with the help and encouragement of 'dippers'. There was a great deal of nude bathing, and extensive commentary on it by cartoonists, journalists and outraged opinion. But the dramatic growth of the towns themselves which remains their most startling feature. Brighton's population was a mere 2,000 in 1760; by 1801 it stood at 7,000, growing to 12,000 in 1811 and doubling again in the next decade.

This development of the seaside towns continued as the century progressed – hastened of course by the arrival of the railways – to the point where the main resorts had become substantial urban areas in their own right. Compared to the inland industrial areas, the resorts seemed a triumph for good order and taste; of course to a large degree this was because they originally catered for those classes which expected more than the mere basics of life. The resorts, like the spas, were designed for the leisured classes of the aristocracy and emergent middle classes for whom style and elegance were a way of life, and the surviving maps and prints reveal the degree to which the physical face of early nineteenth-century seaside towns was shaped by those pre-requisites. It was to be a startling contrast to the seaside growth of the late century.

Those who visited the early nineteenth-century resorts were, in general, the privileged – those anxious to imitate royalty and the upper reaches of society – and those able to afford the costly time-consuming and bone-aching journeys to the coast for long periods in the summer season. Apart from local people, few poorer visitors went to the resorts, but as transportation improved a visit to the coast became the natural aspiration of many of the rising middle class, personified by Dickens's Tuggs family, keen to use their newfound wealth to promote their social rise. From an early date there were clear social distinctions between resorts, and much of the social tone was established by an indefinable combination of clientele and the determination of local landowners not to allow their property to stray into the 'wrong' hands. One major factor in the lowering of the social tone of those resorts along the Thames estuary – never as fashionable as the Sussex coast – was the ease of access. Long before the railways began to carry their passengers from the cities to the coast, the boats (steam after 1815) cheapened and quickened the journey from London down the river. In 1831, in the season, 2,000 people travelled each day from London to Margate whose trade 'is almost entirely connected with the resort of visitors'.

Seaside resorts set out on the whole to appeal to the nation's better-off groups. Even Blackpool, a small remote spot on the Lancashire coast, hoped to attract a superior clientele. In 1785 a local proprietor informed the 'Gentry and Public' 'that he has completely furnished and fitted up a commodious genteel house in an eligible situation and that he hopes by his accommodation to merit the encouragement of such ladies and gentlemen as may be pleased to favour him with their company'. Clearly the local well-to-do could afford to stay in these early Blackpool hotels, but the growing habit of visiting the seaside had spread even to the poor. In 1813 Richard Ayton found in Blackpool 'crowds of poor people from manufacturing towns, who have a high opinion of the efficiency of bathing, maintaining that in the months of August and September there is physic in the sea – physic of a most comprehensive description'.

Transport was a problem, however, and poor visitors generally had to travel to the coast on foot or, if lucky, by cart, and even then only on the infrequent days free from work. 'Most of them [said Ayton] come hither in carts, but some will walk on a single day from Manchester, distant more than 40 miles.' Blackpool and other Lancashire seaside towns were within reach of a number of developing industrial towns and they consequently attracted large August crowds 'of visitors of various classes' even before the advent of the railways.

Railways, with their apparently unlimited potential, dazzled the early Victorians. Dr A. B. Granville, an early historian of the resorts, wrote that 'to afford cheap and speedy means of travelling for the people, is to induce people to travel who would otherwise have staid [sic] at home'. Many of course headed for the coast, and the resorts were among the first to feel the full brunt of the railways when the trains began to deposit their unprecedented hordes close to the water's edge. It was soon appreciated that there was a major market for the low income groups, best illustrated by the success of the early excursions. Throughout the 1840s, the trains bore vast crowds of passengers on day trips to their nearest seaside town. At Whitweek 1850, more than 200,000 people left Manchester by train. And the greatest impact of these numbers fell on the resorts. 'Unless immediate steps are taken [wrote the *Preston Pilot* in 1851], Blackpool as a resort for respectable visitors will be ruined. . . . Unless the cheap trains are discontinued or some effective regulation made for the management of the thousands who visit the place, Blackpool property will be depreciated past recovery.'

Much the same story was repeated whenever a new railway line forged a link between a major city and the coast. Royalty learned the lesson and soon after the arrival of the first trains at Brighton in 1841 the royal family took themselves off to more isolated, and therefore socially exclusive, retreats. The trains also enhanced Brighton's attractions as a residential area and in the decade after the opening of the railways housebuilding in the town increased fivefold, but the town's greatest attraction was for day-trippers from London. Brighton became the 'lungs of the capital' and in 1851 it was noted that 'on holiday occasions, in fine weather, there seldom arrives fewer than 5,000 visitors in the London trains. The number of passengers in one week in May 1850 was upwards of 73,000'. It was above all else the 1851 Great Exhibition which confirmed the significance and importance of the excursion trains.

The debate which always preceded the decision to build or resist a railway line to a resort was generally couched in economic terms but, inevitably perhaps, social considerations were often uppermost. Opponents in Scarborough, for example, had 'no wish for a greater influx of vagrants, and those who have no money to spend'. Much the same complaint was heard a few years later in the new resort of Morecambe, where there was opposition to 'birds of passage whose residence does not extend over more than 2 or 3 days'. As the century advanced it became clear that the visitors, even the trippers, did indeed have money to spend (even if only in small amounts) and it was to cater for this expanding consumer power that entrepreneurial guile and financial initiative began in the last quarter of the century to create new forms of leisure for poorer visitors. Initially, though, the resorts were developed not to cater for the tastes of low-income visitors, but for the more refined and more expensive leisures of the more prosperous who tended to stay for lengthy periods. Thus the development of many resorts, with their hotels, residential facilities, public amenities and fashionable recreations, was aimed at wealthier patrons and, increasingly, prosperous inhabitants. Seaside resorts became desirable places to live in, more especially after the railways enabled businessmen to commute to nearby industrial towns.

New resorts sprang up where nothing had existed before the railways; small villages mushroomed into major towns and even the old well-established resorts of the late eighteenth century found themselves transformed by the railways. There were however unmistakable social differences between, and even within, the resorts, long before the emergence of the distinctively plebeian resorts of the later years of the century. One commentator in 1860 thought Margate 'low, *bourgeois*', satisfactory 'if you are a tired Londoner, not too dignified or distingue'. Ramsgate was even worse, attracting visitors who 'seem to have no more sense of decency than so many South-Sea Islanders'. By contrast, Brighton remained 'that queen of the sea-coast towns', despite having been 'converted into a marine suburb of

London by the iron rail'. In the third quarter of the century, many people felt that the resorts would be able to bring together English people of all social classes in the search for pleasure and good health, in a unique display of collective enjoyment which seemed to cross class lines. This, however, was not to be and a subtle process was already at work at many levels, segregating the English at play as at work.

Distance was the most important limitation on day trips and it was no accident that popular excursions into the West Country came late. When the railways for instance were opened to Torquay in 1848 they were followed not by excursionists but by retired and professional people in search of rest and good health. Much the same story was true of Bournemouth, which had to wait until 1870 for its railway line. Yet although it was true that the excursionists created most *éclat* on a few days each year, it was the establishment and spread of extensive seaside holidays among the more prosperous which characterised the resorts in the years 1850–75.

By the 1860s manufacturers and retailers were directing numerous new products towards the seaside market. Seaside and yachting jackets could be bought from Peter Robinson; D. Nichol of Regent Street advertised Promenade Costumes. In 1867 the Great Shawl and Cloak Emporium announced the Atlantic Yachting Suit, a 'very desirable and pretty suit for seaside wear'. Among those able to afford such clothes and to enjoy extended summer holidays by the sea, the resorts came to have added attractions, for by the 1860s the medical establishment were actively promoting the benefits of life by the sea, though now for quite different reasons. Dr Richard Russell had recommended the sea for good health; a century later doctors were advocating the benefits of sea air. 'In short [said Dr Thomson in 1860], sea air is eminently possessed of those properties which tend to stimulate, and to give a healthy character to the blood, and through it . . . to the entire bodily system.' This growing obsession with the air was in large measure a result of the Victorian concern with pulmonary complaints, particularly tuberculosis which killed one English person in six. Like poverty itself, TB hit the distressed most severely, but it was no respecter of class; the knowledge that it was primarily an urban disease encouraged those who were able, to migrate, often on a permanent basis, to the coast. Throughout the nineteenth century, TB remained a major scourge, and from the mid-century onwards medical opinion turned to the idea that fresh air, by the sea or, if possible, in the mountains, could bring relief, if not necessarily cure. Consequently the sick joined the retired and the elderly beside the seaside, and although the phenomenon of whole towns given over to the aged and sick is much more recent, the pattern was clear in the second half of the nineteenth century. Thus the new English seaside town attracted not merely those in search of leisure for a single day but also more prosperous visitors and residents seeking relief, peace and sometimes better health. 'The restorative properties of the sea have long been fully appreciated [wrote Dr Yeo in 1882], although regular and periodical migrations to the seashore is the custom of modern origin.'

The outcome was that the seaside developed an attraction (resistible only by the very poor) for all classes of English society. To working people with time and money it afforded a welcome, pleasurable, though all-too-brief escape for a day or two from an unhealthy industrial atmosphere. For the middle classes and their superiors it provided either a suburb-by-the-sea or a peaceful retreat into retirement and, with luck, better health. There was also a multitude of attractions, increasing all the time, even before the commercialisation of the more popular resorts. For the middle classes there was, by mid-century the fascination of marine biology and conchology, propagated largely by the works of Philip Henry Gosse whose books on those subjects sold in great numbers among interested middle-class readers. Best remembered perhaps by Charles Kingsley's *Water Babies*, the mid-Victorian preoccupation with marine biology led to a massive upsurge in related publications, both popular and scholarly, and a growth in the popularity of domestic and public aquaria, and of course in the collecting and exploratory habits of well-to-do visitors to the coast. Victorians paddled in their thousands, wading through rock pools and along beaches, in search of shells and weeds (which themselves became a small seaside cottage industry).

The physical face of seaside England changed dramatically from mid-century: a combination of urban development, expanding population and the slow but gradual submerging of mile after mile of natural coastline beneath deposits of promenades, streets, houses and hotels. Among the most striking features was the proliferation of piers, initially designed to cope with steam and paddle steamers, but later built as attractions in their own right. When in 1861 a group of Blackpool businessmen met to discuss provision for 'greater promenading space of the most invigorating kind', it was agreed to erect 'a substantial and safe means for the visitors to walk over the sea at a distance of thirteen hundred and fifty feet at high water'. The piers, like so many of the other seaside attractions, were functions of the Victorian iron age and it was fitting that the first one should have been opened at Brighton in 1823. There and at Southend the piers rapidly established their economic utility, particularly as landing stages. But by mid-century the piers had developed even greater commercial appeal; as they became attractive in their own right the heavy capital investment involved was more than amply rewarded by the returns. Some 10,000 people paid to walk on Brighton's West Pier on one Sunday alone; in 1875 more than 600,000 had paid at the turnstiles. There was in the last quarter of the century a veritable pier-building mania, and of the fifty-four which survive to this day, thirty-three were constructed in the years 1875–1910. Gradually their style changed from the starkly functional to the ornate and often over-elaborate, as more and more commercial attractions were heaped on the basic structure. Booths, machines, mechanical devices, theatres and conveyances were added to the piers which were, essentially, miniature pleasure-lands jutting out to sea. Offering such an array of attractions it was hardly surprising that they seduced ever more of the trippers, who headed for the pier as surely as they headed for the beach.

Slowly the major resorts, attracting the greatest numbers of trippers, became pleasure centres capable of offering the long-stay or casual visitor much more than the once simple pleasures of beach and sea. Indeed the resorts registered, in an acute and specific form, the commercialisation of English leisure which was so noticeable throughout the country in the last years of the century. Theatres, music-halls, swimming pools, zoos, gardens and parks, illuminations and funfairs – these and other attractions sprang up in clusters as the local (and outside) financiers sought to capitalise on the obvious collective wealth of the seaside visitor. At Rhyl, a town virtually created (like Las Vegas) by the railways, the Winter Gardens were opened in 1876, embracing a zoo, bear pit, theatre, seal pond and skating rink. In 1902 when the local Queen's Palace was opened, the entertainments were even more lavish: along with the zoo there was a ballroom for 2,000 couples, and an imitation underground Venice with gondolas. Similar, and often bizarre, developments could be seen throughout the expanding resorts of seaside England.

Music was perhaps the most inescapable of artificial seaside sounds, as visitors had noticed and complained about since early in the century. Musicians, from the excellent to the execrable flocked to the summer resorts, few of which were without their own collection of bands, orchestras, groups and, less formally, itinerant and often irritating players who haunted the beaches and streets in search of a living. Best remembered were the Nigger ministrels who appeared on summer beaches from mid-century and were soon accepted as 'kings of the Beach, the Promenade and the Pier'. Their charm, much of it directed at the children, was a basic family appeal, and their songs and music swiftly entered the nation's collective memory. From the 1890s onwards, however, they faced increasingly stiff opposition from the pierrots who, by the end of the century had become more popular than the minstrels. Clifford Essex, the man who launched the pierrot cult in 1891 did so for overtly commercial reasons, and very soon the pierrots, like other travelling groups of artistes, fell under the control of agents, managers and strings of companies. It was clear that considerable 'showbiz' fortunes could be made simply by catering for people's pleasures beside the seaside.

Theatres and theatre chains proliferated around the coast as investors sank their money in the lucrative world of seaside entertainment. Businessmen from the major cities pumped their funds into the resorts. In 1886, for example, William Broadhead, a Manchester builder, bought Blackpool's Prince of Wales baths, converting them into a theatre and swimming pool. At his death Broadhead owned ten theatres, and his descendants added a further eight. The growth of the seaside entertainment industry was only a part of a much wider theatrical development which saw theatres and music halls spring up in towns and cities across the country, but it is significant that investors thought it worth while to invest considerable sums in seaside theatres which were, in general, only open for four months in the year. Seaside theatres were used much more intensively than their counterparts in the cities; their clientele could after all devote their full time to the pursuit of pleasure. For sixpence the visitor to Scarborough could spend the entire day, from 9 a.m. to 11 p.m., in the local 'People's Palace and Aquarium' and enjoy an endless stream of entertainment. Not all resorts could offer comparable delights, but the better-endowed were able to compound their attractions by providing such treats for the visitors.

Towards the end of the century seaside attractions became bigger and more elaborate (and thus more expensive), often influenced by American and European developments. Blackpool's famous Tower, opened in 1894, was an imitation of the better-known one in Paris. Two years later it was joined by a shortlived 'giant wheel', a copy of the Earl's Court wheel of 1895. Late Victorians seemed unduly impressed by the mechanical marvels of fun made possible by advances in technology and engineering. Roller coasters began to appear, a direct import from the highly successful American leisure industries. At Brighton 'Volk's electric railway', a hybrid between an elevated pier and a tram, trundled through the sea. Indeed the new 'pleasure beaches' which began life, as their name suggests, on the beaches, were influenced by American prototypes, but were more directly dependent on advances in mechanised and electrical power. Electric lighting itself became a major attraction, later enshrined in seaside illuminations, bringing light to piers, promenades and musical gardens, and extending the long summer days well into the night. It was, even at this mundane level, such a sharp contrast to the ill-lit cities of the interior. Electric trams and trolley buses, trains running along the piers, magic lanterns and later films – all these offered the seaside visitor an unusual array of pleasures. All these changes could be found in most of the country's major urban areas but, with the exception of London's West End, few places could hope to offer such a collection of up-to-the-minute attractions throughout the waking hours and even into the night.

Technical changes went hand in hand with shifts in social attitudes to enhance further the national desire for leisure and to increase the provision of cheap and readily obtainable mass pleasures. Seaside towns were obviously not alone in witnessing a remarkable upsurge in popularity in the last twenty years of the century, but resorts, more than any other particular form of entertainment, exemplified the widening commercialisation of leisure and the growing in popular demand for it. The bicycle craze of the 1890s illustrated this pattern perfectly and gave the impression that leisure was undergoing a rapid process of democratisation. Bikes appeared in their tens of thousands throughout the country, and although it is true that mass production led to a sharp fall in prices, they nonetheless remained beyond the pockets of ordinary working people. At the seaside however, the visitor could hire a bike, if only for a short ride or for an hour. Once again, the resorts were able to make available to the poorer visitors a range of material goods, experiences and delight which were generally preserved for their betters. The resorts undoubtedly democratised leisure by providing cheap and widely available amenities; they rented out collective pleasure and entertainment to people who craved for it yet who could afford it only for a moment. For a penny the curious tripper could even enter the world of the upper classes by courtesy of the 'What the Butler Saw' machines which came to dot the piers and promenades. Perhaps the most important technical innovation however was the evolution of cheap photography (itself a growth industry), enabling the visitor to return home with a visual record of an important day by the sea. Indeed some of the best evidence for the social history of the resorts between the 1880s and 1914 can be found in the collections of seaside photographs.

There are innumerable signs of the rapid commercialisation of English leisure, of seaside leisure in particular, but not all of it is immediately obvious. Some of its most telling manifestations are goods which the casual observer would so take for granted as to overlook their significance. Manufacturers for example thought it worth while to produce buckets and spades for children's play on the beach. Publishers issued books and magazines for children and women, specifically for seaside reading. But to a large extent, when the weather was good, the greatest pleasure was to be had in the simple delights of spending hours on the beach, and it is clear that families of all social stations enjoyed this to the full, though they were normally segregated by a complexity of factors into different 'zones' within the resort, or into socially distinct resorts. Arguably the most striking feature of the late-Victorian resorts was the degree to which they offered family-based entertainment for all social classes. Apart from the beach (and church) Victorians tended to enjoy themselves in groups divided by sexual and age differences, but the beach was the place for all the family together.

Beach life seemed relatively cheap and simple, though for the excursionist it had to be close to a railway station. But even at the water's edge a variety of beach entertainers crowded on the visitors for money. Punch and Judy shows, the donkeys (now licensed by local authorities worried about public 'nuisances'), itinerant musicians, hawkers, food-sellers, boatmen and, of course, the hirers of changing huts. Seaside towns were inevitably forced to regulate the activities on their beaches. In 1897 Blackpool began to license beach traders, originally authorising only donkeys, bathing vans and boats, but after the resultant outcry they also sanctioned 'Ventriloquists, Niggers, Punch and Judy, Camels, Ice Cream, Ginger Beer, Blackpool Rock, Sweets in Baskets and Oyster Sellers'. But there were to be no 'Phrenologists, "Quack Doctors", Palmists, Mock Auctions and Cheap Jacks'. Even the poorest visitor, however, could enjoy the simple delights of a day on the beach, weather permitting. Paddling appealed to everyone, as contemporary photographs show, but swimming was generally a more cumbersome and sometimes expensive hobby. Municipal pools, the exploits of Captain Webb in 1875, and the encouragement of swimming in the new schools had together helped to enhance the national interest in swimming. But appropriate costumes were expensive, although manufacturers were currently offering more streamlined costumes, designed both to help swimming and to reveal more of the swimmer's body. Beaches were often segregated for swimming and there was a great deal of nude swimming, much to the continuing outrage of contemporaries. The growing insistence on wearing bathing costumes, often enforced by local legislation, gradually led to the evolution of mixed bathing beaches (though such rules and regulations could scarcely apply to the more isolated beaches).

Victorians were endlessly commenting on nude bathing and the need to control it, though some took a contrary view. The Rev. Francis Kilvert complained in 1874 that 'at Shanklin one has to adopt the detestable custom of bathing in drawers. If ladies don't like to see men naked why don't they keep away from the sight? His concern was not perhaps utterly altruistic and in the following year that frustrated gentlemen, whose diary records the tensions and anxiety of frustrated Victorian sexuality, recorded:

> One beautiful girl stood entirely naked on the sand, and there as
> she sat, half reclined sideways, leaning upon her elbow with her
> knee bent and her legs and feet partly drawn back and up, she
> was a model for a sculptor, there was the supple tender waist,
> the gentle dawn and tender swell of the bosom and the budding
> breasts, the graceful rounding of the delicately beautiful limbs
> and above all the soft exquisite curves of the rosy dimpled
> bottom and broad white thighs.

Not everyone professed to relish such sights however, especially since most nude bathing tended to be male. From Torquay, William Miller complained in 1888 that 'a number of working men (it was Saturday afternoon) whisked off their clothes at the wall on the beach and ran like savages to the water'. Miller complained of female voyeurs at Bournemouth and about female costumes at Yarmouth, while at Ramsgate the sea 'was filled with a heap of mingled pale-faced and rosy nymphs in scanty and dripping attire, and all sorts of little cockneys . . . sans gloves, sans well-brushed hat, sans slender silk umbrella, and sans almost everything'. By the outbreak of the First World War however mixed bathing had become commonplace; in August 1914, for example, *Punch* reported from the Isle of Wight that 'men, women and children have been swimming and splashing joyfully in a most mixed manner'.

One of the most notable innovations of Edwardian England, motor transport, despite its crudity and limitations, had begun to alter certain patterns of leisure before the outbreak of war. Growing numbers of visitors to the resorts took to the roads instead of the trains though the full revolution in road transport had to wait until after 1918. For the wealthy the motor car enabled them to escape from the middle and lower reaches of society more quickly and effectively than previously. It had always been common for the upper classes to leave a resort when it was infiltrated by their social inferiors, and the motor car gave them a perfect means of escape to country retreats and parts of the Continent yet untouched by the trainborne hordes. Despite the obvious trends, there were pious Edwardians who believed that the holidays brought English classes closer together. 'And even if the lower, middle and upper classes fail to mingle freely, they are, at least, brought closer together, and made better acquainted with each other's nature and character. In fact the entire holiday movement tends towards the same increase of knowledge, the same better under-standings, the same realisation of one another's virtues.' The over-whelming bulk of contemporary evidence suggests quite the opposite: at play beside the seaside, as at home, Englishmen were quite sharply divided. Yet this simple statement hides a complex phenomenon for in origin and early development the history of the seaside resorts seemed to augur well; seemed a perfect means of bringing different classes together in the pursuit of common enjoyments. Ultimately however the seaside holiday merely followed economic lines; those with more money and time expected and could afford different residential and recreational facilities beside the sea. If the excursionists proved too numerous, too noisy or too close, the well-to-do simply distanced themselves from the crowds – going to Hove instead of Brighton, Lytham instead of Blackpool, Scarborough south shore rather than the centre of town. Despite the superficial similarities between resorts, they were in fact remarkably different from each other. One only has to visit those resorts today to see the fundamental, qualitative differences. And the major distinction, as Harold Perkin has shown, took the form of nuances of social tone. From an early date and even when close together, English resorts were easily distinguished by their different social tone.

The most important restraint on popular visits to the seaside was, inevitably, financial. Edwardian gentlemen could afford to pack off the families to the seaside for the whole summer period. Osbert Lancaster remembered that 'each summer at the beginning of August

I was sent with my nurse to an admirable boarding-house kept by an old governess of my father's at Littlehampton, where in due course I was joined by my parents'. Working-class visitors had, by and large, to rest content with a day trip. To make matters worse, in the years immediately before the 1914–18 war the British economy began to stall (this was reflected in the rise in union membership and militancy), and wide sections of workers found their wages inadequate for all but life's essentials, and sometimes not even for those. Even regular employment was not in itself a sufficient guarantee of the enjoyment of holidays. Above all, the ability to save was crucial and although most industries provided guaranteed breaks from work, few offered holidays with pay. By the early years of the twentieth century, however, the concept of holidays with pay had become a common union demand and was to be found as an increasingly common concession offered by management. Union adoption of holidays with pay is extremely revealing and constitutes no less than a *volte-face* by organised labour which had, on the whole, doggedly resisted the idea of paid holidays. By the early twentieth century, however, so common had holiday-taking become that it was appreciated that working people had a right both to time off work and to adequate finances to enjoy it. The direction towards holidays with pay was pioneered in the last twenty years of the old century by a number of private paternal firms who came to appreciate the potential benefits to be gained from paid holidays. One prominent company noted that: 'It was always desired that a man should go away from home for his holiday, in order to get a thorough change. Yet it appeared that in a very few cases did he do so, and enquiries elicited the statement that he could not afford to go away and take the family, and that if he went away alone he left very little money for the housekeeping.'

The numbers of firms providing holidays with pay steadily grew, though usually linked to an insistence on prompt and regular attendance throughout the rest of the working year. Sometimes the holidays were financed by special funds of company shares. The Manchester engineers Mather and Platt set up £10,000 of company shares for one such scheme. 'It has occurred to me [wrote the chairman in 1910] that the annual holiday might be thoroughly enjoyed as a means of healthy recreation out of town.' With the help of the new fund it was hoped that it would henceforth 'be easier for wife and family to share in a husband's recreation in the summer holiday'. This and other schemes proved highly successful, so much that the Trades Union Congress itself resolved in 1911 to press for holidays with pay for all workers. Although it is true that the main thrust of union activity before 1914 continued to be the basic demands for regular work and better pay and conditions, it is nonetheless the case that the establishment of holidays with pay as a plank of official TUC policy marked the coming of age of a new attitude towards working-class leisure. It was no longer thought adequate merely to secure free time;

leisure time should also be financed. The struggle for general holidays with pay was however to be prolonged, interrupted by the more pressing considerations of war, and later by slump and depression. Even when the long-sought-after legislation was finally enacted in 1938 yet another war delayed its effective implementation until the late 1940s.

On the eve of the First World War those working people who wanted to visit the seaside had in general only one way of financing their trip, namely by saving for it from their scarce spare cash. Of course working people were unevenly divided in their ability to do this. The young and uncommitted, if in regular work, were in a better position than married workmates with large families to support. Children tended to benefit from the charitable trips organised by local institutions or benefactors, while young married, childless couples could often finance their own way to the resorts. It was, inevitably, families with young children (often in large numbers) who found these trips most difficult to finance. Yet so much of the seaside's attraction appealed to the young. Trips to the coasts before 1914 may seem to modern eyes to have been relatively cheap, but for many contempories they involved great sacrifices and efforts. And although all the evidence suggests a late-century increase in the numbers visiting the resorts, there were clearly many, perhaps a majority, left behind, unable to afford even the most cursory trip to the seaside.

Finance also dictated which particular resort a person tended to visit. The wealthy could pick and choose, but less prosperous people had on the whole to opt for the nearest. The resorts thus came to rely for their clientele on the people from the towns and cities in their immediate hinterland, more especially those with good rail connections. Oddly enough distance itself was not always paramount. Blackpool for example is some miles closer to Leeds than Scarborough, but the latter town was the natural target for West Riding working people, largely because the railway links were more direct. It is also clear that traditions and customs developed which were important in establishing the popularity of a resort among people in a nearby town, and thus helping to create its social tone. Morecambe was developed later than Blackpool and consequently could never capture the Lancashire textile workers to the same degree as Blackpool. Southport, closer than Blackpool to some of the Lancashire towns, was nonetheless able to maintain a slightly superior air (in part because of the town's deliberate land-holding policy). Skegness was created by the new railway links to the East Midlands. Scarborough, though appealing to working-class visitors, could (like Brighton) cater for all social classes, though admittedly it did so in separate sections of the town.

In 1888 William Miller found Scarborough 'a good deal frequented by clerks and others who got a week's holiday, or care to spend as much as a week's holiday costs'. Yet even here, the Scarborough south shore was as fashionable as anything to be found in the more exclusive resorts. Hastings was equally crowded. 'The railways bring multitudes of day excursionists from London and elsewhere which, added to the lodgers who come for a week or more, make the beach . . . black with their throng.' Brighton too 'on Sundays and holidays is filled with crowds of excursionists'. Ramsgate seemed to exemplify the popularity of the resorts. 'The shore was a mass of confused gatherings from the great metropolis, tumbled upon it and packed as thickly as they could sit or stand, as if all London had been thrown upon a cotton handkerchief.

It was the sheer boisterousness and rowdiness of the popular resorts which so disturbed refined sensibilities.

> It cannot be denied [complained the magazine *The Queen*] that numbers of persons of the 'robustious' temperament feel themselves exhilarated by all these accessions – niggers, musical performers of varying degrees of discord, overcrowded wagonettes and steam trips, pier entertainments, and the rest, which affect adversely those with finer nerves. . . . Then there are the young ladies, perfectly decorous and well-behaved in London who give themselves up to abandon on piers and other public places which is astonishing.

The English seemed united, almost obsessed, in there summertime rush to the sea; they travelled to the coast like lemmings, and behaved oddly out of character on arrival. But beneath the surface similarities, they were divided in their enjoyments at the seaside. They undoubtedly went down to the sea in droves, but they went along different routes, for different periods and to sharply contrasting resorts and enjoyments.

7 The rise of organised sports

By 1914 the English regarded themselves as a sporting nation, and much of the people's leisure time was filled by a great variety of sports. Organised games had been traditional since time out of mind, but hitherto on a local and informal basis; within the space of fifty years these pastimes had become almost unrecognisable, evolving into a collection of nationally organised recreations, each with its own sophisticated bureaucracy, finances, armies of players, officials and spectators – many even had their own publications.

By the early years of the twentieth century sport had developed an international status, familiar to the modern eye, with international committees controlling the development and playing of sports which reached an unprecedented level of intensity all over the world, attracting millions of participants and spectators: even the great days of Greece and imperial Rome had not seen such complexity. Many of the mass sports which now dominate the scene were fashioned in the second half of the nineteenth century: soccer, rugby football, athletics, cricket, cycling, skating, rowing, tennis, even croquet, were transformed into the major sports of today.

If the trip to the seaside exemplified the growing national and individual desire to enjoy oneself by the sea, the emergence of organised, spectator and participatory sports represents a major revolution in social life. It is significant that people began to speak of 'national games', which for England meant soccer in the winter, cricket in the summer. Again, this process originated in major social and economic changes, rather than in the history of the sports themselves. Few were more revealing or fundamental than the story of soccer. While various forms of ball games known as football had been common throughout pre-industrial societies, there they were largely informal and generally disorderly and violent. Rules, regulations and good order were apparently rare, though where the game was used to celebrate a local or national event or holiday, the passage of time tended to add shape and regulation to the conduct of the game. Location varied, teams were of indeterminate size (though generally young and male) and aims were ill-defined. But the ball (usually an inflated animal bladder) remained unchanged until manufactured balls appeared on the market in the 1870s.

English football was for centuries denounced by men of authority, both as a threat in itself and as an occasion for collective boisterousness among young men. There seems no doubt that at its worst, pre-industrial football caused serious damage, injuries and sometimes death, and its early history could be written in terms of official efforts (largely unsuccessful) to curb it. As late as the last years of the eighteenth century, Shrove Tuesday football at Derby was denounced as a custom 'disgraceful to humanity and civilisation, and subversive of good order and Government and destructive of the Morals, Properties, and very Lives of our Inhabitants'.

Turbulent, unpredictable and, worst of all, normally played on the sabbath, pre-industrial football was the game of the common people, the game most disliked by their superiors. Yet this game, played in both town and country, began to fade from the land in the late years of the eighteenth century, a victim of urbanisation, of the enclosure movement and of the growing control being exercised over the wilder pre-industrial sports and recreations. Writing in 1801, Joseph Strutt remarked of football that 'it was formally much in vogue among the common people of England, though of late it seems to have fallen into disrepute, and is but little practised'. One major explanation was the growing scarcity of spare commonland – a blight on many popular recreations. 'Football [wrote a contemporary in 1838] seems to have almost gone out of use with the inclosure of wastes and commons, requiring a wide space for its exercise.'

Ironically, football was to survive throughout the years of greatest urban change, not in the areas of its strongest traditional allegiance, but within the small band of public schools – Eton, Charterhouse, Harrow, Rugby, Shrewsbury, Westminster and Winchester – which, educationally, by the early years of the nineteenth century were quite unsuited to the changing needs of a rapidly changing society. Brutality was commonplace in those schools and it was consequently reflected in their sports. Their varieties of football (each one different from the other) were remarkably similar to the turbulent popular games which, at the same time, were disappearing from the country at large. Yet it was from these greatly differing games that late nineteenth-century soccer and rugby football were to emerge to become the nation's winter games.

The long process of taming the games (and the pupils) was set in train by Dr Arnold at Rugby and later perfected (to a degree he would have found intolerable) by his followers, whose 'muscular Christianity' helped to convert the idea of 'godliness and good living' into 'godliness and manliness'. Central to Arnold's ambitions was the prefectorial system which helped to confirm the existing order of authority within the schools while making it directly responsible to the Head. As a result, Arnold was able to extend his control through sports, more especially football in winter and cricket in the summer. Football, once codified and disciplined within a school, had enormous virtues: it absorbed large numbers of boys in energetic play, inculcated the virtues of manliness, selflessness and teamwork. In short it was responsible for helping to mould the 'character' of the English public school man. Though the process was common to all the schools (and to a growing number of new public schools) each still had its own particular brand and rules. The result was that, while more and more public school men left their schools keen to play their favourite sports, they tended to be different from those played by their contemporaries at other schools.

The Clarendon Commission of 1864 confirmed the role of sports within the public schools, noting that 'the cricket and football pitches . . . are not merely places of amusement; they help to form some of the most valuable social qualities and manly virtues, and they hold, like the classroom and boarding house, a distinct and important place in public school education'. Furthermore ex-public-school men set themselves the task of converting the nation at large to their own newly defined games, and the degree to which they succeeded counts among the many positive public school contributions to the emergence of modern British society. Before the century was out, however, different social groups had effectively colonised a number of these sports and made them into an expression of their own cultural values and ideals.

From mid-century onwards the most notable change in public school sports was their codification and dissemination throughout the country. The inspiration was simple, for those former pupils, now at Oxford, Cambridge or working in London, who were anxious to play their old school sports needed agreement on rules and conduct. So too did the schools themselves, for their teams began to travel around the country playing other schools. Old boys' were crucial in the spread of the games (and indeed often adopted their old school name for a team name). Old Rugbeians and Marlburians played against each other whenever they could, but when in 1840 Old Rugbeians played the Old Etonians at Cambridge the latter 'howled at the Rugby men for handling the ball'. Slowly, codified rules evolved, particularly at Cambridge, enabling teams to play on agreed terms. But the differences between conflicting allegiances, between those who followed the Rugby-inspired game of running while clutching the ball, and those who favoured dribbling the ball – led to a growing divergence between the two games – a divide accentuated in 1863 by the establishment of the Football Association. The Association game which evolved thereafter derived its structure, inspiration, bureaucracy, teams, competitions and ethos directly from the public schools. Not surprisingly when, in 1872, the FA Cup was inaugurated to encourage competition among the growing number of soccer teams, for the first decade the finalists were uniquely ex-public-school teams.

Adherents to the other football game, inspired by Rugby, were similarly influenced by the urge for codification, using laws drawn up in the 1840s and depending for their growing popularity on the missionary work of their former pupils. Spectators of a game among Old Rugbeians in Liverpool in 1855 were asked if 'this new sport was a worthy manner for gentlemen to employ themselves with on a Saturday afternoon as a change from the common one of rabbit coursing'. By then the game was becoming well known. At the 1851 Great Exhibition Rugby School had a stand where they displayed, among other things, goalposts and a local ball, described in the official catalogue as 'No 187. Gilbert W. Rugby, Manu.:- Footballs of leather dressed express for the purpose'. Gilbert was in fact the Rugby school shoe and boot maker, and his prototype for encasing an animal bladder in leather rapidly became the norm both in rugby and soccer. The game of rugby remained in a confused state however though there was a large number of teams which regularly played on London's parks. Growing public concern about the level of injuries in the game led in 1871 to the formation of the Rugby Union. But the links with soccer were still quite close, for among the founders of both rugby and soccer the spirit of their respective schools shaped the direction and ethos of the two games, at least until the 1880s when newer, more plebeian voices began to demand a different say in the running of the games.

Among football's apparent virtues, according to its public school proponents, was its emphasis on physical fitness. Within the schools the cult reached absurd proportions, yet there was little doubt that in all the nation's great cities there were armies of people desperately in need of exercise and improved physical condition. What became known as 'the Condition of England Question' began to preoccupy the Christian middle- and upper-class conscience, and it was endlessly debated in print and in private. One immediate result was the determination of growing numbers of public school men, many of whom were teachers and ministers, to undertake missionary work among the nation's needy. And in their sports, these men discovered qualities which seemed ideally suited to the task of bringing large-scale physical exercise into the cities. The games were national, with clearcut rules and an ethos suitable for the job in hand. As a result, in the 1860s public school men began to promulgate the virtues of their own games among people of a lower social station, a task facilitated after 1870 by the introduction of a national school system which made it easier to organise and marshall the nation's young.

Ministers and curates, school teachers and Sunday school teachers, industrialists and financiers – all helped to spread a popular interest in sports. Their success with football was remarkable. Their timing was perfect for their urge to introduce atheletic activity into the lives of poorer urban people, particularly men and boys, coincided with the growth of more free time in many industries. Free Saturday afternoons and a little spare cash enabled growing numbers of working men to take part in the newly disciplined team games. The new sports were unlike old pre-industrial games: disciplined, regulated, controlled by nationally agreed rules. They formed a sharp contrast to the indiscipline and irregularities of older sports, even those from which they had emerged. Yet these changes merely reflected the more fundamental changes in society at large for by the last quarter of the century the working population had itself become disciplined and attuned to the rigours of a clock- and machine-dominated life. The games they turned to (and ultimately colonised) were in keeping with that discipline.

The most prominent *entrée* into working-class life for the public school games was through the churches, whose ministers were often men anxious to bring their school's benefits into the industrial areas. Few sports were as convenient or attractive as football; played in a limited space, needing only a minimum of equipment, its skills and excitements could attract both the individual and large groups. And unlike its forebears the new form of football was no longer a threat to law and order and could be allowed as a street game. Churchmen consequently had great success in transplanting the game, which mushroomed dramatically throughout the country in the last quarter of the century. In Liverpool for instance, from 1878 onwards, football teams proliferated from churches, led by St Domingo's, St Peter's, Everton United Church and St Mary's, Kirkdale; by 1885 twenty-five of the 112 football teams in the town had church connections; similarly in Birmingham in 1880, eighty-three of 344 clubs had religious affiliations. As might be expected, there were major exceptions to this pattern, more particularly in Bristol and a large number of football teams were secular-based. What seems to have happened is that following the lead of a pioneering football club, other local institutions – unions, factories and schools – established their own football teams. Sunday schools (Fulham), local YMCAs (Burnley), as well as the efforts of prominent individuals, often spawned new clubs. Schools, particularly, after the 1870 Education Act, turned to football as a major recreation for boys, and the game often became the mainstay of extra-curricular activity. Old boys from Blackburn Grammar School (1874), Leicester's Wygeston School (1884), King's School, Chester (1889) and Droop Street School, London (1885) formed teams which later became professional clubs (the last being Queen's Park Rangers).

The post-1870 school system was crucially important for the expansion of football, ensuring that football would within a few years become a major sport among schoolboys, and that it would be perpetuated from one generation to another. Schoolboy soccer became a major enterprise in itself, with its myriad of local teams, leagues, competitions, trophies and even 'caps', mirroring the developments of the professional games. By the last years of the century not only was football the commonplace game among young men and boys, it was also watched by hundreds of thousands of spectators. Some as H. E. Meller has shown, even felt that sporting zeal had gone too far.

Our school competitions in football and other sports have now become a severe tax on the strength of any boy, and particularly on the poorly-clad and ill-fed. . . . In many cases a team from a poor district has to compete with a team in a better neighbourhood, where the boys are better fed, and much evil must result.

Like the schools, the workplace was an obvious place to establish football teams and, like the schools, has to this day remained one of the great strengths of the game in Britain. Once again, many of the teams survived in trasmuted form, to become the professional clubs of the present day. The 1863 North Staffs railway team became Stoke City; a Manchester railwaymen's team of 1880 later became Manchester United. Workers at Morton's factory in Millwall formed that team in 1885. Munition workers at Woolwich Arsenal formed a football team; in 1895 employees at the Thames Iron works founded a team (partly financed by the company) which subsequently became West Ham United. It was inevitable that the football club should spring from existing institutions in working-class life, in whatever free time was available on Saturday afternoons. It was also noticeable that whereas many clubs were the conscious creation of men of a superior social station, determined to introduce their own sports into working-class life, the process rapidly became self-generating. Clubs sprang up independently from working-class institutions. Even when the clubs were guided by others, control was soon wrested from their grasp.

Football and other sports were thought to be ideal vehicles for bringing together the country's distinct and conflicting social classes, and for a short while the rise of mass football seemed to have aided this process of social unity. Rapidly, however, football developed a plebeian and commercial tone, with its encroaching professionalisation, heavy capital investment in new stadiums, and armies of fiercely partisan supporters. Many men from the old schools who were deeply wedded to the essential amateurism of football and to a conflicting ethos of sporting behaviour were slowly drawn away. The changing social context of football was reflected in the history of the FA Cup, which for its first ten years was won by ex-public school teams. In 1883, however, the working-class Blackburn Olympic team defeated the Old Etonians, returning home in triumph to a brassband welcome.

Rising football popularity, in the north and Midlands was directly responsible for the emergence of professionalism; to pay for the new grounds (teams having moved from the municipal parks and cricket grounds) the clubs began to charge admission fees. Their funds (and entrepreneurial backing) were then sunk in costly new stadiums and the growing complexity of play, which involved leagues, competitions and travel, all of which created further costs, wider interest and an awareness among a new generation of players that they possessed a commercial value. By the late 1880s, professionalism in this, the greatest of English spectator sports, had become a *fait accompli*. Public school teams retreated into their own sporting world of strictly guarded amateurism, and, even further away, into the yet more appropriate world of rugby union.

Increasingly, public school men scoffed at the mercenary nature of soccer, arguing that henceforth rugby was the bastion of fair-play. It was according to Bishop Carey, 'a game for gentlemen in all classes but never for bad sportsmen in any class'. Unhappily for the union, the threat of professionalism even raised its head in rugby. Rugby enthusiasts, like soccer fans, were faced with growing financial problems as the game began to demand ever more time and money to prepare and travel. It was obviously unreasonable to expect working men to lose precious earnings simply to play rugby, but those men who were able to play irrespective of cost found the consequent requests for wages to be subsidised tantamount to a plea for professionalism in the game. It was in fact a similar argument to the one which for years had dogged the debate about the payment of MPs. Used effectively to keep out working class MPs, a similar argument restricted working-class rugby players. When in 1893 pressure from northern clubs failed to persuade the union to sanction the payment to players for 'broken time', a movement was launched which resulted, in 1895, in the establishment of a breakaway rugby league, based primarily in the north. By 1898 not only had it become hugely successful and popular among fans in Lancashire and Yorkshire, but it was also professional. Rugby union (with the obvious regional exception of Wales) remained strictly amateur and non-plebeian. Like football, rugby had become by the turn of the century a sport divided on class lines.

Amateurism survived in certain quarters, more especially in the upper bureaucratic reaches of the FA. On the field however it was best represented by the Corinthians, a team of gentlemen who refused to meet as a team before a game, arriving in top hats and carrying canes. But by the early years of the century football was best represented by players and supporters who wore cloth caps. In 1895 a commentator noted: 'The nation, we are told, is a democracy, and the game of the people must be accepted as the game of the nation.' Football was seen, by the British and outsiders, as the national game. 'It is simply monstrous to what a pitch this football-playing has arisen,' moaned one Liverpudlian (of all people). Such a state of affairs could of course be only partially explained by the intrinsic attractions of football itself, and it is worth remembering that football was not the only organised sport to be enjoying undreamed of support in the early years of the new century.

Many new recreations had been made possible by the increased provision of municipal parks, the absence of which in the early century had been a common complaint in most English cities. Led by Manchester and Birkenhead, municipalities and prominent individuals in the cities began to set aside open space for the leisure pursuits of local people. London, with its ancient parks and heaths and its commercial gardens, had been particularly well endowed for open space. Liverpool on the other hand was especially blighted.

When municipal parks began to appear late in the century they were often accompanied by municipally sponsored leisure and recreational facilities, baths, recreational grounds and gymnasia, all of which were part and parcel of the emergence of a new late-century commitment to civic pride. Unfortunately the open spaces needed for rest and recreation in an urban environment were, by contemporary standards, extremely expensive, and many towns depended to a large extent on the contributions of money and land from local benefactors. Local authorities were hard-pressed to provide even the most rudimentary of social services but there was money to be made by providing the right kind of leisure facilities and the sports stadiums which began from the 1880s to dot the outer fringes of Victorian cities were, by and large, monuments to the commercial potential of mass sports. The men who financed these football, cricket, athletic and cycling grounds were, like those who financed the physical amenities of the seaside leisure industries, anxious to capitalise on popular consumer power.

Entrepreneurs and manufacturers were among the first to spot the commercial potential of sporting equipment. Footballs, boots, shorts, shirts, goalnets, turf and seeds, medicines and rubs, sailing wear, cricket equipment, skates, croquet sets, tennis rackets – these and a myriad related items were readily available in the new multiple stores throughout the country. Of all the commercial investments in the growing English commitment to organised leisure perhaps the most notable was in the field of publishing. By the turn of the century few sports were without their own newspapers or magazine, in addition to the growing space and prominence given to sports in the local and national press. The press indeed provides the best index of the public's interest in sports and sporting competitions. To a considerable degree this coverage was a function of emergent popular literacy and, as we have seen, late-century compulsory education had helped to establish a wider reading public at a time when technical innovation cheapened the spread of the printed word. In an age without radio or TV it was the press which accentuated and spread knowledge and interest in the major sports. Fixtures, venues, times, prices, teams, travel arrangements, stories about the 'stars' (themselves largely a creation of press coverage), and of course the results of matches, were readily within the reach of most people through their newspaper or, for the more committed, through specialist magazines.

For those sports which were played on a national basis, and watched by increasing numbers of paying spectators, transportation for players and fans was crucial. The national railway system had, from mid-century, clearly enabled teams to travel long distances; it had revolutionised horse-racing. But in many respects it was the great strides in cheap *city* transport, particularly by tram, which enabled thousands of spectators to be deposited at the various stadiums on the edges of cities. Travel within the cities and across the country was undoubtedly encouraged by the emergence of the mass spectator sports, which in turn were only made feasible because of a highly efficient transport system. Yet all these developments were utterly dependent on the economic condition of participants. The ability to buy sporting equipment, to travel to games, to pay the admission fee and all the ancillary costs generated by such games was the central determinant of the rise of mass sports. Without popular consumer power the transformation of games into a major feature of English social life in the late century would not have been possible. They would doubtless have remained securely within the purview of charitable works, made available to large numbers of people solely through the efforts and goodwill of local benefactors.

Football may have epitomised the rise of mass sports, but it was only one of an extremely varied range of games which were common-place in English cities. While the games differed, the history of their development was often very similar. Cricket, like football, had an ancient history and strong popular roots, particularly in Yorkshire and Kent; and again, its development was inextricably linked with the public schools, where cricket thrived, was perfected and passed on to genera-tions of cricketers who went into the outside world determined to play their favourite summer game. Ironically, the initial impetus towards taking cricket to the people came from William Clark, a joiner brick-layer, who from the 1840s onwards toured the country with an All-England XI and helped to encourage the development of local interest and teams. Similar tours, and the work of cricketing schoolmasters and ministers, produced great enthusiasm in the counties. The process was aided by the first publication of Wisden's *Cricketer's Almanack* in 1864 and culminated in 1873 in the development of the county champion-ship. The idea of such competitions, as with football, was directly attributable to the public schools' athletic competitiveness. From an early date, however, there was in cricket a marked divide between gentlemen and players: gentlemen and professionals. It was, in the words of R. Mason, 'largely correct to say that the quality of amateur cricket was determined in the public schools and the universities and that of the professional game in the wandering circuses and counties', but there were links between the two sides, for professional cricketers were employed by the public schools as coaches and groundsmen (known to pupils simply by surname).

At times there were close links between cricket and football. A number of prominent and influential public school footballers were equally renowned for their cricketing skills. Before the development of special football grounds the older cricket pitches were often used by emergent football clubs, until it was appreciated how much damage was caused to the playing surface. The first Cup Finals were played at the Oval. Moreover many football clubs sprang up as the winter sport for a cricket club. Derby County (1884) originated in the local cricket club; men from Preston Cricket Club formed a football team in 1881, later to become Preston North End; Sheffield Wednesday (1867) came from a cricket club and Sheffield United (1889) emerged from the Yorkshire County Cricket Club. The development of cricket was clearly well ahead of football, but the long duration of cricket matches (three days in county games) and the expense of the equipment, prevented it gaining the genuinely popular spectator following of the shorter, cheaper sports. (In this respect it is significant that it was the proliferation of one-day cricket tournaments in recent years that has brought a football-like following back to the cricket clubs.) Despite the growth of professionalism within the county teams, cricket before the First World War was at its cavalier best, dominated by the famous amateur teams which emerged from the public schools. Cricket was furthermore well ahead of other games in being played at an international level as early as the 1860s, with an English tour of Australia. In succeeding years while football was putting down local and organisational roots in the urban areas, cricket was already exported by public school men to various parts of the Empire. Other sports soon followed in becoming international phenomena, and the early years of the twentieth century saw the creation of organisations to govern sports internationally. The Imperial Cricket Conference was formed in 1909; The International Association Football Federation (FIFA), in 1904; and the International Lawn Tennis Federation in 1913.

Tennis emerged as a major sport in these same years, again having its roots in ancient forms but finding itself transformed into a recognisably modern pattern in the last twenty years of the century. Perfected in the 1860s by Major Wingfield (who patented the rules and equipment), in 1875 it found its home henceforth at Wimbledon. The local All England Croquet Club (formed in 1869) suggested in that year that tennis should be offered as a commercially attractive sport, and thus help to pay the club's high rent; by 1877 the club's name was changed to the 'All England Croquet and Lawn Tennis Club'. The tennis championship introduced in that year was devised specifically to raise funds and has proved to be the highlight of English tennis to this day.

In the case of tennis, cricket, football and rugby (both varieties) it is clear that competitions were designed primarily for financial reasons, but in their turn, such competitions proved enormously influential in promoting the growth of the specific sport. In tennis, yet again, public school men were present in the organisation and conduct of the game. The first Wimbledon championship in July 1877 was arranged to end by Friday to enable everyone to move on to watch the Eton and Harrow cricket match at Lords. Symbolically the first Wimbledon winner was an old Etonian (the second was a tea planter from Ceylon); as with cricket and football, the English soon exported the game to Europe, the colonies and to North America.

In one major regard tennis was unlike other games: it soon became a game for women as well as men (though female clothing severely restricted their mobility). Women's tennis, mixed tennis, local, regional and (from 1892) international tennis, helped to spread the game. And, as in other sports, the players from public schools and Oxford were the most influential in the evolution and growing popularity of the game. Throughout the major sports of the late nineteenth century, the public schools (and the element of competition) were vital ingredients which made possible their emergence as mass spectator and participatory occasions.

Women were able to make their mark in tennis, but the most notable female sporting presence (except perhaps horse-riding) was in cycling, which in the 1890s became something of a national obsession. The story of the bicycle is in itself fascinating, evolving slowly throughout the century but hastened from mid-century onwards by technical improvements and cheapened by mass production. For many women however the bicycle involved more than mere sport when, from 1870 onwards, a fierce political debate arose about the propriety of women cyclists. Cycling was thought to be unladylike (originally, of course, only ladies tended to ride); it was claimed to be unhealthy, producing various unspecified gynaecological effects, and indecorous, resulting in changes in female clothes. American women had already shown the attractions and possibilities of cycling, developing the scandalous 'bloomers' specially for the purpose. Bolder spirits in England insisted on following the American (and French) example, wearing the new clothes and embarking on cycle races.

By the early 1890s women had generally won the argument by simple force of habit, and the craze was heightened by the manufacture of women's bicycles, though hardier women insisted on sticking to the older 'male' models. In the words of the *Northern Wheeler* in 1893: 'Woman has taken her stand, and her seat in the saddle, and like the author of the historic phrase, we men can only say – This is not a revolt, it is a revolution. I am tolerably certain that the net result will be that woman will take her true position as man's equal.' Women's cycling clubs proliferated, with the interesting by-product that some women's clothing became more practical – a move encouraged by the 'Rational Dress Society', but only fully completed by the exigencies of industrial work during the 1914–18 war. By 1895 cycling had become a national craze and cyclists often usurped the place of horse-riders in fashionable London parks. Aristocratic ladies, middle-class ladies and fashionable society in general vied with each other to be seen astride a bike; poorer women could only hope for a ride at the seaside, where bikes could be hired for a short spin. It is symptomatic of the craze that in the 1890s bicycle hire became a commonplace feature among seaside recreations. As with other sports, cycling was carried along by entrepreneurial guile, and propagated by a spate of cycling publications.

There was growing belief that sporting activity ought to be available to all, irrespective of sex. 'Legitimate sport or exercise for the grave and gay [wrote the sports editor of the *British Argus* in 1887] for the young and old, for the rich and poor, for the male and female is the great order of the day.' There were however major social practical and financial difficulties facing female sports and in consequence provision for them lagged badly behind those for men. Moreover in working-class communities the problem was even more acute because there, women with families tended not to enjoy even the minimal extra earnings and free time of their men folk. Middle- and upper-class women could on the other hand enjoy certain sports – tennis and cycling as we have seen, and croquet on the lawns of large houses or private clubs. In the last years of the century ice-skating also became favourite recreation among women. This modern sport originated in the colder climate of North America and northern Europe, and its development in Britain depended on the technical ability to create an artificial ice-rink. Following the opening on a Manchester rink in 1877, similar ice-stadiums were opened throughout the major cities in England, Europe and North America. They, like so many other contemporary sports, involved considerable investment in sporting equipment, and constitute still further evidence of the continuing attraction for leisure in the business world.

Swimming too was open to women, particularly because of the proliferation of municipal pools – themselves a function of the move towards municipal provision of recreational facilities. Again, it seems unlikely that such pleasures came the way of poorer women whose time and efforts were often totally consumed by family life and whose recreations, as contemporary photographs show, took place on the crowded streets and alleys where they lived.

Clearly a number of major recreations were open both to men and women, but the major sports of the late nineteenth century were, in general, for men and boys; many of these games had already been male-dominated in their pre-industrial form. The chances of women breaking into sports in a society convinced of the essential masculinity of such activities were remote, and most sports became progressively masculine by having passed through the proving grounds of the English public schools. With the possible exception of cycling (which was an individual rather than team sport) women were an insignificant sporting presence by the early years of this century. This is not to say that particular women did not excel, or that women were not at the forefront of the development of certain games. But in national terms, whether seen as a participatory or spectator phenomenon, the mass sports of the late nineteenth century were male-dominated. Yet within this generalisation there were major exceptions, determined largely by class; upper-class women were for obvious reasons much more likely to be able to participate than their poorer contemporaries, whose lives were dominated either by work or the family. The masculinity of English sports in the early years of the century tells us a great deal about the social and economic factors which determined their contemporary appeal. Even when some women made determined efforts to enjoy new forms of recreation (as in cycling) they met dogged resistance from both men and women who had come to share the prevailing philosophy that sports ought to be masculine.

The importance of the public schools' influence on games in the last thirty years of the century is hard to overstress for their ethos went far beyond the mere evolution of rules and came to represent the very essence of Victorian sporting spirit. Ultimately, however, the evolution of more plebeian games and, eventually, professional forms created a divide. Public schools undoubtedly created many new sports, and even more sportsmen, but the changes in social and economic fortunes among low income groups enabled working men to colonise some of these sports. Equally important in the spread of sports was the spirit of competition which derived directly from the schools. The leagues, championships, trophies, cups and caps which were soon a feature of most major sports originated in the public schools. Competition itself proved remarkably influential in generating interest; designed to raise money, competitions gave direction and shape (in many cases lasting to the present day), and in some cases became a game's most distinguishing feature. And the organisations and bureaucracies which controlled the major sports were often in the hands of public school men anxious to control the evolution and direction of the particular sport. Indeed the proliferation of sporting organisations – the bureaucratisation of sport – was a major feature of the new age. Generally centred in London, the major sports had clear-cut rules and regulations and a firm bureaucratic dominance over the conduct of the game. Many of these bureaucracies burgeoned into major business enterprises (though often debilitated by an uncompromising amateurism).

Sport was not simply a national phenomenon: it had become an international concern. Many sports soon developed their own international organisations to control the rapid growth at both amateur and professional level. It was in these same years that the modern Olympic movement was established. The inspiration behind the Olympics was the French aristocrat Baron de Coubertin, whose views about education and physical recreation, rooted in classical ideas, paralleled those of the contemporary English public schools. Like those schools, he was disturbed by the encroachment of professionalism and commercialisation and in 1894 he set in train the events which two years later culminated in the first modern Olympics, in Paris. Thereafter the story was one of prodigous growth, though the scale, veiled professionalism and commercial involvement of modern Olympics would surely have saddened the good Baron.

Long before the First World War, organised sports had become a major industry. They were played by millions, often thanks to the new school system which placed growing emphasis on physical recreation. The major games were watched by millions, whose money was the livelihood of the sporting world. And, as major industries, they generated capitalist interest and spawned a vast range of ancillary industries. Not since the classical world had sporting endeavour represented so much, both good and evil. But even the classical world would surely have been surprised at the scale and intensity of early twentieth-century sporting efforts. To many millions of people the fortunes of their local teams, their national heroes, the achievements of their children, had become major facts of life. Playing and, increasingly, winning, had become major ambitions for millions; watching others play had become equally important for millions more.

It was in effect little less than a social revolution, and as such represented a major shift in social attitudes, for the games which now attracted armies of players and spectators, and which so often originated in pre-industrial forms, were as regulated, ordered disciplined and controlled as their forebears had been beyond control. Such sports perfectly represented the emergence of leisure among an advanced, industrial and disciplined labour force, whose lives were characterised by the very qualities of discipline so essential to their sports. We have seen how the emergence of an industrial society had slowly purged the people of their pre-industrial foibles and 'weaknesses'. Urban life was now ordered as never before and the games which in the late nineteenth century became the major recreations, thanks to available free time and more money, were as ordered as urban life itself. Their spirit, rules and ethos were consonant with the needs and interests of industrial society. This is not to claim that sports were mere ideological tools of a prevailing economic order; it was simply that both had emerged from similar economic and social circumstances.

8   The sound of music

Of all forms of leisure, few were so ubiquitous among all age groups and classes and throughout the year as music. It would be difficult to overstress the role of music in England before 1914. From informal singing in the home and the handing-down of scarce-remembered folk songs, through to the late-century set-piece epics performed by brass bands, choral societies or orchestras, the sheer range of musical entertainment was staggering, and is witnessed by the large numbers of instrument makers and music publishers. In music in its various forms the English people found a pleasure and a recreation which surpassed all others, and it was not to be seriously dislodged until the inroads of broadcasting and cinema after the Great War.

Musical enjoyment can be either individual or collective: it is the collective, communal nature of nineteenth-century music-making which was so distinctive. To a large extent this was encouraged in the late eighteenth and early nineteenth centuries by the emphasis on choral music in the expanding nonconformist (particularly Methodist) churches. Inspired by the hymns of John and Charles Wesley the Methodist churches placed great importance on congregational singing. 'I want [said John Wesley] the People called Methodists to sing true the Tunes which are in *Common Use* among them.' As his followers proliferated throughout the north and the Midlands, so too did the range and the quality of church singing, more noticeably among the poor. Performances of Handel's *Messiah*, thanks to the emergence of choral singing, became a major cult by the early nineteenth century. It is significant that when in the summer of 1846 Alfred Novello advertised 'THE CHEAPEST PUBLICATION EVER OFFERED TO THE PUBLIC', to be sold in twelve monthly parts, it was a serialised version of *The Messiah*. By the late 1850s the complete version could be had for one shilling an example of the cheapening of music publishing made possible by technical change and Novello's acumen. Demand for performances of sacred music grew to epic proportions by mid-century, as the *Musical Times* noted in July 1865:

> In tracing the course of the widely spread love for sacred music, it must be remembered that Novello's cheap series of Oratorios not only supplied the demand which was caused by the constant

performance of these works, but actually created a public of its own, by circulating, at the price of a commonplace ballad, the entire Oratorios amongst the audience; so that, not only were they enabled to follow every note during the presentation of the works, but a library of standard sacred music was almost unconsciously formed in thousands of homes, leading to the establishment of private and public choral societies, which have increased year by year.

Handel's music appealed to the Victorians because it was both enjoyable and elevating, and it became a prominent feature of Victorian middle-class life and of their attempts to generate holiness through music among their inferiors. But in fact, large sections of working-class, mainly nonconformist life independently turned to Handel and other prominent writers of oratorio with a similar zeal and in similar numbers. The crowds drawn by Handel's music surpassed those at all other forms of organised leisure; the Crystal Palace Handel Festival of 1857, 1859, 1862 and 1865 attracted a total of more than a quarter of a million people. Furthermore Handel's grip on popular choral music was much firmer than even these figures suggest for performances of his music were regular features in working-class communities, particularly those dominated by nonconformity in the north and Midlands.

While nonconformity lay behind much of the impetus behind early nineteenth-century choral music, the Church of England also took a hand from the 1840s onwards. The long-standing battle between those who wanted to see church music the preserve of a small, often professional minority and those who wanted to see congregational singing, was slowly won by the latter group, and by the late 1840s, Church of England congregations were no less vocal than their nonconformist rivals. One important consequence was the work of peripatetic choir-masters who helped to establish a crude choral uniformity, as well as encouraging skills and interests in choral music. All this took place at a time when formal instruction was generally absent from large numbers of working-class communities. Local organists played similarly important roles in local musical education, conducting music lessons and choral instruction throughout the parish and often encouraging non-church music. While it seems undoubtedly true that the level and quality of Church of England music was of 'unsurpassed dullness', concerned as much with lofty virtues and sobriety, it is nonetheless the case that its practitioners were responsible for promoting wider interest in music.

The Anglican revival reinforced a long-held conviction that music held great potential in education and up to the Education Act of 1870 (and within the state school system thereafter) determined efforts were made to use music as a means of educating the people. Music, it was thought, was capable of imposing on the listener or player a moral tone and certain worthwhile attitudes; as a result, in

Victorian England inordinate stress was placed on the words in order to achieve this 'uplifting' effect. Arguably the most influential proponent of education through music was the social reformer Dr Kay-Shuttleworth, who, influenced by the example of music in continental schools, actively encouraged its development in England, with the invaluable help of John Hullah. Hullah's work and disciples spread rapidly throughout the Sunday and day schools of mid-Victorian England. Their results were remarkable. In 1839 it had been claimed that music was virtually non-existent in English schools, but by 1870 it was to be found in some form in most schools. Needless to say music made inroads into the public schools, despite their prevailing philistinism, and their committed pupils spilled out into a great variety of influential positions in the musical world. These were, after all the years when the 'school song' of the English public school became established features of a school's ethos.

For those musical missionaries who felt that their most pressing task was to convert the masses to musical involvement the major obstacle was the technical difficulty of teaching music. This was partly overcome by the Tonic-Sol-Fa system, a system of 'sight-singing' which, inspired by continental models, substituted syllables for musical notes and was promoted in various forms by John Hullah and John Curwen. There were imperfections and weaknesses in the system but it was nonetheless responsible for the musical training of tens of thousands of pupils from the mid-century onwards. Moreover the decision of 1872 to establish compulsory music in state schools, using the Tonic-Sol-Fa system, was responsible for increasing further national musical interest. But it is revealing to note that much of the impetus behind Tonic-Sol-Fa was educational/inspirational. 'The method [wrote Curwen's son] was the indirect means of aiding worship, temperance, and culture, of holding young men and women among good influences, or reforming character, of spreading Christianity.'

Musically, Tonic-Sol-Fa is often thought to have had a deadening effect, but it was undoubtedly responsible for creating vast numbers of choral singers and choirs. Size rather than quality seems to have been the prize aim, and size was conveniently suited to Handel's major pieces. Educationally, however, particularly after the 1870 Act, more children seemed to learn to sing by ear than by any real method, though often of course their teachers were Tonic-Sol-Fa disciples. People can after all, sing without any formal musical education. Music had been since time immemorial a central aspect of human societies and continues to be so in societies which lack formal education. Listening, watching, participating: these, more than any other factors were perhaps responsible for spreading the nation's musical interests. Nonetheless it has to be stressed that what encouraged this expanding interest was the growing proportion of the people, particularly among the young, who were organised within institutions – Sunday schools, day schools and after 1870, state schools – where they could be taught in large numbers. The conviction among the growing band of music teachers that music ought to be a basic part of education, and their ability to reach ever increasing numbers of pupils was largely responsible for a massive (and growing) commitment to music.

This was merely one aspect of music as leisure; there was also a wide spectrum of musical activity much of which was informal and self-taught. Among the most striking features of nineteenth-century music is its scale and its rapid commercialisation. Long before the Victorians' games and sports had been commercialised and professionalised, large areas of English music had fallen victim to, or had been made possible by, commercial enterprise; even those branches which wished to remain rootedly amateur found themselves, because of their sheer growth, drawn into commercial activity. Choral societies provided a classic example of the way growth inevitably paved the way for commercialisation. By the late nineteenth century there were thousands of them, but their numbers belied their relatively recent history: they emerged rapidly from obscure origins. The first mention of a Yorkshire choral society was in Halifax in 1817, the next in Bradford in 1821, and it is significant that a movement which appears to have begun in Yorkshire should, as the century progressed, be best represented in numbers and quality in that county. With understandable pride the *Yorkshire Post* commented in 1853 that local choral societies 'not only possess the best voices we have yet heard from any English choral body, but sing better in tune, and with great precision and oneness of tone and feeling than any others with whom we are acquainted in this country'. The number of choral societies in the north might be explained by the connection with local nonconformity, a link found also in other regions where the choral tradition flourished.

Beginning as small groups committed to song, and to self-improvement through song, the societies rapidly became major concerns, possessing large musical libraries, having extensive local, regional and, later, national engagements and inevitably burdened by the expenses of bureaucracy, travel, equipment and the hiring of halls, to say nothing of the cost to individuals of having 'respectable' clothes for performances. The Huddersfield Choral Society founded in 1836 was designated for 'the improvement of the talent and taste of this town and neighbourhood, in the performance of Sacred and Choral Music, Overtures etc'. And whereas Huddersfield's rule IX specified 'that on the monthly nights each member shall have allowed 3 gills of ale, bread and cheese', the Oldham choir (founded in 1842) was thought to be 'a great improvement on some of the musical clubs in this neighbourhood, where two-thirds of their money is spent in liquor, instead of upon music, as it should be'.

As the choral societies grew in size and numbers, concerts, exhibitions and contests became a major feature of the musical calendar, ends in themselves, for which the choirs trained, but also means of financing their growing organisation. There was also the added incentive of the interest shown by local philanthropists, businessmen, politicians and local municipalities, all of whom realised the social and cultural potential of such popular musical activities, dominated as they were by sacred music. (Handel still remained the most popular and most commonly-played composer. The *Messiah* for example was played forty-one times by the Bradford Choral Society between 1856 and 1906.) Choirs and singing groups tended to develop on a narrowly local basis and those choirs which bore the town's name were, in general, only the largest and best remembered of the myriad of singing groups in the town. These bigger choirs involved expensive operations, and from mid-century large-scale festivals, competitions and concerts were organised to raise finance, often by local men of substance anxious to encourage this 'useful' form of recreation. It was moreover one of the few forms of Victorian leisure in which women could participate on equal terms with men.

The north did not of course have a monopoly on such musical activity and choral societies proliferated in the Midlands, east, south and west, and everywhere the pattern was similar. When in 1844 shopkeepers in Guildford resolved to close their shops early in the evening, it was hoped that 'the young men would employ their time profitably to themselves, and with satisfaction to their employers', and invitations were extended 'to join the Choral Society as one of the means to that end'. In 1849 the choir at Bungay sang before an audience of two hundred, 'most of them working people, servants and apprentices, etc; but with a considerable proportion from the classes above them'. Often membership fees were extremely high. The Bristol choir charged a fee of two guineas a year; Exeter's cost half-a-crown entrance fee and a shilling a month subscription. Such fees were clearly prohibitive for low income groups, though it was often the case in the north that choirs made exceptions for poorer, sick or unemployed members.

Despite such problems the choral societies presented growing numbers of local concerts, but their best efforts were reserved for the choral festivals which, in attendance, quality and public interest were accepted by contemporaries to be among the highlights of late nineteenth-century social life. Indeed the crowds they attracted were in many cases equal to the major contemporary sporting events and, like those sports, their sole limitation on audiences was the seating capacity of the municipal buildings and concert halls where they met. As the century advanced halls specifically designed as a suitable venue for popular, though culturally 'sound' activities were constructed throughout the country. As early as 1845 Birmingham Council had ordered that the Town Hall organ should be played once a week for the benefit of the labouring population – at a charge of threepence, but it was in the 1850s that popular concerts became a really prominent aspect of city life. By and large the reason was straight-forward, for the provision of concerts and choral facilities came in direct response to the emergence of leisure time among local operatives. Another powerful inspiration was the important temperance determination to sever the age-old connection between spare time and drink. There was in addition a widespread keenness and a desire for music, as one man discovered in Bradford in 1848: 'Such was the thirst for relaxation and recreation among the working people, that, on a Saturday night, whenever there was a sound music to be heard, however offensive and contaminating the atmosphere might be, there a crowd of people was collected.'

Essentially, the choirs, festivals and concerts which sprang from the joint forces of popular interest and parallel middle-class determination to steer leisure into 'better' channels, where fiercely respectable. The Huddersfield Choral Society rules of 1842, for example, declared that: 'No person shall be a member of this society, who frequents the "Hall of Science" or any of the "Socialist Meetings", nor shall the Librarian be allowed to lend any copies of music (knowingly) belonging to this society, to any Socialist, upon a pain of expulsion.' This 'respectable', politically Conservative impulse also sought to guide popular musical interest away from the place of drink, which so often tended also to be the subversive place of radical politics and union meetings. It is not surprising that 'respectable' proponents of the movement began, from mid-century, to fear the subversive threat of the expanding network and popularity of the commercial music hall. Indeed 'peoples' concerts' were organised in West Yorkshire specifically to undermine the influences of local music halls. Significantly, it was the 'rational' alternatives to the more boisterous 'Casino' music hall which soon collapsed through financial indifference.

The numbers of choirs grew rapidly, but their social composition is much less certain. It often varied greatly from one region to another. The Leeds Festival Chorus of 1895 was thought to be 'mostly of factory workers', but more detailed analysis reveals 161 women, 47 of whom were housewives and 67 had no specified occupation; 25 were teachers and only 22 were shop or factory girls. Of the 184 men, 21 were factory workers, 49 tradesmen and shop assistants, 18 traders, 56 clerks and travellers, and 40 shopkeepers or warehousemen. Current research suggests that the great majority of members of northern choirs were likely to be 'aristocrats' of labour, or from the lower reaches of the middle class. It is also clear that in large measure the belief that the choirs were working-class stemmed from the assumption of southern critics that anyone with a northern accent (in speech or song) must necessarily be working-class. Whatever their composition, the choirs and choral societies, with their links into the schools, Sunday schools and local communities, were extremely influential in creating and expanding the national interest in music.

Victorians were increasingly subjected to the sound of outdoor music, indeed they could not escape from it. Bands, orchestras, wandering groups and peripatetic musicians plied their trade throughout the streets of Victorian England. The inescapable sound of street music, much of it appalling, was a frequent complaint among contemporaries. Writing from Broadstairs in 1847, Dickens complained: 'Unless it pours with rain I cannot write half an hour without the most excruciating organs, fiddles, bells or glee-singers'. London was bedevilled by such noise, but the worst abuses were reserved for the seaside towns which were the mecca for any aspiring musician in the summer season. Again, they were a constant source of complaint and, later, municipal regulation. In 1877 a correspondent in *Punch* complained that, at the seaside, he was 'regaled with music of a German band attempting to get through the overture to Zampa with a clarinet, a cornet, a trombone, all more or less beginners', and the evening was completed by the 'Town band dreadfully noisy and awfully out of tune'. Londoners were assailed throughout the year by 'mechanical' musicians, many of them Italians, with their barrel organs, piano organs and hurdy-gurdies. Persevering musicians such as these penetrated even the grimmest of urban slums. According to *Chamber's Journal* in 1881 'the mechanical organs and pianos which penetrate into the remotest slums and alleys spread musical culture even among the dregs of the people. They are, in effect, so many perambulating *conservatoires* teaching the masses the most accepted music of the day.'

It was the bands which made the best of the open-air music. From the 1840s the Sunday performances of bands in the parks were a source of bitter contest between sabbatarians and those anxious to enhance the nation's leisure facilities. Whenever band music was played, crowds flocked to listen, adding more fuel to the sabbatarian feeling that such performances were undermining the nation's commitment to the church. 'The strains of martial music [wrote Edward Baines the Leeds MP] cause the pulse to bound, and fire the imagination, and they are wholly out of accordance with the sacred repose of the Sabbath.' The gradual evolution of free time on other days of the week, and the emergence of new kinds of bands, gradually wore down the sabbatarian lobby. As the century advanced, outdoor music came to be equated with the brass band – the best supported of all forms of Victorian outdoor music; and the brass band movement was rootedly plebeian.

In 1847 Alfred Novello, on one of his business journeys to the north, reported on a Whitweek temperance festival in Leeds; 'We were both surprised and gratified by the manner in which several brass bands and wind bands executed a variety of opera and other airs. We understand the performers to be almost all workmen in the factories, many of the mills have their own especial bands.'

To a significant degree the emergence of the brass band movement was made possible by the technical innovation in instrument manufacture, coupled with the determination of many employers to foster this 'useful' and elevating recreation in their labour force. But, like so many other sponsored recreations, the brass band was soon taken over by working men, who made it their own. The growth of the movement was phenomenal. By 1887 there were an estimated 40,000 brass bands throughout the country, and one instrument manufacturer alone had 10,000 bands on his books. The bands sprang from every conceivable institution in working-class life – from the place of work, the union, the church, Sunday school, co-op, temperance society and political organisations. Indeed those new evangelical societies of the late century which sought deliberately to penetrate into working-class communities, notably the Salvation Army, Band of Hope, Boys' Brigade and Boy Scouts, often did so through the brass band. It was no accident that the sound of brass band music could be guaranteed to raise interest and support whenever it struck up; moreover it soon came to represent a great variety of social and political aspects of working class life; it characterised the interval at the local football match, it dominated the union parade or political gathering, and at holidays and high days it simply entertained the community.

Brass band instruments were simple to master, relatively cheap to buy (assisted by rudimentary hire purchase agreements between manufacturers and bands), ideally suited to playing out of doors even in uncertain weather and the bands proliferated. Like other forms of recreation, they were rooted in and made possible by competitions. Beginning near Hull in 1845, brass band festivals fostered that competitive spirit which in its turn extended musical interest, a closer regard for musical excellence and a general appreciation for brass band music. By the 1890s there were 222 such festivals throughout the country, the most important held at Belle Vue, Manchester, and watched by many thousands of spectators. The centre of gravity of brass band music was to be found in the Midlands and north but the south too could offer considerable competition. In 1900 the Crystal Palace brass band festival attracted twenty-nine bands; by 1903 there were one hundred and seventeen taking part, and 60,000 people attended the 1908 contest there. By then the more famous bands were also playing in Europe and North America; like football, cricket and tennis, the pattern of development had, under the stimulus of competition, become nationwide; and the improvement in performing skills, the rise in public (and thus commercial) interest was followed by the determination to export the music abroad.

Brass bands, in common with other recreations, gave birth to a spate of their own publications: *Wright's and Round's Brass Band News* (1886), *The British Bandsman* (1887), *Musical Progress* (1907) and *Cornet* (1893). The bands of course relied on their own industry (a major one), while outfitters were kept busy designing and making the splendid uniforms which became so important a part of a brass band occasion. Yet the musicians were overwhelmingly working-class, despite the fact that the expense of belonging to a band was high. Rehearsals and live performances were equally expensive of the bandsman's free time. Such costs and demands could only be met by men whose work yielded surplus cash and considerable free time. Often of course, time and facilities were provided by the institution (the firm for example) anxious to gain credit from the achievements of their own music makers. In the years after the Crimean War the brass band movement began to make inroads into the armed forces and today many of the country's best bands are military. Even outside the armed forces it is noticeable that bands took on a military air, their uniforms, discipline and often the music, striking an unusually militaristic note.

With massive and increasing support the movement became one of the nation's major leisure industries. To raise funds for instruments and equipment, the bands played in public, and the competitions were lucrative both for the bands and for their backers. Brass band music through its growing popularity began to attract serious composers who had earlier thought it an inferior *genre*, but now wrote specifically for brass bands; this in turn led to its critical re-evaluation. Thus a movement which had such plebeian roots had, by the early years of the twentieth century, become respectable, international, and attractive to all classes.

Nowhere did this music seem more at home than beside the sea where, in the summer months the municipal bandstands, parks and piers were filled with crowds, listening to the brass bands and orchestras. Even inland cities made great efforts to provide their residents with cheap, accessible band music, generally in mixed classical and popular variety. But it was the seaside band which was the best remembered, its popularity enshrined in the words of the contemporary song, 'Oh I do like to be beside the seaside'. Much of that music was of course free to the thousands who stood or wandered close to the bandstands; by the late century however, much more sophisticated musical offerings could be enjoyed at the resorts.

Like other features of seaside life, much of the musical entertainment was inspired by the spas, where orchestras were a traditional part of the attractions. By the late nineteenth century there were a number of excellent orchestras dotted around the coast, in the new pavilions, winter gardens and piers, offering an amazing variety of musical entertainments to residents and visitors. No self-respecting resort could be without its orchestra or band; some possessed several, quite apart from the musical entertainments available in private hotels. Led by Bournemouth, a number of seaside municipalities established their own orchestras and often built a place for them to play. Like the brass bands, the repertoires of the seaside orchestras were unusually varied; classical music was played alongside selections from the current hits of musical comedy and American imports. When an Englishman paid a visit to the summer resorts, he assumed that music would be a basic ingredient of the entertainment. Musical style differed from one resort to another, the more respectable and residential, the less 'popular' the music on offer, but the modern reader is struck by the sheer range of music played. Some orchestras were very large; that at Eastbourne in the 1880s was fifty strong; smaller resorts such as at Whitley Bay, Saltham, St Anne's and other even smaller places also had their own. It is a striking feature of the surviving photographic evidence that seaside orchestras and bands are well represented. There are literally hundreds of them, posed in the stiff, unbending postures demanded by late Victorian photography, as reminders of the armies of contemporary music makers. Many contemporaries, particularly German critics, complained that England was 'a land without music'; the reality was quite different.

Resort bands and orchestras were not the first to offer varied musical entertainment; following the example of musicians in Paris and Vienna, similarly mixed programmes had already been presented in London. It was the pioneering work of Louis Julian in mid-century which confirmed the popularity of what one historian has called the 'resort tradition' of mixed musical programmes: Beethoven, Haydn, Mendelssohn and Berlioz were played side by side with ballads, polkas, quadrilles and musical comedy. A similar programme was presented by Henry Wood in his first Promenade Concert (the term itself symbolic) in 1895; only later did the Proms become primarily symphony concerts. From this mixed, highly popular musical tradition, played by bands and orchestras throughout the country, generations of eminent conductors were produced. It is worth remembering that in 1925 the young Malcolm Sargent began his career on Llandudno pier – to modern eyes perhaps an incongruous start, but in fact it was perfectly fitting that such centres of musical diversity and excellence should both attract and produce men of talent.

Public musical tastes were enormously varied and mixed at all social levels and it is often difficult to distinguish 'high-' from 'low-' brow music, though this is not to say that all kinds of Victorian and Edwardian music were equally good. Inevitably music had its fads, snobberies and class distinctions, yet in terms of performance and offerings, English music was more flexible, varied and catholic than we might expect today. The one exception was, as we shall see, the late century music hall.

Most of the music discussed so far was played in public but music was also the mainstay of a great deal of domestic Victorian entertainment and leisure. To be able to sing was the simplest and most easily acquired of musical assets. Singing was a national pastime and was, as we have seen encouraged at home, in the school, church and choir. It is significant for example that soldiers' songs of the Great War – often popular songs transformed and vulgarised to suit the needs of wartime – remain among the most telling and poignant of its documents. It is equally significant that the Second World War did not produce a similar popular musical culture: the difference perhaps lies in the fact that the soldiers of the Great War had a readymade choral tradition to draw on.

In 1870 *The Child's Guide to Knowledge* asked the question, 'What musical instrument is now seen in almost every household'; the answer, exaggerated but revealing was, 'The pianoforte'. Domestic Victorian and Edwardian music so often centred on the piano which, as mass production and rising consumer power increased, spread throughout the nation's households. It even penetrated the better-off sections of working-class life, thanks again to hire purchase, but in general, the poor could only enjoy music and join in the accompanying singing in local pubs. The history of the piano takes us back to an earlier period, but by the Great Exhibition of 1851 it was sufficiently well established and popular (in large measure because of royal patronage) to warrant a major position at the Crystal Palace. Improving technology, growing popularity and the massive expansion of production in Europe and, significantly, America, led to cheaper pianos. Whereas manufacture and demand had originally centred on London, the century saw a spread of the trade into the provinces, with a corresponding growth of the retail outlets specialising in selling musical instruments. The revolution wrought by the American Steinway company transformed the market for, and availability of, the piano, though it was the late-century German pianos which eventually captured the British market. By 1914 one out of every six pianos bought in England was German. The evidence suggests that by 1910 there were at least two million pianos in the country. As new pianos were bought, the older models simply passed down to less exalted stations.

The late-Victorian passion for pianos became nothing less than a mania, encouraged by a music industry but, like other manias, denounced by some observers. In 1899 the *British Medical Journal* complained: 'All – except perhaps teachers of music – will agree that at the present day the piano is too much with us.' It was even claimed that 'the chloroses and neuroses from which so many young girls suffer' was due to excessive piano lessons, and it was felt that 'an ordinary intelligent girl will learn half the languages in Europe in the time given to her abortive struggles with an art she does not care for and cannot understand'. Despite such criticism the piano afforded young women of the lower and upper middle classes a form of recreation which was as welcome as it was rare. (It is noticeable that when a new form of leisure emerged which was thought to be suitable for women, it was seized and soon became a mania – a sign perhaps of the general absence of recreation in their cloistered lives.) Women took both to the piano and to the bicycle with a zest born of a desperation for leisure activity. There was clearly a wider significance to the con-temporary female addiction to the piano. According to one clergyman,' 'a good play on the piano has not infrequently taken the place of a good cry upstairs', a statement perhaps more perceptive than it appears at first sight, for in a society famous for its repression of women, their life was often one 'of feeling rather than action . . . and society, whilst it limits her sphere of action, frequently calls upon her to repress her feelings'. These were not of course, women of the lower orders, but obviously belonged to those households able to afford a piano; families where domestic musical entertainment, for guests or family, frequently centred on music. Magazines for middle-class girls in the later years of the century often portrayed the heroine playing the piano; and it was to provide for this massive and expanding market that music publishers poured forth great quantities of piano music.

Like so many other forms of contemporary leisure, the piano cult was a consequence of rising consumer power, and this was also manifested in the explosion in music publishing and the rapid rise and cheapening of piano lessons. Even the poor began to aspire to owning a piano. In their respectable corner of a Salford slum, the family of Robert Roberts bought a battered piano before the First World War. The £2 'Collinson's Sweetone Parlour Model', delivered on a handcart, proved to be a wreck, filled with straw and dust, and untouched for ages, but it was promptly repaired by a band of friends and workmen. Even then the instrument was thought to be 'buggered really', though it might be 'all right for the children to learn on'.

Sheet music was everywhere, thanks to the progressive decline in its price. The score of *The Messiah* which cost two shillings in 1837, cost only one shilling fifty years later. Publishing costs in general had fallen following the abolition of the paper tax in 1861, thereafter the proliferation of sales outlets across the country made all forms of publication more widely available, though music publishers – in common with others – faced the nightmare of pirated versions, a practice stopped only in 1906 by new legislation. The explosion in choirs, orchestras, bands, music halls and domestic music in the last twenty-five years of the century stimulated (and was itself made possible by) this massive rise in reproduction. 'The Lost Chord' for example sold 500,000 copies between 1877–1902; 'In the Gloaming', 140,000 in the 1880s. 'The Holy City' sold 50,000 annually throughout the 1890s. Sheet music was both an industry and an art form, and the work of prominent contemporary illustrators decorated many of the sheets. Piano teaching also grew dramatically, though often attracting bands of frauds and charlatans (who like acrobats and escapologists often took the self-imposed title 'Professor'). By 1881 there were an estimated 26,000 music teachers in the country; by 1911 the number had risen to 47,000.

The piano represented much more than the emergence of a new kind of musical cult; it also captured the search for respectability by many groups anxious to improve their social status. Few material objects could so instantly confer respectability as the acquisition of a piano, often enshrined in the front parlour, a room, even in crowded homes, which itself became the symbol of a search for respectability and was consequently only used for special occasions such as holidays, family celebrations and, of course. for laying out the dead. A Yorkshire miner told a select committee in 1873 that 'We have got more pianos and perambulators', but the former was 'a cut above the perambulator'. Perceptive workers on Charles Booth's surveys noticed the wall advertisement in a poor community 'What is home without a piano?' It is impossible to know precisely how far down the social scale ownership actually went, but there is no doubt that it became commonplace even in working-class areas and was reflected in the massive success of hire purchase in the last twenty years of the century, to say nothing of the snobbish hostility against HP. A critic in 1881 noted that the popularity of the piano had even attracted 'the poorer classes to a sense of the virtues of a household orchestra', urged on by a 'spirit of emulation for the possession of . . . that highly respectablising piece of furniture'. The resulting HP, embryonic and without firm legal guidelines or protection, led to regular scandals, invariably at the cost of the working-class consumer. All this merely compounded traditional snobberies about working-class aspirations. Slowly however HP seeped down the social scale, adapting its terms to suit the peculiarities and needs of low-income groups. Long before the 1914–18 war it had reached well into the middle strata of working-class life. As HP spread, so too did cheap and better pianos, and by the end of the century it was no longer true that the cheaper models were greatly inferior. The years before the war have been described as 'a golden age' for piano buyers, and it was in these years that possession of a piano enhanced both the owner's social status and the family's recreational potential. Respectability went hand in hand with domestic recreation.

Respectability was the last quality generally associated with the most popular of all late Victorian musical cults – the music hall. In origin the music hall was metropolitan, growing out of the song and supper rooms, which early in the century provided variety and song as well as drink and food. Their popularity grew enormously; by 1868 there were twenty-eight in London, and some 300 in the rest of the country, varying in size, style and offerings both of food and artistes. Organised by sharp-eyed entrepreneurs but restricted by penal licensing laws, the early music halls presented a variety of entertainments, including extracts from ballet and opera, but as the years passed there was a shedding of the more 'serious' side as more popular acts and music rose to prominence. New halls were designed specifically for the purpose and their growing popularity began to yield rich returns for investors. The economic pattern was much the same as that found in the world of major sports, and the rising income of the halls was used both to enhance their appeal and to pay the rising salaries of their stars. The West End of London developed increasingly lavish theatres and offered staggering salaries to the most famous artistes, while a great chain of theatres, linked by owners and theatrical agents, spanned the country. Music halls were at their peak in the years roughly between 1890 and 1912, attracting millions who sought their fun. But they remained anathema to the more respectable, much of whose criticisms were directed against the halls' obvious links with prostitution and the open vulgarity and bawdiness exhibited on the stage.

The glamour of the halls was often merely a façade. The great majority of the performers were paid a mere pittance and it was in keeping with the political climate of the times that in 1906 the artistes began to organise themselves into a trade union. The halls' problems were not solely economic however; their life was notoriously rootless, and had a reputation for broken marriages and drunkenness. In their heyday, however, the stars who shaped their image, songs and style received astronomic salaries. Harry Lauder could command £500 a week; so too could 'Little Tich', who also performed for Edward VII at Sandringham. Marie Lloyd earned £240 a week, and even in the provinces the principal stars could command unusually high salaries. Yet behind these major figures there were legions of less famous artistes whose efforts held the shows together throughout long hours in return for a minimal wage.

Through the music halls' years of prosperity the cost of operations rose sharply as wages and theatrical expenses escalated. Not surprisingly the ownership and management of the halls were always keen to attract new income by means of more eye-catching schemes. Aquatic displays, semi-nude shows (partly inspired by French example), ugly artistes, freaks, tended to blur the hall's main attraction which, until 1914 was the songs. Many songs readily remembered today were popular in the great years of the halls. 'My old man said follow the van', 'Oh Mr Porter', 'The man who broke the bank at Monte Carlo', 'Lily of Laguna', 'My Old Dutch', 'Any old iron', 'Tipperary', 'I love a lassie', 'Roamin' in the gloamin', 'Stop yor ticklin' Jock', 'Keep right on to the end of the road', 'She's a lassie from Lancashire' – these and countless more could be sung without any great effort by millions of people who were born long after the halls had died away. It is difficult to explain why such songs, invariably sung by the more famous stars, should stick so firmly in the collective memory. Whatever the reason, the facts are not in dispute; the music hall before 1914 spawned a variety of songs which outlived the context in which the words were comprehensible.

The halls and their songs were formative in the evolution of popular choral music throughout the first half of the twentieth century. As early as 1899 George Gamble, in *The Halls*, claimed: 'From the music-hall come the melodies that fill the public mind; from the music-hall come the catch-words that fill the public mouth. But for the fecundity of the music-hall, how barren would be the land, how void the chit-chat of the drawing rooms, the parlours, the sculleries!' The bulk of the lyrics were about day-to-day events, of love and domestic problems, commentaries on current events and, much more rarely, political issues. Research on surviving sheet music in the BBC library provides a revealing picture of music hall songs, the majority of which were concerned, not with politics in a specific sense, but with much more commonplace and everyday affairs. Perhaps this common appeal was part of their great attraction, their ability to appeal directly to the experience of most people in the audience, rich and poor alike. Predictably, such music was denounced for its mundane, everyday triviality. Sir Hubert Parry complained in 1899 that,

> The modern popular song reminds me of the outer
> circumference of our terribly overgrown towns. . . . It is for the
> people who live in these unhealthy regions, people who have the
> most false ideals, who are always scrambling for subsistence, who
> think that the commonest rowdyism is the highest expression of
> human emotions; for them, this popular music is made, and it is
> made, with a commercial object, of snippets of slang.

Music apart, the music hall created yet another considerable leisure industry and became a massive employer of labour, both skilled and unskilled; commercial fortunes were to be made (and lost) within the halls. As with organised sports, it was entrepreneurial skills which converted this industry into a major force. Manufacturers produced the material goods to satisfy growing demand; pianos, mechanical instruments, brass and silver instruments, printed music, ancillary industries of music teaching, theatrical design and construction, agencies to handle the unusually complex web of music hall interests, all blossomed from the fertile soil of popular music before 1914. To illustrate the size of the operation on Sunday, when artistes switched from one theatre to another, there were an estimated 142 trains employed in ferrying them around the country. There was even a special category of landladies in most towns, specialising in catering for the peculiar needs and hours of music hall people. Yet all these were only the most obvious battalions of people whose economic well-being ultimately depended on the success of the world of music as a commercial enterprise. There were thousands of others who were equally dependent but much less noticeable; those who worked behind the scenes, in the halls and concert halls, and those who lived like parasites on the names and commercial appeal of the artistes.

English music very quickly became international and by the last years of the century orchestras and bands, singers, choirs, and the songs, were travelling to Europe and North America – and to the British colonies. To a degree this can be explained in terms of the widening of British commercial and imperial horizons; wherever the British traded or ruled, they exported prominent features of their culture, both high and low. Just as their games were played and watched by growing numbers of people around the world, so too did their music and musical stars find favour abroad. Not surprisingly, the rise of a British overseas presence and all its complications (more particularly the case during and after the Boer War) registered itself in popular music. Music was after all a major barometer of contemporary feeling and attitudes and it was inevitable that Britain's growing international stature should find a number of reflections (not all of them political or jingoistic) in contemporary popular music.

In recreational terms it was the USA which apparently held out so much promise for the future. To many Britons (and Europeans in general) the USA was an image of the future already at work. Music hall stars and concert celebrities were quickly seduced across the Atlantic. The Americans were, in commercial terms, already helping to satisfy the demand for diverse leisure products in the late nineteenth century, the most notable and ultimately most successful being the cinema. Even before the outbreak of war films had begun to lure English artistes to the more prosperous climate of California, and thus to undermine the music halls, many of which were well suited to conversion. But the early films were silent and it is significant that when shown they were accompanied by a pianist. In the home, pub, theatre, music hall, and now, the cinema, it was impossible to escape from the sound of the piano.

The sound of music not only epitomised much of English leisure at all social levels, it also accompanied other forms of recreation. The English went to church and sang; they watched sports, with intervals for music; their dominant theatrical form was saturated with music, weekends were often highlighted by music on the streets, in the parks and pubs; holidays were dominated by it. Even inside the home music was a regular part of English home life in the years before 1914. Moreover all these musical dimensions were in addition to the powerful folk tradition of song and dance. Deep-rooted in certain areas it was revitalised by the 'discovery' of folk music and the founding of the Folk Song Society in 1898, and the collecting and editing of English folk songs by Cecil Sharp. Perhaps the most durable and important feature of this revival was the Christmas Carol. All told, no other form of English leisure before 1914 was so all pervasive, so influential and so nationwide as the enjoyment of music.

9 Treats and children's games

The need to relax, to enjoy oneself, to get away from it all, was not new, nor could it be satisfied solely by the new recreational industries. There was a multitude of individual and personal ways in which people chose to spend their free time, often far away from the crowds and noise of organised leisure. Moreover the need for a change was not peculiar to the urban poor, tied as they generally were to the cities. The Victorian and Edwardian rich were as determined as any to escape, and their wealth made it easier to do so. Indeed considerable parts of their wealth and even more of their energy went into the pursuit of pleasure. To that end large new retreats were constructed away from the crowds, particularly in Scotland and northern and southern France, many of which remain as monuments to the contemporary upper-class need to escape as far as possible from the thousands pressing on their old recreational preserves. There were only a few sports which could still be enjoyed away from the milling crowds. The most exclusive members of society followed the royal example and took up yachting, establishing in the process the popularity of the sailor suit worn by children of all social classes in the years before 1914. Equally secure in their isolation were the shooting parties and weekend houseparties, their development and popularity encouraged by the invention of the motor-car. Even before the war motor transport had begun to redirect the recreations of the English upper classes.

Leisure was at its most ostentatious among the wealthy – itself a commonplace and traditional fact – but before 1914 it was transformed by the sheer scale of upper class enjoyment and the vast numbers involved. Moreover it was in many respects an international phenomenon, spearheaded by Europe's ruling houses who helped to define the nature and style of upper-class European leisure before the war. In these same years the Americans too, thanks to their already legendary wealth and the improvement in trans-Atlantic communications, were beginning to cut a style in the leisurely world of the European upper-classes.

Americans had become familiar sights in European cities, their open opulence perhaps yet another stimulant – if any more were needed – to regard the USA as the country of the future. But towards the end of the century, America offered much more than a supply of tourists, for its untapped potential continued to attract armies of European immigrants. The major American cities proved highly attractive for British entertainers. Bands, orchestras, choirs and actors, footballers, athletes and music hall stars crossed the Atlantic, more often than not on tour but also frequently tempted to try to make a more lucrative career in a more prosperous nation. The flow was not only one way for, though the Old World undoubtedly fed a great deal of its talent and initiative into America, the products of that maturing industrial giant flooded back.

American pianos had, as we have seen, democratised piano music. Much the same process was at work in other recreations, more especially where technology was harnessed to the need to cater for new demands. From the 1890s onwards American technology and entrepreneurial guile pointed the way towards new mechanical pursuits. Along the east coast of the USA a string of leisure facilities and parks were established, often by local transportation companies who (thanks to the tram) were able to carry hordes of people from the cities to the new developments. The resulting 'pleasure beaches' – exemplified, though by no means dominated by Coney Island – were monuments to mechanical fun, the power of electricity and the revolution in urban transport (all dependent on the consumer's spending power). Artificial representation of foreign civilisations, the construction of giant towers and ferris wheels, and lavish displays of lighting which dominated the pleasure beaches and gardens of major American cities in the 1890s soon found their way on a smaller scale into England. Blackpool's tower and wheel, Scarborough's short-lived tower, Blackpool's pleasure beach, even Rhyl's imitation underground Venice complete with gondolas, were all pale reflections of brasher, bigger, more spectacular American versions. English resorts and music halls attracted famous American stars, from Caruso and Buffalo Bill to the ageing Blondin. Long before the First World War the American influence on English commercial leisure activities had become apparent as the beginning of a process which was accelerated in later years by the cinema, recorded music and, later still, by TV. Even when the Americans copied a European form of leisure, they invariably made it bigger, more spectacular and, often as not, more lucrative.

This was most clearly the case with the circus, which began in its modern form in England in the 1760s. Limited to the theatre in the early nineteenth century, the circus spread throughout Europe and North America, its main attraction initially being horseborne acts. Gradually the repertoire became more varied; menageries were incorporated, followed in the mid-nineteenth century by growing numbers of trapeze and high-wire acts. At the same time, circuses became peripatetic, thanks largely to the perfection of large 'big top' tents, which were developed in the USA. And it was in the USA that the new railborne circuses, heralded by amazing publicity stunts and street parades from the railway sidings, took on their modern form. To a large degree the initial success of the American circus was the work of pioneering publicists, none better than P. T. Barnum, whose eye for the commercial appeal of the big top was surpassed only by an eye for freaks and wonders of men and animals which paraded at his shows. When Barnum teamed up with John A. Bailey they established the 'greatest show on earth' and their outrageous style and panache soon became the model for circuses everywhere. One circus even had the audacity to attach itself to a procession of Queen Victoria through London. And like sports, circuses began to appear throughout the western world in the twenty-five years before 1914.

In England, the appeal of the circus was heightened by the late Victorian obsession with empire and the curiosity about unusual creatures to be found there. Not all circuses however were as spectacular as their publicity suggested. The Rev. Kilvert recorded the pathetic scene when 'Wombwell's Menagerie' travelled to Hey from Brecon Fair. 'The elephant, a very small one, and three camels or dromedaries came shuffling and splashing along the muddy road in heavy rain looking cold and miserable and shivering as if they were wet through. The camels were being towed by the caravan.' For the rest, the show consisted of a lion, a wolf, a laughing hyena, a black sheep and a three feet dwarf who 'stirred the beasts up with a long pole and made them roar'. Doubtless it impressed the locals. When in 1872 'Mander's Menagerie' visited Woodstock, the parade was led by 'carriages drawn by elephants, camels, dromedaries, zebras, mules etc., and accompanied by a brass band'. Major towns had their own familiar circuses; Wild's and Banister's in the north and Midlands, Saunders' Cooke's, Somerwell's and Clarke's in the south, east and west. By modern (and by contemporary American) standards most were small and their performances brief, but the animals and artistes were kept at work as long as people filed into their seats. And there were even smaller circuses which, like the one seen by Kilvert, toured the remoter and less profitable areas.

Circuses, or merely displays of freaks and unusual animals often appeared at fairs. And in many respects the English fair provided generations of people with a brief (often annual) taste of pre-industrial enjoyments. Few parts of the country were without their local fair, feast day, wakes or holiday festivity. Such events had (and in many places continue to have) an important role; the horse, cattle, sheep, hog, cheese, hardware, and hiring fairs provided an important economic focus in pre-industrial society. Normally fairs were also the occasion for organised pleasures, and hence attracted a range of recreational facilities, drinking and musical activity which enhanced their importance for local people. Business and pleasure mingled easily as Dr Asplin recorded in his diary at Prittlewell, Essex, in 1826; 'The fair is a very decent one. An exhibition on our right of a Giant, Giantess, and Albinos, a native of Buffin Bay, and a Dwarf – very respectable. We had a learned Pig and Punch on our left and in front some Theatrical Exhibition. All in very good order.'

Fairs and wakes, with a multitude of local and regional variations, were generally events to be enjoyed and were invariably linked to the patterns and rhythms of local economic life. Many rural fairs survived throughout the nineteenth century, though their bloodier, less disciplined recreations disappeared, as Professor Malcolmson has shown. In Northamptonshire for example there were more fairs in the 1850s than a century before, and it seems that those which mixed business with pleasure were the most likely to survive. Those whose status declined found themselves under attack. In 1875 two fairs at Sawbridgeworth in Hertfordshire, were criticised as being 'of the smallest conceivable worth in a commercial point of view . . . ' and having become, in their critics' eyes 'the prolific seed plots and occasions of the most hideous forms of moral and social evils – drunkeness – whoredom – robbing – idleness and neglect of work'. Many of the old fairs simply disappeared, the most notable casualty being Bartholomew Fair (in 1855) but in industrial areas new fairs were created to provide urban people with traditional pleasures. Manchester's Knott Mill Easter Fair and the summer and winter fairs at Leeds were good examples. So too was Oxford's St Giles's Fair where, in the word's of the *Oxford Magazine* of 1883 'every class was fully represented except gentlefolk'.

Often a fair was a very small, mere parish or village gathering, but nonetheless important in the lives of the local people who prepared for weeks for it. Processions, bands, flags, church services, races, dancing, stalls for food and entertainment, all helped to transform a village into a fun fair for the day. It was to such fairs that travelling entertainers were attracted, moving, like their modern descendants, from one to another throughout the season. Roundabouts, swings, shooting galleries, Punch and Judy shows, menageries and performers of all conceivable kinds, converged on the fair from their last engagement. In the 1870s, at the Highworth Fair there were 'exhibitions . . . of beasts and birds, waxwork figures, model machinery, glass-making, cotton-spinning, picture galleries, and all sorts of things besides. . . . A great Zulu and several negroes performed the war dance.' Flora Thompson, whose account of rural life is invaluable evidence, describes a North Oxfordshire parish show:

> The crowning event of the . . . year. . . . From ten o'clock in the morning onward a stream of villagers and their friends . . . might [be] seen making its way over the greensward towards the big marquee flying the Union Jack and the smaller but no less exciting cluster of show booths, coconut shies, and gingerbread

stalls by which it was surrounded. A brass band was engaged to play for the day, and the steam roundabout had an organ attached which was permitted to play by arrangement at such times as the bandsmen felt in need of refreshment.

Prizes and awards – such as being king or queen for the day – would sometimes crown these memorable days in the toiling lives of local people, and those who failed to carry off a prize, at the shy, or even for the best bunch of wild flowers, could enjoy the games of football, cricket and dancing which invariably developed. But it was the unusualness of the fairs and their distinctive, eye-catching attractions which lived in the memory and which, significantly, were remembered decades later by young people grown old. Pamela Horn writes of one visitor's recollections of a fair at Ramsey in the 1880s:

> where you could buy things to eat, like hot pies in a basin, or a dish o' whelks, or a packet o' brandy snaps. . . . There were the Fat Lady, all dressed up in spangles, a mountain o' flesh and blood, and a couple o' tiny dwarfs called Tom Thumb and his wife. . . . In another booth there were the conjurers, and in another the performing fleas, that I remember being in chains. Then there were a boxing-booth and a waxwork show, where when I was ever such a little girl I see the sad sight o' Queen Victoria and all her children round Prince Albert's death bed.

Whatever economic purposes such fairs may have had, it was memories of their unusual glamour and colour which lingered longest in the public mind, and whenever old people were asked to remember their late century childhood, they invariably dug out these colourful scenes from their youth, largely perhaps because such events formed such a sharp contrast to their everyday life. Their memories were often of much less spectacular enjoyments – a visiting band, a dancing bear, a 'one-man' band or a charitable feast provided by a local benefactor.

These delights were not restricted to rural people, for the travelling folk set up their stalls and shows wherever the need arose, in town or country. At the Slaithwaite (Yorkshire) fair held 'between the Crimble Viaducts and Spa Mill Terrace' there was the usual array of enjoyments, 'the swings, hobby horses, switch-backs, dry-land sailors, and two bazaars . . . also a brandy snap and coco-nut, and ice-cream stall, and a pea saloon.' Even in the heart of Robert Roberts' Edwardian Salford slum, a May Pole was erected each year for the ritual fun and games. Twice yearly, a travelling fair set up shop on a vacant lot. 'It brought us tattered gaiety and a music at times so plaintive that, heard in the dark approaching lanes, it filled one with a sort of infinitive regret. . . . Under bursts of naptha light, the 'croft' ran alive with Lowry-like figures.' Whatever the peculiarities of local features of such fairs, they gave local people rare glimpses of the colourful and the bizarre. For the poor, unable to afford a trip to the music hall or to the seaside, the visiting fair, showman, itinerant musician or dancing bear came as a reminder of the better things in life. Even in the most squalid areas of English cities there was an occasional, but all too rare, glimmer of colour and enjoyment.

London was renowned for the depths and extent of its squalor, yet even the capital could lay on a splash of colour for the poorest of its people, and had its own special occasions, apart from the carnival which attended Royal occasions. The Oxford and Cambridge boat race (a much more democratic event that it is today) annually drew all classes to the water's edge. 'LISTEN! THE GUN! There is a heaving of the entire mass: a low, full murmur rolls along the river banks. A spasm of intense excitement passes through the two or three hundred thousand people who have packed themselves along the shores to see the prowess of a few University lads.' And this description can be seen in Gustav Doré's sketches of the teeming riverside scenes.

Competing with the boat race for the capital's favour was the Derby. On the rare holidays and, according to Doré and Jerrold, 'on the two national race-days – the boat race and the Derby – London is not the old, familiar, hard-working, solemn-visaged place of every day.' Most of the city seemed to rise early and head for the Epsom Downs in May. The teeming thousands heading to the races, the congested scenes and roadside incidents, the carnival atmosphere on the Downs and the heady excitement of the races themselves were colourfully captured by Doré and Jerrold. Poor and rich alike enjoyed Derby Day when 'all classes are intermingled for a few hours on the happiest terms'. Ribald, drunken, thieving, the poor of London frolicked to and from the Derby, pressed alongside the carriages of their betters, on whom they heaped the vulgar, funny insults of the world's poor towards those above them. It was an unusual and distinctive occasion, though the century also saw the emergence of a similar racing carnival at the Grand National Steeplechase in Liverpool.

These interludes were available to all, irrespective of social station and money. At the fair, few people enjoyed themselves so thoroughly and more vigorously than the children. Children's recreations could, on the whole, take place without any of the concessions of free time and spare income, though armies of the Victorian young were denied proper recreation by the needs of their crowded families. 'Never no time to play,' one poor London child told Charles Booth. Children had, since time out of mind, found enjoyment in their own games, songs, rhymes, inventions, imaginary worlds, and reconstructions of the real world. Both in town and country, the nation's young enjoyed a recreational world which survived from one generation to another, often despite the changing circumstances around them.

Children's games were remarkably durable and, with local

variations, nationwide. The evidence of oppressive economic conditions for millions cannot mask the fact that children managed to create games and enjoyment from the most unrewarding of circumstances. Indeed from mid-century onwards photographic evidence is often dominated by children; they seemed to fill the urban areas and dot the spaces – an indication of their overall numerical significance. Throughout the second half of the nineteenth century, some 36 per cent of the population was under the age of fifteen (figures comparable to developing countries today). In 1871 the census recorded, 'The people of England, which calls herself old, are younger than the people of many other nations.' Family photographs, like street and seaside snaps, convey the impression of a nation with an unusual abundance of young people. This youthful presence had repercussions on all aspects of society, on economics, employment, housing, and of course, on leisure. Particularly before the introduction of compulsory schooling, it was impossible to escape from the bands of children at play, the older ones often looking after their brothers and sisters, and thus fulfilling an economic function even when at play.

The recreations of English children differed enormously, not merely along local and regional lines but more especially along class lines. Poor, overcrowded homes afforded none of the play space so common in wealthier houses, and consequently poor children tended to play on the streets, and in alleys and clearings in their immediate neighbourhood. It was in those unpromising circumstances that children kept alive, as the Opies have shown, the cultural heritage of childhood which went back for centuries. Pre-industrial children's culture survived the impact of urbanisation largely, one suspects, because children were not so divided from their traditional recreations in the way their parents were. Children's games adapted themselves to the circumstances of urban life but more remarkable still were the continuities, for many of the catching, guessing, chasing, daring, hunting, pretending, and countless other games of Victorian children had originated hundreds of years before. While their parents' recreations underwent major change and sometimes disappeared, children's games remained remarkably longlived.

Games in the countryside were even closer to pre-industrial life than those in the cities. Country children continued to be important to the economic wellbeing of their families, yet even when at work, guarding animals or crops and helping on the land, country children found time to play with hoops, ropes, tops and marbles, and to go bird-watching, nesting, fishing and hunting. Long summer days saw the upsurge of those games popular in towns; 'Oranges and Lemons', 'London Bridge is falling down'. For boys there were the increasingly important games of football and cricket, both of which had traditional rural roots. Poor children may have lacked the expensive toys of their betters, but there was no shortage of imagination in fashioning toys and games from whatever materials were available. Home-made bats and balls, rag and straw dolls, were just as much fun as the more costly versions. Robert Roberts recalled his own poor childhood:

> They bought us no toys, we hung no stockings, yet none of us felt in the least deprived. . . . We built hamlets of thatched cottages, roofing gas mantle boxes with wisps of straw, sticky with albumen from the egg crate. We borrowed lumps of washing soda from a sack under the counter to make cliffs, gorges or the Rocky Mountains, using flour, sugar and salt sweepings from shelves to scatter creations with snow and ice, people it with figures carved from pop bottle corks. . . . My two older sisters Elbe and Ada . . . once erected for me a splendid Greek temple from half-pound block of Sunlight loaf . . . and carton board, with rows of candles for columns – all based on a picture in Harmsworth's Self-Educator.

Games long-popular among pre-industrial children continued well into the nineteenth century. The slaughter of animals tradition-ally provided new material for games, as one Victorian recalled 'As children we hung around waiting for the bladder, which when drained we blew up with a clay pipe stem, and then would use it for a football.' An upturned table was an adequate alternative for a boat at sea; children unable to buy expensive fireworks sometimes managed to buy ingredients to make their own. These and countless other twists of invention brought endless fun to children who seemed on the surface to be denied the more obvious forms of material enjoyments.

Most English children enjoyed a variety of seasonal games and enjoyments. Shrove Tuesday, which had since the Middle Ages been a day for games, was the day for tops and shuttlecocks. April Fools' Day, then as now, generated its own plethora of fun and collective amusement. Halloween was a similarly mischievous night, and of course Guy Fawkes's night has to this day continued to be an occasion for childhood enjoyments. In many respects it seems pointless to illustrate the diversity and range of children's games, because so many of them would be familiar to readers. Yet it is important to underline the remarkable endurance of children's recreations, even when times were hard. Moreover, there was a growing commercial interest in children's leisure. A great deal of commercial activity concentrated on the thriving market of children's leisure – football, cricket, seaside visits, toys, children's literature and countless other aspects. The pantomime, which emerged late in the century as an annual Christmas treat, owed much of its continuing popularity to its appeal among the young. Indeed it was striking that large numbers of entertainers focused on children; nigger minstrels, pierrots, Punch and Judy shows. And of course visits to the seaside had become a major treat for English children (or an ambition among the poor).

Not all children were, like Robert Roberts and the armies of the poor, obliged to rely on stray bits and pieces for their fun and games. For the more privileged, recreation was provided by the outpourings of the growing children's industries. Children's books and magazines flew off the presses, some of their writers being among the nation's best-selling authors. For those able to afford such relatively expensive items there were also consumer goods to fill the nursery. Many toy makers, while interested in a mass market, were equally concerned to produce works of quality and educational value. Many Victorian toys thus demanded intelligent use; there were cut-out games and toys, jigsaws (introduced in the 1870s) and chemical sets. Dolls became more varied and more sophisticated, though rag and woollen ones remained popular with Victorian children. Dolls' houses and toy theatres complemented the array of make-believe people lining the nurseries and bedroom walls. It was into this world that Lewis Carroll, Hans Christian Andersen and others wove their webs of fantasy. Yet this more privileged child's world was not totally divorced from that of their poorer contemporaries for, particularly in the country and among the staff 'below stairs', wealthier children had friends and contacts in a world which was as austere and barren as theirs was plentiful. So many poor children, living in overcrowded quarters. were forced on to the streets and open land for their games by sheer pressure of numbers and shortage of space. And it was there that they lived out an independent recreational culture which was older than living memory.

Informal children's games were not thought to be a sufficient recreational diet by growing numbers of Victorians and, in the last decades of the nineteenth century, they began to change as a result of the encroachment of compulsory education, which embraced physical education as well as the three Rs. The most obvious consequence of compulsory education was the long-term impact on popular literacy; it was no accident that the arrival of mass education coincided with the expansion of the national press. Equally important, the new schools began slowly to provide facilities for recreation as part of the syllabus. Leisure, particularly those forms conducive to 'good health' and 'social discipline' came to be seen as important as the three Rs themselves.

Inevitably perhaps, the recreations of the new schools were fashioned from within the public schools. Commenting in 1861 on rural schools in the south west, the Rev. James Fraser told a Parliamentary Commission, 'good games need to be taught as well as lessons. And I do not think that the encouragement of healthy athletic sports, such as cricket, football, etc., has yet found the legitimate place in the education of this class [rural poor] which public school men would desire'. These complaints were stifled by the new state schools' provision for games; indeed very soon recreation became a major attraction of school life. By 1888 it was asserted that:

It cannot be doubted that good playgrounds attached to schools have a perceptible influence on the inclination of children to go to school, especially in the case of boys. Those whose physical restlessness leads them to absent themselves from school, whenever they can do so, finds their wants met by the games which take place in the playground in the intervals between classes.

By the mid-1890s another commentator felt that 'the work in the playground [is] a very important part of a child's life'. And even in those schools which, particularly in the cities, lacked a playground or playing-field, the introduction of 'military drill' ensured that, by the mid-1890s compulsory recreation had become a part of school children's lives.

Girls however were ill-served by the new schools for, while most Victorians were in agreement that recreation ought to be provided, the games and drill they encouraged were designed for boys (yet another suggestion of the Victorian view that athleticism ought to be masculine). It is nonetheless true that by the turn of the century many children's recreations had been subsumed within the school system. They may not all have enjoyed the schools' games and drill, but, with the exception of the unfit and unsuited, most of the nation's children were provided with the means, however limited, and the encouragement to take part in recreations. Yet it is significant that when people recalled their late-century memories, they remembered, not the school games but their own informal play and the occasional colourful visits from fairs and travelling shows. Charitable efforts and, in the last years of the century, state endeavours, had striven to bring enjoyment and fun (in conjunction with better health) into the world of the Victorian child, particularly the poor. But in terms of enjoyment and lasting memories, they scarcely matched the colourful provisions of more traditional pleasures, or even the commercial attractions of the new mass sports.

As the century advanced, more and more philanthropic efforts were directed towards providing children with 'treats', and though such efforts had been common in the early years of industrialisation, there was a noticeable late-century increase in charitable provision of facilities. People were now thought to have the right to leisure and considerable efforts went into providing it for those in harsh circumstances. Hordes of children were packed into trains for visits to coast and country, onto steamers for trips down river or round the bay. Schoolmasters, clergymen, social workers and others with access to poor quarters, rallied willing armies of children for these trips. In 1887 a Glaswegian businessman treated some 15,000 of the city's poorer children to an outing to Rothesay; in 1895, 7,617 poor children from Newcastle enjoyed a charitable day at Tynemouth (in both cases serenaded by local bands). With similar aims in mind 'the Fresh Air Fund' was launched in 1892 by C. Arthur Pearson; by 1909 it had financed day trips for more than two million children. While the seaside was the most popular destination, children were also frequently taken into the countryside – Epping Forest was a favourite spot for Londoners. But in both cases the determination to deposit gangs of needy children beside the sea or in the country was inspired by the feeling that everyone ought to have a healthy break. And to bring home the point to the wealthier (upon whom these ventures ultimately relied for finance), the Fresh Air Fund published a telling poem in 1909.

> Pity the children of the poor
> Who've never plucked the daisies
> Who've never watched the skylark soar,
> Or heard it singing praises;
> Who've never trod the fresh green sward,
> Or rambled by the river,
> They need a holiday, ye rich –
> may God reward the giver.

Organised charitable trips were not reserved solely for children, for philanthropy was extended to providing treats for thousands of people, not all of whom were needy. Shops and factories, employers and owners, often made lavish arrangements for their employees to enjoy a treat at the company's expense. By the late century such trips were commonplace and added a new dimension to the recreational lives of employees. Wealthy industrialists opened the grounds (and sometimes the doors) of their stately homes to the curious gaze of their employees, who were ferried into the country by fleets of trains and coaches. The day was usually filled with sports, brass bands, tea in the marquee, and dancing. Catering for the enjoyment of the assembled thousands was a major and costly undertaking, yet industrialists thought it a worthwhile expense. For many employees, the activities (and food) must have provided a rare and welcome taste of enjoyment they would otherwise never have known. In 1897 Lever Brothers treated 2,300 employees to an excursion: to London for the Queen's Diamond Jubilee, and 'although the expense of the outing was tremendous, each employee will be paid his or her usual wages without the deduction of a penny.' In 1909 the staff of W. H. Smith's warehouse in Fetter Lane travelled to the countryside at Pinner, where they enjoyed dinner, tea and a cricket match. Many such trips were epics of organisation on an almost military scale. In June 1914 Huntley and Palmer ferried 7,000 workers from Reading to Margate, Ramsgate and Portsmouth.

In Edwardian England trips such as these – sponsored by factories, schools, private organisations and benefactors – had become commonplace. But their wider significance lies, not so much in the vast crowds involved, but in the attitudes which lay behind such ventures. Employers had come to the view that these costly ventures made commercial and social sense and that the expense was more than offset by the advantages and in many companies they continued well into the century. Day trips were of course partly inspired by a desire to whip up corporate identity; more often than not speeches and thanks were made in praise of the boss or the company. The company was seen to be caring for its employees' wider interests, giving them pleasure and unexpected vistas, quite apart from employment. It is also important to remember that these outings were available to women and children; many were family occasions, doubtless helping to reinforce the wider sense of family loyalty to the place of work. Indeed it would not be too fanciful to see such entertainments as the peak of industrial paternalism in Britain. But such scenes of collective enjoyment must be set against the marked deterioration in industrial relations, and the related upsurge in syndicalism, in the years before 1914. Works outings did not end in 1914, but they represent a particular type of corporate Edwardian attitude between master and man in certain employments. It is of course hard to know how effective such outings were in cementing loyalties to the firm but it would be wrong to suggest that this alone was the sole inspiration behind their provision. Even among men of powerful economic vested interests, concern for the wellbeing of their employees was genuine and commonplace, personified by the Rowntrees of York. While the most obvious answer to this concern was to provide more adequate wages, it is nonetheless true that these paternalistic gestures brought enjoyments which would otherwise have remained mere aspirations.

Outings from the cities or to fairs in the country were mere splashes of colour for millions of people whose lives were dominated by work. Yet, at the turn of the century there were many more such occasions and events for people to enjoy. Victorians and Edwardians were constantly looking for an opportunity to celebrate their own achievements, and as the Queen got older, and her empire larger and more impressive, the occasions for national self-congratulation became more frequent and grandiose. Of course the 1851 Exhibition, a monument to mid-Victorian achievements, set the pattern which was to last, in changing form, throughout the following century. Exhibitions of all kinds, to celebrate manufactures, foodstuffs, imperial conquests and national greatness, were regularly organised in London and other major cities; many of their awards are still recorded on the promotional claims of foodstuffs. The London Exhibition of 1862, The Great International Fisheries Exhibition of 1883; Empire and trade exhibitions, and the displays to celebrate royal anniversaries, birthdays, visits or, increasingly, a major sporting event, produced visitors to the capital by tens of thousands. Travel had by then become easier and more comfortable, and so too had accommodation. Indeed the very fact of travel on such an epic scale in pursuit of pleasure and fun was itself a Victorian invention, and the train or coach ride, the boat or steamer trip were pleasures in themselves. Travelling was half the fun of the excursion to the seaside, country or capital, and has remained so to the present day. For people whose lives (even with the improvements of shortened hours) were dominated by work, travel was itself exciting. Often on a day trip it took longer to get to the chosen spot than the time spent there. Simply to get away from the home environment was enjoyable, and the mythology, popular songs and ditties about the journey, its upsets, late and non-arrivals, missed connections and mishaps, were widely popular and provide an insight into the excitement afforded by travel.

There was a major upsurge in late-century travel, in large measure because there were many more people (particularly in the cities) in need of transportation simply because of the population rise. Moreover these same years saw the coming of age of the concept of leisure. While it is true that there was still a distinct 'leisured class', it was now widely accepted that leisure was no longer the monopoly of that class. By the turn of the century, partly as a result of the proliferation of facilities, it had become generally accepted that everyone had a right to the enjoyment of leisure. Many of the new types of leisure had penetrated even into the slum streets of the major cities. This is not to suggest that everyone was equal in the pursuit of leisure or that all forms of leisure were comparable; to have a good time, to enjoy oneself, however briefly or humbly, was thought to be everyone's legitimate right. Whenever the chance arose, English people of all classes made the most of enjoying themselves, no matter how simply.

Part Three

Leisure in war and peace
1914–1950

10 The Great War and after 1914-1939

Few events in modern history have had such shattering repercussions as the Great War of 1914–18, its most immediate and
long-term consequence being the appalling casualties. The figures
themselves make terrible reading. During the four and a quarter years
of fighting there was a daily average of 1,500 British casualties; the
peak days were of course much worse, and the apparently endless
lists of dead and wounded published in contemporary newspapers
stand as monuments to the daily suffering. On the first day of the
battle of the Somme in July 1916, 20,000 British soldiers were killed.
Yet hostilities had begun with scenes of jubilation on the streets of
Britain and Europe as the people rejoiced at the prospect of war.
Those public displays of collective joy were not to be seen again until
November 1918 and then only among the 'victors'. The human consequences of the war were manifest throughout the succeeding
years. Whereas in 1911 in England and Wales there were 155 males
aged between twenty and forty per 1,000 of the population, by 1921
there were only 141. The proportion of females rose; the 595 per
1,000 aged over fourteen in 1911 had risen to 638 in 1921. The proportion of widows rose from 38 to 43. Yet such statistics merely hint
at the individual and collective agony of the war years.

In the early months of hostilities there was popular rallying to
the flag, a symptom of that distinctive public attitude which persisted
throughout the war in defiance of the evidence from the front and the
words of the men who returned. The gulf between the popular
acclaim for the war and the realities of life in the trenches remained
unbridgeable. While the man in the front line endured a life of
unprecedented horror, the discomforts of many at home were tolerable
and seemed insultingly minor. After a year of war, the Editor of the
Daily Express wrote in his diary, 'No cricket, no boat race, no racing'.
There were of course more onerous restrictions on wartime life, and
they increased as the war bit deep into the nation's economy, but the
pursuit of leisure seemed singularly inappropriate at a time of national
emergency. Leisure activities suffered accordingly, both under the
pressure of outraged opinion and, more directly, because of the
draining of physically fit men into the armed forces. But the cessation

of sporting activity was uneven, for those sports which tended to cater for the middle and upper classes ordered an immediate halt to their proceedings. Cricketers, according to the MCC secretary 'now look for their heroes on the great field of battle'. Other sports were slower in accommodating.

Association football, followed by the masses, commercial and professional, continued to be played throughout the first eighteen months, though the ruling FA, like all private organisations, put its organisation and money behind the war effort. The FA gave away its money, indiscriminately, to war charities, opened its London offices to the army and, most important of all, put its national bureaucracy at the service of troop recruitment. The FA agreed that clubs should be 'requested to place their grounds at the disposal of the War Office on days other than match days, for use as Drill Grounds. . . . Where football matches are played arrangements [are] to be made for well-known public men to address the players and spectators, urging men who are physically fit, and otherwise able, to enlist at once'. The amazing outcome was that by the end of 1914, of 1,186,337 volunteers some 500,000 had come forward through footballing organisations. Despite such efforts, which inevitably went largely overlooked at the time, the footballing fraternity was the object of vituperative attack by spokesmen of those other games who had stopped playing on the outbreak of war. Insulted in the press, attacked in the Cabinet, football finally succumbed and decided to abandon the professional game after the Old Trafford Cup Final of April 1915. Lord Derby, presenting the Cup, urged the players; 'You have played well with one another and against one another for the Cup; play with one another for England now.'

In the eyes of many people, the war ought to have been a total war requiring the civilian population to make sacrifices to complement the even greater sacrifices of the troops. Those who tried to carry on apparently non-essential business were denounced. Complaints similar to those against football were directed against horse-racing. In May 1915 *The Times* commented: 'It is the business of the country to see that the movements of its fighting men are not inconvenienced by the rush of racecourse crowds. . . . Racing still presents its saddening contrasts to the patriotism of those who have devoted themselves to the service of their country.'

Racing men had convincing answers; in the north racing had indeed been abandoned so as not to interfere with war work, while the facilities of the grounds had been put at the army's disposal. In some cases local pressure had led to cancellation of race meetings. As a last line of defence, the proponents of racing urged that the sport continued, not for amusement, but largely as a major employer of labour. In fact football and racing were the exceptions to the general abandonment of major sports, and even these had to battle against dwindling crowds, public hostility and inconvenient railway facilities.

Foremost among the complaints against them was the confusion and strain they caused on the hard-pressed transportation system. Pressure on racing built up. In 1915 the Duke of Rutland withdrew his horses from Epsom and Ascot, finding it offensive to pursue pleasures in wartime; the railway companies were persuaded to withdraw excursion tickets, the press was filled with anti-racing letters. Under government pressure, in May 1915 (a month after football's termination) the Jockey Club bowed to the inevitable; the surviving *ad hoc* meetings were finally extinguished in 1916 by application of the Defence of the Realm Act (DORA). Racing stables however had a much wider importance, in maintaining bloodstock, and with that in mind there was a relaxation of the ban late in the war and in 1917 and 1918 limited racing fixtures were held. The pressure on sporting organisations in wartime had been considerable; their players and spectators had joined up, their funds depleted, their property often put in government hands, and travel made extremely difficult. But perhaps even more important was the extreme political pressure which castigated the pursuit of pleasure as an affront to the patriotic and a hindrance to the single-minded conduct of the war.

It would be unreasonable to expect to find consistent wartime behaviour throughout the population; to find everyone enduring the war years with rigid abstemiousness and a consequent self-denial of leisure. The domestic shortages and sacrifices seem, in retrospect, minor compared to the tougher days of the Second World War. But there was an undoubted climate of hostility towards the more overt forms of pleasure, and although that hostility was largely successful in helping to curb the public's organised pleasures, there was nonetheless a continuing subterranean groundswell of public fun. Whenever such enjoyments came to the attention of the newspapers a thunderous correspondence in the press inevitably followed. Following stories about a crop of dances throughout the country in February 1917, *The Times* satisfied itself 'that there are whole circles of society, both in London and elsewhere, in which the spirit of sacrifice is utterly unknown, and "pre-war conditions" still flourish without the smallest regard for the exhortations of the Prime Minister and the Food Controller'. It was, said *The Times* 'nothing less than life and death to this country that there should be no exceptions to the rigorous rule of self-denial which has been willingly undertaken by the great mass of our people'. Despite these pronouncements, correspondents continued to inform *The Times* of transgressions against self-denial, and to provide instances of open self-indulgence and consumption. In March 1917 there was a bitter complaint about private supper parties and dances with excesses of food and drink. 'At a dance of this kind recently in a London gathering, an unlimited supply of champagne was provided. . . . There were oysters for each of the hundreds of guests, and salmon and lobster mayonnaise. Fowl, quail, pheasant and other game were to be had in unfailing supplies.' *The Times* and its supporters were clearly right in feeling that such lavish entertainments were both inappropriate and offensive to millions of contemporaries.

The Times did not reserve its antagonism for upper-class extravagance. They and their readers were equally offended by the newfound wealth and its manifestations among workers whose earnings had increased dramatically, largely through having to work long hours in war industries. The Times spoke of 'those well-paid industrial communities which are said to be enjoying the war'. They even had the effrontery to write that 'Fur coats have come to be known as "munition overalls"'. The Times called on its readers to visit working-class areas of London to see the flourishing state of trade – butchers, provisions, furniture, drapers stores – even jewellers – all of them enjoying unprecedented business. 'It is not without significance that pears are displayed in a fruiterer's shop in Walworth Road at 3d apiece and grapes at 5s a pound. But it is also significant that every picture palace is crowded night after night, and that some people visit different halls three or four times a week'. One thing alone disturbed that thunderous newspaper more than middle- and upper-class enjoyment, and that was fun and material consumption among the working class. There was of course no doubt that many working people, more especially women drafted into the factories, were enjoying unprecedented wages and yet their conditions and long hours were unlikely to persuade them, for instance, that their hard-earned cash ought to be sunk entirely into government bonds. Many people who throughout their lives had been able merely to press their noses against shop windows, now found themselves able to go inside and buy the goods. To do so however was to offend the sensibilities of those who saw material self-denial and the national refusal to enjoy oneself as a fundamental principle of the war effort.

Seaside resorts continued to attract the seasonal visitor in wartime but the atmosphere was more restrained, and the clientele had changed dramatically. It was difficult to travel abroad, so wealthier people tended to take their holidays at home. Certain resorts became less popular. The German raids on the east coast in December 1914 (killing 137 and wounding 592 in Hartlepool, Whitby and Scarborough) put a blight on that region. South coast resorts however were crowded, as The Times noted in the summer of 1915: 'The hotels and boarding houses are full; indeed they are fuller than in most years.' But even when crowded the resorts had changed in style and character. 'The long front at Eastbourne is crammed with people who in ordinary times would have avoided Eastbourne as dressy and dull. At Littlehampton you may see gowns and hats that look as if they were made for Trouville. . . . Brighton is very full – but for Brighton very quiet.'

The reason was not hard to find; 'There are men about these places – perhaps one in ten. . . . At Brighton and everywhere else the crowd is quiet, all except the children'. Holidays, like sports, were thought to be inappropriate to wartime, though the hard efforts of the industrial nation in the first year of the war certainly qualified the people for a refreshing break from their work. Many people were reluctant to visit the seaside for fear of enemy bombardments and raids. In January 1915, for example, a U-boat blew up a steamer off the Blackpool coast and the lights rapidly went out on Blackpool's funmaking, a process made more effective and nationwide by DORA. Some resorts, with their tens of thousands of extra beds, proved ideal emergency billets for the troops, and they did again in 1939. Yet despite the restrictions and sober atmosphere the resorts continued to lure people throughout the wartime summers. Even when in 1917 railway fares to Blackpool were raised by a staggering 50 per cent, the town's traditional clientele overcame the expenses by taking to the complex system of trams linking the industrial towns and the coast. Travelling all day from Leeds and Halifax, these committed holiday makers, not to be put off their annual seaside trip by the war or the railway companies, found a way of getting to Blackpool for 2s 10d instead of 7s 8d. Resorts for their part tried to pretend that it was 'business as usual', but there were few places in those troubled years where business could be usual. And as the war dragged on the largest group of men to be found at the resorts were often the bands of wounded soldiers. Hospital blue and military khaki became standard colours whenever a seaside crowd gathered. In the summer of 1918, at a charity cricket match at Lords, these colours dotted the crowd, just as the team sheets were dominated by military personnel.

Everyone was agreed that in general the English people were now less noisily boisterous when enjoying themselves. Bank Holiday on Hampstead Heath in 1918 was noticeable, said *The Times*, because 'The noises of the old pre-war days were almost unheard'. Even the cricket crowd was more silent than before. It was in keeping with this more sombre mood that the quieter, more refined pleasures boomed as never before, perhaps, as Arthur Marwick has suggested as a result 'of the heightened emotional responses stirred by the war'. Music enjoyed unparalleled popularity because, in the words of Sir Thomas Beecham, 'the temper of a section of the people became graver, simpler, and more concentrated' and music (less of it German, more English) became one of the 'antidotes to a troubled conscience'. Galleries too enjoyed boom years; the crowds at the National Gallery in 1918 were so large that on certain days the turnstiles were put out of commission. There were other notable cerebral pleasures which flourished between the wars. Many more people developed the habit of reading, partly through the growth of book clubs and also, following the initiative of Allen Lane in 1935, through the establishment of paperbacks. Despite the increased availability of conflicting attractions, the English read more books (and borrowed more from libraries) than ever before; and they were already known as a nation of ewspaper readers. Yet not all enjoyments were so cerebral. London heatres boomed, to a large extent because of the sheer numbers of roops passing through the capital in the course of the war. The mpty seats of the first few months of the war were soon filled and hroughout the war years the theatres enjoyed a boom which was to last into the 1920s. But the most significant change in entertainment was the evolution of the cinema.

Cinema came of age in the war years, though by 1914 there were already 3,000 throughout the country, and they had begun to eat away at the unique position of the music hall. Ranging from the garishly opulent to the local 'flea-pit', the cinemas began to offer a range of visual excitements unknown before. Many of the new stars, like Charlie Chaplin, were British exports to the American film industry. Indeed it is significant that a popular front line soldiers' song was 'The moon shines bright on Charlie Chaplin'; already the stars had entered into popular mythology. Long before the war had nded the cinema had begun to extend its appeal. Thought initially be 'the poor man's theatre' it soon appealed to all social classes, and a commission looking into the cinema in 1917 concluded that ightly speaking, half the entire population, men, women and children, visit a cinematograph theatre once every week'. By 1919 ne half of the population went to the cinema twice a week. Equally mportant, the great bulk of cinema audiences did not attend other aces of entertainment.

For the poor, the local cinema was an incalculable benefit. As a don magistrate noted: 'For the few hours at the picture palace at corner they can find breathing space, warmth, music (the more better), and the picture where they can have a real laugh, a cheer sometimes a shout. Who can measure the effects on their spirits bodies?' Many thought that one advantage of the cinema over music hall was the absence of drink, though some critics felt this was outweighed by the fact that 'the darkness encourages ecency'. The cinema became the obvious place for courting uples to meet, and it was commonplace in the East End to say that ou take your "bird" to the pictures'. Films were equally important mong the troops and were similarly responsible for establishing the great popularity of the cinema after demobilisation.

There was initially a snobbish resistence to the cinema, but wartime saw a gradual erosion of that attitude. Charlie Chaplin's anti-German films, for instance, wore down the early resistance towards him as a young Englishman not 'doing his bit'. Apart from the comedy and drama, cinema audiences were introduced to news-reels of the war in Europe and the Near East; enterprising cinema managers projected photographs of local men at the front, royalty began to attend, in 1919 a film was shown in the House of Commons – and gradually the social resistance diminished. There was however a residual distrust of 'American vulgarity', but the sheer size and commercial pressure of American contribution in the 1920s prevented the fledgling British cinema industry from making any more than a brief impression on the virtual American dominance over the British cinema. Throughout the 1920s films were silent, but they represented little short of a social revolution which extended beyond the world of leisure. The queues which ringed the cinemas consisted not solely of men as those at the sports ground generally did, but also of whole families.

Many women found in the cinema one of their first majo collective escapes from home or industrial drudgery, though it is clea that female efforts in the war itself, working in most areas of th economy, had already produced fundamental changes in women perceptions of themselves and of the outside world. It was no acciden that American film-makers produced films specifically for wome viewers. Ultimately too the cinema was to cut great paths through tl popularity of the churches and the pubs. Indeed it offered most of tl virtues which throughout the nineteenth century had been four primarily in the pub; it was a meeting place, cheap, war entertaining, and it could also be educational. It can be argued tha along with the newly established radio, cinema was the catalyst f the great social change of the twentieth century (with the exception war itself). Born into the hedonistic days of Edwardian Englan cinema came of age in the years of wartime suffering; it was to susta millions of people throughout the endemic troubles of the inter-years. As times got harder, the cinema was always on hand, almost always open, to provide a refreshing glimpse into a diffe and often amazing world.

The initial post-war optimism and post-war boom was transformed into the troubles of the 1920s, which in their turn overwhelmed by the even more fundamental problems of the y 1929–31. Yet the nation's economic misfortunes were not unexpec and most major politicians and businessmen faced the prospect peace with trepidation. The debts and costs of the war were to we with nightmarish weight on the inter-war economy and imaginatic Those debts were to be paid most painfully by the swelling ranks the unemployed, and the bitterness of the economic woes felt mc acutely by workers in the old industries, led by the ailing coal industry Strikes, violence in London, Liverpool and Glasgow, lengthening line of the unemployed, bitterness towards management and government, and the sour taste of unfulfilled expectations by men who fought the war both at home and abroad, these were the features of the new decade of peace. And despite the brief success of the first Labour government in 1924, economic ills and their social consequences were to be the staple diet of British politics until the declaration of war in 1939.

It seems ironic that modern leisure, which had been born in the improving conditions of the late nineteenth century, should thrive and continue in the new, harsh conditions of the slumps of the 1920s and 1930s, but the reason was straightforward. As we have seen, leisure was now regarded as a right of all the people – irrespective of economic circumstances. People in the most desperate of circumstances could always find relief, even if only in their local 'flea-pit'. New stars, animated cartoons, the vogue for cowboy films, the masculine attractions of Valentino and Fairbanks, the female charms of Swanson and others, and the hilarity of a host of silver-screen comics (still led by Chaplin), all these and more could be relied upon to bring colour, fun, excitement or romance into the meanest of streets. Even the recreational culture of the nation's children was complemented by the heroes and heroines, locations and mythologies of the films. It was an all-pervasive medium, more profound in its social impact than even its ternest critics could imagine.

The theatre in London rallied from the initial shock of the cinema, branching out into new light musical reviews and comedies, some of the most successful written by English writers (led by Noel Coward) but, here again, American products made major inroads into the English stage. There was no escaping from the American influence in the musical and visual arts in the inter-war years. Both on stage and screen, and also on the wireless, products of the highly successful and imaginative American entertainment industry became standard fare for a hungry British public. It was apt that the most important breakthrough in the cinema – the talkie – was an American invention. Henceforth American cinema was linked to new forms of American music. Symbolically the first talkie in 1927 was Al Jolson's the *Jazz Singer*; the blacked-up son of a Jewish cantor conquered the the world with songs from the real and the make-believe South.

Critics could be forgiven for feeling that the Americans had conquered Britain; their plays and music were among the West end's favourites, their film stars held the nation captive in their cinema seats, and their music, much of it black in origin, transformed English ideas of popular music. *The Jazz Singer* was only one of many forms of music which thrilled its followers as much as it appalled its opponents. To make matters worse it was associated with new forms of dancing which, like jazz, seemed utterly alien to an English audience reared on Edwardian musical treats. Long before the war, American music and dance had already made a major impact on Britain, but it was the war years, with their need to find a frenetic outlet (particularly in the capital) which saw the main flourishing of the ragtime bands. This tendency was accentuated in the last years of the war by the arrival of waves of American troops who confirmed the craze for American music and dance – a craze which long outlived their military presence. Hotels and dance halls led by the new Hammersmith Palais de Dance in 1919, provided a forum for the growing number of American and American-influenced bands. Just as the war saw the relegation of the more sedate music of

Edwardian England (much of it played by German and Austrian bands), so the peace heralded a new kind of restless, free-and-easy music and dance. 'If these up-to-date dances, described as the "latest craze" are within a hundred miles of what I hear about them [said one vicar in 1919] I should say the morals of a pig-sty would be respectable in comparison.'

Men of authority, with that moral fervour they so often reserve for the inconsequential, thundered forth against the wickedness of these new musical forms. Bishops and surgeons wrote to *The Times* specifying the moral and physical dangers inherent in the foxtrot, the tango and dancing to jazz. Journalists wrote of 'Nights in the Jazz Jungle' and, even more amusingly, proclaimed that 'The shimmy is shaking suburbia'. And the craze for wild dancing was accentuated, from 1923 onwards, by the success of the Charleston (which arrived in England in 1925). Criticisms were, once again, more strenuous than the dance itself, though now all the nastier because of the overt racist antipathy. It was thought to be 'freakish, degenerate, negroid'; the *Daily Mail* thought it 'reminiscent only of negro orgies'. Equally extreme was the attack by a Bristol vicar on the Charleston: 'It is neurotic! It is rotten! It stinks! Phew, open the windows.' Despite these and other outbursts, the new music and dance became increasingly popular (though restricted in the more genteel of dance halls).

Contemporaries were troubled by the attitude of many young women to this music, for the new dances, like the cinema, offered them an escape from the more restricted styles of pre-war days. The wartime liberation of women produced, not merely the vote in the 1920s but also a freer and more widely accepted role in leisure, particularly in the cinema and dance hall. For all the undeniable prevailing inhibitions there was a clear thawing of relationships between the sexes and this was well represented in the new styles of dancing. It would be a mistake to see these changes as the monopoly of the over-privileged; those unpleasant, narcissistic *enfants d'orés* who left such an indelible mark on the nation's literature in the 1920s and 1930s. Dancing, like the cinema, became a national pastime and spread through the country by the efforts of business chains who constructed dance halls in most major towns. Theatres were converted to dance halls, but it was the custom-built dance hall, the *palais de danse*, which became, like the new cinemas, architectural symbols of the new leisure form, and remain to this day as classic monuments to the period. It is of great importance to remember that many of the finest features of Victorian, Edwardian and inter-war architecture were built for the pusuit of pleasure; seaside piers, football stadiums, music halls, theatres, dance halls, pubs and cinemas.

Paradoxically the upper and middle classes who originally led the way in pioneering the new dances were soon left behind, for they tended to dance in restaurants and clubs, which inevitably had smaller dance areas, while the working- and lower-middle-class dancers could enjoy the expansive (though crowded) facilities of the new urban dance halls. This, in the words of the social historian of dance, explains the situation 'where skill and grace in ballroom dancing came to be in inverse proportion to social status'. Yet these were the years when unemployment reached its highest ever and even the Prince of Wales made reference to the unemployed in his Christmas speech. It seems ironic that frentic enjoyment and desperate economic circumstances had become, not mutually exclusive, but uncomfortable bedfellows.

One innovation above all others ensured a further qualitative change in English leisure in all social classes: the wireless. 'Broadcasting' was born in the 1920s, a monopoly under the aegis of the BBC, and even more firmly in the control of John Reith, a tough Scottish Calvinist whose aim was to offer over the airwaves 'all that was best in every department of human knowledge, endeavour and achievement'. Inspired, if that is the right word, by Reith's assertive and often intolerant control, the BBC, in the words of A. J. P. Taylor, 'came to be regarded as an essential element in the "British way of life".' Within the first four years of its existence, the BBC began to revolutionise British social life, despite the fact that Reith and his fellow founders had a socially conservative view of the role of broadcasting. The profundity of the impact of broadcasting ought not to have been surprising, for the signs from America were already unmistakable, as they had been in so many areas of leisure. In the USA broadcasting had become a means of enormous commercial competition. More important still perhaps, it was seminal in creating whole new areas of 'taste' and popularity in entertainment, the likes and scale of which could scarcely be conceived. Its potential was not unlike the cinema but with the crucial distinction that the wireless could reach into every home. The wireless set rapidly became a distinctive piece of household furniture, quickly to replace the piano as the focal point of domestic entertainment, with all the attendant consequences for self-entertainment. In 1922 there were 35,744 wireless licences issued; by 1926 the figure had grown to 2,178,259. The wireless industry and ancillary electronics, became major and pioneering industries, as did the retail outlets which catered for the growing demand. To buy a wireless set was, as the *Radio Year Book* for 1925 said, a great occasion; 'when we first get the wireless set from the shop there comes the first thrilling moment when the set is to be operated and the family delighted with music. This, like the wedding day and the first ride on a bicycle, gives a thrill such as we seldom feel in this unromatic age.'

Critics abounded. Some believed wireless would render the nation passive and uniform, and it was felt that the English people were about to be rendered culturally homogeneous. Few could deny however that this new vehicle for pleasure was creating a home-based market of unprecedented size. Whereas earlier entertainment had aimed at peak audiences of thousands, the wireless could capture millions. Of course the possession of a wireless was more commonplace among the better-off, but, despite the prevailing economic conditions and the formidable ranks of the unemployed, the wireless began to permeate British society, though curiously it remained less common in mining communities. Furthermore, for every household which owned a wireless set, there were many more who visited their friends, relatives and neighbours simply to listen to the radio. The wireless set became both cause and occasion for friendly visits, and helped to establish a social custom of visiting which outlived the early novelty.

Growth continued at a remarkable rate. In 1927 the BBC employed 773 people; by 1939 they employed 5,000. In those same years the numbers of licence holders grew from 2,178,259 to 9,082,666. On the eve of the Second World War the BBC, according to Asa Briggs 'was catering for the majority of the British public'. The BBC differed remarkably from the American version, more especially in refusing to become entangled with commercialism and the consequent promotion of other technical changes (films, gramophones and cars for instance) which were so transforming the face of the country. Nonetheless the BBC's influence was indisputable and seminal. It was symptomatic that the changes in popular dancing styles coincided with the inauguration of the BBC. The wilder, fashions of the im-mediate post-war years gave way to more sedate dances; new versions of the waltz, quickstep and foxtrot soon became the nation's favourites. Much of this change was a result of the BBC's light musical programme. Classical music in the mid-1930s remained at the fore-front of the BBC's offerings, reaching audiences far wider than any conductor or orchestra could previously have dreamed of, but it was 'light music' which dominated the air. The BBC was sufficiently powerful to generate its own entertainment industry, with orchestras, bands, singers and comedians, shows and stars, all of whom owed their fame to the wireless. At the same time broadcasting helped to reinforce the popularity of outside performers. Certain bands became national institutions thanks to their wireless introduction. Indeed the very concept of a person becoming 'a household name' is itself confirmation of radio's grip on a domestically defined culture.

While the Corporation steadfastly resisted overt commercial-isation, there were incalculable and seductive pressures which permeated the nation's popular culture, and which were in consequence reinforced by the radio. American dance music and popular songs, American stars of cinema and records, inevitably found their way on to the air. Dance bands in the late 1930s adopted the American 'swing' music – an influence exaggerated and confirmed in the Second World War by the arrival of American GIs (a reprise of 1917). Swing, and, from Cuba, the rumba and the indigenous 'social dances' (the conga and the Lambeth Walk) – all these in the 1930s were responsible for the slow transformation of both English dancing and popular music. By and large, the BBC broadcast British songs and, overwhelmingly, British singers. But even their greatest popular star, Al Bowley, was remarkably like Bing Crosby and his music had a major influence on British taste, to be replaced in the early years of the war by another American, Frank Sinatra. Indeed it could be argued that from the 1930s to the 1950s the most influential popular singers, copied by dozens of indigenous British performers, were Americans. From the 1950s onwards Rock and Roll added a new dimension to the scene.

It is of course difficult to weigh the balance of cultural influence and yet it seems, inexorably, to tip towards the Americans. While local popular musical talent before and more especially during the war, was represented by Vera Lynn, Al Bowley and the bands of the Squadronnaires, Geraldo, Joe Loss, Ambrose and Billy Cotton, the Americans could counter with Crosby, Sinatra and Glenn Miller. There is no easy answer to this complicated question of popular cultural influence, since so much depends on taste, but there seems little doubt that the American entertainment industry was, on the eve of the Second World War, exercising an unprecedented and increasing influence over British leisure. And it was to grow more pronounced in succeeding years.

In America, big business had both created (and been generated by) various branches of entertainment. In the inter-war years however, the most notable feature of commercial entertainment was the degree to which different branches of entertainment came together within one organisation; this also happened, in a non-commercial way, in the BBC. The drift towards entertainment monopoly – the amalgamation of radio, gramophone, broadcasting and film interests – occurred in both countries. The manufacture of radios (sales of which were spreading throughout the population, thanks to the growing acceptance of HP), gramophones, records and films and the construction of cinemas and cinema chains, were all functions of a complicated social phenomenon. This was partly a consequence of enterprising commercial investment in, and public demand for, entertainment, but its prime cause lay in the ability of increasing numbers of people to pay for these pleasures. This again highlights the connection between prosperity and relatively costly forms of leisure. For millions of people times were undeniably hard, and for them the new mechanical forms of entertainment were correspondingly less common.

Nevertheless HP, though not totally respectable in certain quarters, enabled even luxury goods to appear in poorer communities and was largely responsible for the massive upsurge in the consumption of clothing, furniture and electrical goods, particularly in the 1930s. Its use multiplied four times in the period 1918 to 1938, accounting for perhaps two-thirds of all mass-produced articles, and absorbing about £50 million at any one time. While HP made possible sales of a variety of goods, its promotion of the wireless was unique.

Henceforth 'the world was now in men's homes instead of being outside them'. The rise of wireless paralleled a major decline in many of the older leisure forms; church, chapel and other more cerebral activities declined markedly, though it is impossible to say how much of this decline was caused by the radio.

Certain forms of leisure were positively encouraged by broadcasts. Serious music for example reached unprecedented heights between the wars, attendances at London concerts reached new records; the Proms had never been so popular, thanks in large part to Sir Henry Wood's conducting, while the work of Sir Thomas Beecham was largely responsible for the widening interest in British composers. For the better-off the gramophone made it possible to enjoy orchestral concerts at home. This, too was aided by the BBC whose concerts were significant contributors to the upsurge in serious music in the 1930s. This interest in music was not restricted to the capital, for in Manchester the Hallé orchestra became a major international orchestra.

Remembering Reith's puritanical attitudes, it is ironic that the BBC was also to some extent responsible for the success of a new form of gambling – the football pools (though it did this unconciously) by bringing instantaneous reports into the home. The pools enabled millions of people to gamble legally and anonymously. The football authorities (and successive governments) had tried since before 1914 to stamp out gambling on football matches, but the new companies, aware of the legal loopholes, continued to offer their customers the fantasy of massive wins for a small stake. By the mid-1930s, 16½ times as many people gambled on football as watched it, pumping £800,000 a week into the pools companies. Upwards of 7 million people spent £30 million a year on the pools, the graph of their spending traced in the upward swing of the sales of sixpenny and shilling postal orders. Even so the pools attracted only one-fifth of the money spent on horse racing. When it came to gambling, the nation seemed to have no shortage of spare cash. New forms of gambling were introduced to satisfy the hunger for it (the first greyhound racing-track for instance was opened in Manchester in 1926). The total annual amount spent on gambling was more than £200 million – amounting, according to *The Economist*, to the nation's second largest industry. But the football pools alone remained the one legal form of betting which could be indulged in without fear of moral condemnation by neighbours and friends, thanks to its anonymity via the post.

Many of the inter-war changes in leisure were, like many other social changes, a function of technical innovation, hastened by the war itself. Motor transport epitomised these changes and the car, coach, char-à-banc and lorry began to transform the face of English society. Photographs form telling evidence of the impact of motor transport; where once the streets and landscape had been dotted with people, by the 1930s, those same scenes were choked with vehicles.

The 500,000 of 1920 had grown to 1½ million by 1930 and more than 3 million in 1939. There followed a related revolution in transport, retailing, wholesaling and general travel, even for the poor whose lives had previously been dominated by trains and trams. While the aspiring middle class saved for their cars (emulating the style of their betters before 1914) working people took to the roads in motor coaches and char-à-bancs, heading for favourite haunts and new delights, more often than not in the company of neighbours (the coach had the advantage over the train of being able to pick up people at their own street corner). For millions it was a major emancipation, even when enjoyed only on the occasional day.

The motor trip even penetrated the poorest of communities, Robert Roberts has told how, after the war, his parents 'for the first time in a quarter of a century . . . spent a holiday together, and one of a brand new kind'. The upper sections of working class life began to take coach tours round Britain, to the consternation of the middle- and upper-class residents of hotels. Robert Roberts provides some of their reactions. '"How in the world do they *do* it, my dear?" "Well some of them did very nicely out of the war, you know – munitions!"' A friend of Roberts' father, Bob Owen, a mechanic, paid for his trip by saving his overtime in the Post Office Bank. 'And the missus does a cleanin' job, see – Fridays at a chip shop.' The astonished listener to these comments, a lady resident of a south-coast hotel, could only reply, 'Well! Well! Really! I must tell my husband! How *very* industrious.' But for Roberts' mother, this holiday proved unsettling and 'strengthened my mother's longing to be off anywhere out of the slums of Salford.'

The commonplace sight of traffic congestion was first felt in its most acute form on the summer roads leading to the coasts. The Preston to Blackpool road – the busiest holiday route in England – experienced a sevenfold increase in traffic between 1914 and 1924. There and elsewhere local authorities began to construct ring roads (architecturally as distinctive of the inter-war years as ribbon development) to cope with the increase in traffic. To make matters worse the holiday period was wedged firmly in the period July–August, with vast movements of people on Saturdays in those months. The railways were taxed to the limits; in the 1930s rail traffic increased threefold. Motor transport was more flexible and the commercial grab for the holiday market produced fierce competition between road and rail companies and a substantial fall in travel costs for excursionists. Seaside municipalities, inundated with coaches and cars, began to channel large sums into problems of traffic control and parking. And like the train excursions a century earlier, the 'chara' trip became a holiday experience in itself, filled with games, songs and 'whip-rounds' for the driver. It also meant that trippers could now visit previously inaccessible parts of the country. As a result large parts of the nation's natural beauty spots were laid bare to motor-borne tourists – the beginning of a phenomenon which ever since plagued the country's rural assets.

More adventurous and prosperous holidaymakers began to turn to remoter spots for their holidays – renewal of the old pattern of movement to more distant places as transport improved and money became more plentiful. After the 1914–18 war foreign travel began again for the more prosperous, with organised trips to the battlefields. Major new travel firms developed, specialising in coach travel to Europe, and by 1930 some one million Britons took their holidays in Europe. Thereafter for a time the economic crash drove the English back to their old haunts beside the English sea.

In the 1930s holiday-making came to be discussed as a 'problem'. It crippled the railways, choked the roads, sometimes halted industry; it created ribbons of urban development along the British coastline and forced seaside municipalities to spend millions of pounds in local amenities. And all for a mere three months a year. In a decade when investment in civic amenities was crippled by economic retraints, the resorts had no trouble in finding substantial sums to enhance their appeal; upwards of £4 million each year was spent on sea front facilities, giving still further concern to the architectural and urban planners, who realised that the erosion of the coastline cried out for firm control. Understandably, some resorts tried to extend their seasons by the introduction of 'illuminations' in the autumn.

All forms of holidays in the 1930s increased markedly, in spite of the fact these were years not normally associated with material wellbeing. One survey after another showed that people expected to have holidays; those too poor to afford them were often catered for by charitable efforts. Travel firms, particularly those catering for low income groups, flourished; seaside entertainments thrived, though changing rapidly to suit new tastes; dancing and cinema replaced the music hall; resorts established their own advertisement and promotional departments. And many of these changes were enjoyed by low-income groups whose savings, both by individuals and through group schemes, were directed towards the need to save for the day trip, or, if lucky, a week by the sea. By the late 1930s, some fifteen million people, about one in three of the population, were spending at least one week's holiday away from home. In the words of the Industrial Welfare Society in 1938 'holidays are now part of the standard of living aimed at by nearly everyone'. New types of holidays sprang up; camping and hiking became popular, as did the new vogue for holiday camps, perfected though not pioneered by Billy Butlin. On the eve of the Second World War some half a million people annually spent their holidays in one of over a hundred camps around the country.

There was also an upsurge in outdoor recreational activity. Enjoying the fresh air became a national obsession among certain social classes, partly encouraged by the older scouting and guide movement but, ironically, given a filip by the success of the German 'Strength through Joy' movement. Organisations proliferated to cope with the growing numbers of walkers, climbers, campers and cyclists; so too did the manufacture of their specialised equipment.

One major consequence of the increase in holiday-making was the buoyancy of the resorts; they grew ever larger and their facilities improved. Their population, often transitory and under-employed, increased. In search of leisure some seven million people annually went to Blackpool in the mid-1930s. Even Eastbourne could attract one million. An interesting change was that English holiday-makers now went in search of the sun, as inter-war seaside postcards clearly show. Edwardians had hidden from the sun but the seaside trippers of the 1930s consciously sought it. Henceforth a 'tan', aided by the new cosmetic creams, was the most prized souvenir of a holiday, a fact reflected in the new styles of swimming constumes, designed for more sun-bathing as well as swimming.

The summertime rush to the sea was perhaps the most notable feature of the national urge for leisure evident in all classes, and had been made possible on such a massive scale by rapid increases in holidays granted with full pay. Private holidays-with-pay agreements between employers and workers proliferated throughout the 1920s and 1930s, and despite the slump, holidays-with-pay became a major industrial negotiating point. It was appreciated however that for millions of working people this could only be attained through legislation. The resulting campaign did not succeed in pushing legislation through Parliament until 1938, and only then after a Royal Commission. The outbreak of war prevented its effective implementation for those 10¾ million working people who, at the time, were not yet receiving holidays with pay. But by the later 1930s, from the TUC downwards, it was widely accepted that a paid holiday was the right of everyone. On the eve of the First World War the concept of a holiday as a social right had been accepted, twenty-five years later, it was the holiday *with pay* which had been conceded, and guaranteed by Parliament.

All this is not to claim that the 'other England' had disappeared in a flood of wellbeing which found its best expression in leisure time pursuits. Football had reasserted itself as the national game in the inter-war years, but it continued to thrive most strongly in, and to draw its players from, those areas of the country where economic distress was worst. Unemployment, poverty, bad housing, inadequate education, poor health, and few prospects for improvement, continued to dominate whole regions of working-class England, – areas unknown and neglected by those for whom the slump meant merely newspaper photographs of distant bedraggled men. Leisure pursuits of course thrived even in the most depressed of places; northeast mining communities maintained their culture of pigeon and whippet racing, allotments and the traditional recreations of home-made music and bands. But there, and for millions of other urban poor, the flashier delights of the 1930s were as distant as the prospects of employment. The rise of the new leisure facilities must have posed an insulting contrast to those whose lives were shaped by the need to keep body and soul together.

This world of abrasive contrasts, of poverty and the uglier remains of a Victorian industrial past set against the delights of the new leisure industries, offended many contemporaries. No one captured this mood more aptly than the man who became the spokesman for the period, J. B. Priestley in his *English Journey* of 1933:

> This is the England of arterial and by-pass roads, of filling
> stations and factories that look like exhibition buildings, of giant
> cinemas and dance-halls and cafés, bungalows with tiny garages,
> cocktail bars, Woolworths, motor coaches, wireless, hiking,
> factory girls looking like actresses, greyhound racing and dirt
> tracks, swimming pools, and everything given away for cigarette
> coupons.

It is remarkable to reflect how many of the features which caught Priestley's eye, belonged to the newer gaudier leisure interests of the English people.

11 Austerity and after 1939-1950

In 1914 news of the outbreak of war had been conveyed to the people through the newspapers and the newspaper placards. Significantly, in 1939 the nation heard the news of war on the wireless. Neville Chamberlain's voice entered the people's homes and explained what had happened. And it was to be round the radio, in the most unusual of wartime circumstances, that the nation huddled throughout the war to hear of disasters and victories, and to listen to Winston Churchill, the first politician in modern British history to use the radio to its full potential, encouraging and inspiring the British people as he insulted and threatened the enemy, all through the courtesy of the BBC. An instrument of major recreational change in the 1920s and 1930s, broadcasting became an invaluable vehicle for news and propaganda, and a branch of wartime policy itself. In the dark days of May–June 1940 when British fortunes were at their lowest ebb, Churchill's broadcasts to the nation were incalculably inspiring; so, too, in a different way, were those of J. B. Priestley.

The BBC served the people well in the war, providing serious coverage with the right mixture of light relief – an important factor for people kept indoors for long periods. And the BBC's importance could be measured in its phenominal wartime growth. In 1939 it had 4,233 staff and 23 transmitters; by 1945 these numbers had risen to 11,417 and 38. Slowly entertainment reasserted itself, reaching its popular peaks in ITMA (It's That Man Again) and the Tommy Handley cult, his northern voice and humour establishing him as a national figure. Handley's colleagues, catch phrases and jokes entered into the nation's vernacular and cropped up in every theatre of war. And as the War progressed, more and more light entertainment programmes were devised, to be heard in factories and canteens and at armed services depots. For a nation desperately in need of fun, good news, and a reminder of distant loved ones, the BBC presented all forms of enjoyment. While it would be difficult to pinpoint any one single contribution, there seems little doubt that Vera Lynn captured the sentimental mood of divided families just as ITMA satisfied the need for irreverent humour. Yet not all BBC entertainment was so light. These were the years when the 'Brains Trust' had its greatest success, and its participants became popular celebrities (an unusual distinction, in the case of Joad, for an academic philosopher).

It had long been appreciated that this war would be a total war, involving civilian populations as never before. The resulting need to summon up every available human and physical resource led to state intervention in practically every walk of life. Industry and labour, food and clothing, and the detailed movements of the people became the subjects of the most minute government scrutiny and restriction. Any form of leisure seemed at first sight to be out of place in such a climate and although it is true that initially most forms of leisure were 'frozen', it is significant that practically every form of enjoyment rapidly reasserted itself, or was put on a more organised footing. Theatres and cinemas were closed, but re-opened within weeks. Sporting performances were cancelled and the players drafted into the armed forces (where many were suited to the difficult task of establishing physical fitness among the vast ranks of conscripts). Football and cricket grounds, courses and holiday camps were rapidly converted into military quarters or even turned over to agricultural use.

Seaside resorts were among the first to feel the effects of war. Those on the south and east coast, most exposed to the threat of invasion, were evacuated and turned into military defences. Others, on the west coast, received tens of thousands of young evacuees from the cities, and became major camps for the hastily recruited armed forces and relocated government offices. The availability of large numbers of beds, and the ease of catering for sudden arrivals of people made some resorts ideal reception areas for the waves of troops and civil servants. Seaside ballrooms, theatres and promenades made good makeshift conditions for marshalling, training and organising tens of thousands of troops. In the course of the war, for example, some three-quarters of a million RAF recruits passed through initial training in Blackpool. Transport was put on a war footing and regulated for military needs. It was thus extremely difficult, initially, for people to travel for pleasure. 'Is your journey really necessary' was a constant official reminder. Potential trippers to the coast found it hard to head for their favourite resorts on the crowded and infrequent trains, and often found all beds taken by the troops and civil servants. Yet it is remarkable testimony to the English commitment to the seaside that they persisted in visiting the seaside in the most trying of circumstances, knowing that they might even have to sleep in the open.

Paradoxical as it seems, the British people in wartime spent an increasing proportion of their income on leisure. Between 1938 and 1944 money spent on entertainments increased by 120 per cent. There was an increase in beer drinking, despite its necessary wartime adulteration and dilution, and, after the initial ban, a rise in cinema attendance; some 30 million seats were sold each week and it has been calculated that 'probably most people over forty saw at least fifty first feature films every year'. Oddly enough, though wartime saw a dramatic fall in the number of home-made British films, critics generally felt that their quality greatly improved. Some became major successes, both commercially and for allied propaganda. Inevitably perhaps, Hollywood continued to make its overwhelming impact on the British cinema, notably with its epic *Gone With The Wind.*

Entertainment, in keeping with the rest of the nation's needs and interests, was put on an organised footing, particularly for the armed forces. Millions of men were scattered across the world and it was primarily for them that ENSA (the Entertainments National Service Association) was created, to organise visiting groups of entertainers to every theatre of war. Although the country's major singers and comedians worked hard for ENSA, often in the most difficult of conditions, the bulk of the entertainments were provided by amateur talent which would have been hard-pressed to survive in peace-time. In addition there was a wide dispersal of entertainment talent throughout the country; musicians, theatres, ballet and orchestras performed in places in the provinces previously ignored. Concerts, for example, were performed, and became very popular, in the most unlikely of places: in theatres, music halls, cinemas, galleries and even in factories.

Sports similarly adapted themselves to the peculiar conditions of wartime. National competitions were abandoned, and substituted by local and regional competitions. But even this was made difficult by the departure of most of the healthy men into the armed forces. Football clubs were stripped of their players and could often play their games only by using visiting players passing through the town *en route* to a military posting, or even by asking for volunteers from the sparse crowds. The tannoy asked for volunteers to fit the available sizes of boots; in 1940 when Manchester United played Blackburn (at Stockport's ground) four spectators filled the Blackburn gaps. One of them, 'Little Hallam', could hardly play the game, but for him it was a memorable occasion. 'It was something to have worn the colours of one of the most famous clubs in football history for an afternoon.' Millwall once fielded their fifty-year-old manager; one English international player made his debut – for Wales. It was an unusual sporting world, where the main ambition was to field a complete team. The quality of the play was inevitably patchy, with the exception of teams from the armed forces which were in effect international teams.

The official attitude towards major sports had changed substantially since the First World War. Now the government and local authorities made great efforts to encourage football and other games, without interfering with the war effort. Sunday football was sanctioned; the Board of Trade allowed the use of scarce leather and rubber to manufacture footballs. Gradually as the war advanced and the danger of aerial attack diminished the limits on the size of crowds were loosened. Again unlike the First World War, football was now put to good use in raising money for wartime charities, with great success.

By 1945 sporting organisations had raised some £3 million for the Red Cross and St John's. Cricket too continued in its new form, though it was generally played for much shorter periods than the traditional three-day games.

Wartime Britain became an unusually polyglot society, with hundreds of thousands of European, imperial and American troops preparing for the invasion of Europe. Each group introduced elements of its own culture into a receptive society, eager and keen for anything exotic. American baseball was played in Oldham; West Indian cricketers, American footballers and exiled Europeans, all brought their own traditions and colour into the country. Black American troops and American swing bands helped to reinforce the popular interest in American music. Cumulatively there was little doubt that wartime recreations and leisures of the British people, often enhanced by foreign visitors, did much to enable a beleaguered people to endure the harshest of times. Oddly enough, whole sections of the nation were, in material terms, better off than ever before, for despite war-time taxation and excessive working hours many working people enjoyed a rise in living standards. Rises in wartime living costs were outstripped by rises in earnings. By 1944, though the cost of living was 50 per cent higher than in 1938, weekly wages were 81½ per cent higher. 'Broadly speaking,' said A. J. P. Taylor, 'the entire population settled at the standard of the skilled artisan.' And with a carefully regulated and adequately measured diet, many poorer groups were enjoying a balanced, though unexciting diet. Thus the rise of material wellbeing, in conjunction with the rigours of wartime life, positively encouraged an interest in leisure.

Moreover the government became more perceptive of the need to provide people with a healthy balance of rest to counterbalance their work, and consequently tried to encourage a sensible attitude towards their leisure pursuits. Their suggestions were not always heeded; people refused to listen to the government's advice to take their holidays at home. Many travelled to the coasts and to the races, often when transport was needed for essential war supplies. The out-come was that the government (sometimes at Churchill's suggestion) had to compromise – even with forbidding powers at its disposal – and allow 'unnecessary' pleasures to take place. It was as if leisure had finally come of age and been accepted as an essential part of the national effort, and it was sometimes allowed precedence over more pressing matters. It was clearly accepted (though not by everyone) that leisure was vital to the conduct of the war. People at war, ironically enough, enjoyed themselves as never before. But they were even more determined and enthusiastic about having a good time when the war ended.

Peace was ushered in by the kind of ecstatic scenes which in 1914 had marked the outbreak of war. In retrospect these wild scenes in cities on both sides of the Atlantic foreshadowed a more prolonged pursuit of pleasure in the years to come. Yet the post-war years were, like wartime, dominated by austerity and hardship, made all the more unpalatable for some by the expectations that a victorious peace would see improvements. It seemed an unusually high price to pay for victory, yet it was perhaps because of the continuing hardships that enjoyments became a national obsession in the late 1940s. Moreover the commitment to provide more adequate leisure facilities became a political issue. In April 1945 the Labour Party issued its publication *Let Us Face the Future*, with a firm commitment to enhancing the nation's leisure facilities.

> National and local authorities should co-operate to enable
> people to enjoy their leisure to the full, to have opportunities for
> healthy recreation. By the provision of concert halls, modern
> libraries, theatres and suitable civic centres, we desire to assure
> to our people full access to the great heritage of culture in this
> nation.

The material provision of such facilities had in fact to await the improvement in material conditions on the 1950s. In the meantime existing forms of recreation (notably resorts, sports stadiums and cinemas) were crowded as people spent their wartime savings in a flush of enthusiasm. Despite the rationing, despite restrictions on transport, the English people set out to enjoy themselves, with the result that the immediate post-war years were a boom period for British leisure industries. In the case of holidays the boom was hastened by the effective implementation of the 1938 Holidays with Pay Act. By 1945 some 80 per cent of the working population were paid in their holidays. Partly as a result, there was an upswing in holiday-taking and whereas in 1937 some 32 per cent of the population took a holiday away from home, twenty years later this had risen to 47 per cent. After the war approximately three-quarters of all holiday-makers went on holiday as families. Still travelling in the peak periods of July–August, holiday-makers headed for the coast in growing numbers, but as the years passed they began to switch to road transport, although cars began to carry more people to the coast than trains only in the late 1950s.

Blackpool, which for all its distinctiveness in many respects symbolised the nation's seaside instincts, enjoyed an amazing post-war boom. On the 'Wakes' holiday of 1945, the LMS carried record crowds to Blackpool; in 1949 a record 500,000 visitors travelled by motor coach to Scarborough; in 1948 the all-time record figure of 625,000 visitors had travelled to the Isle of Man. By 1949 some 30 million people took their holidays on the coast, a growing number of them, thanks to motor transport, away from the traditional resorts. Nonetheless the poor, more particularly those with large families, continued to be held back and as late as 1949 three-quarters of all families with three or more children were, obliged to spend their holidays at home. Despite the proliferation of holidays with pay, it was clear that the low-income groups would benefit only marginally. Social investigators were aware that nothing short of a major improvement in overall living standards would bring the more expensive leisures within the reach of the poor. Even the 'prosperous' 1960s were to show the limitations on the diffusion of leisure to the poorer groups in society.

In economic terms the post-war seaside holiday was quite a bargain, for the inclusive costs of a boarding house life had not fully kept pace with rising costs, at a time when incomes and wages had made notable advances. Rationing had made inroads into the amounts and kinds of foods available but this was balanced by the fact that government control of some of major hotels was not relaxed until the early 1950s, giving a fillip to seaside landladies.

The resorts, like industry at large, were dreadfully run down and in need of massive investment and improvement. Yet to a debt-ridden, economically depressed Labour government anxious to secure a more equitable society through its welfare legislation and to stabilise the economy, the pleas of the leisure industries, particularly the resorts, for favourable treatment could scarcely take precedence over the more pressing demands of industry and commerce. When better times returned and the leisure industries were able to modernise themselves it was again largely through the efforts of entrepreneurial initiative in league with municipal authorities.

The most striking post-war seaside development was the rapid expansion of the holiday camps, pioneered and popular before the war but only confirmed as national institutions in the post-war years, largely because of the efforts of Billy Butlin. Initially these camps were too costly for working-class visitors, who comprised a mere fraction of visitors in 1947. Butlin's unparalleled success as a publicist firmly established the camps and guaranteed that when better times arrived they would become more widely popular.

All forms of social enjoyment soared in the post-war years. The cinema, so important in the war itself, enjoyed boom years. Its record attendance of 1,635 million was in 1946, when only 24 per cent of the people did not go to the cinema and cinema-going was commoner and more frequent the lower one went down the social scale. Yet the cinema did not seduce the nation totally away from the printed word, for social surveys of the late 1940s showed that the British continued to be avid readers, particularly of newspapers (which had enjoyed rising circulation since the late 1930s). The national sport of football similarly provided a useful indicator: attendances at professional games reached a peak in the late 1940s, rising from 35.5 million in 1946–47 to an all-time record of 41.25 million in 1948–49. These were the golden days of soccer, when crowds were often determined solely by the capacity of the stadiums. Five hundred clubs employed 7,000 professional players and there were an additional 30,000 amateur clubs. Even the amateur FA Cup Final was so popular that it was switched to Wembley, attracting 90,000 people in 1949. Money flooded into the game (though government regulation prevented a corresponding investment in new facilities). The pools expanded with the end of wartime restraints in 1946 and whereas in 1935 they had attracted £20 million annually, the post-war years brought an even greater participation in football gambling, with an estimated eight million pools punters, whose investments yielded some £12.5 million in taxes and £2 million into the Post Office. Gambling on all forms of sporting activity, still led by the turf, had become so important (with major repercussions on employment in certain towns) that it wore down the moral objections which had so haunted the previous history of gambling in Britain.

Given the British obsession with sports, it was fitting that the first post-war Olympic Games should be held in London in 1948, though British performances did not match the nation's willingness to watch. It is significant that in the late 1940s the nation was keen to spectate in its moments of leisure. It was as if, collectively, the people wished to sit back from their efforts of recent years and enjoy themselves simply by watching others put in the hard work. This was to change markedly in the mid-1960s, when participatory sports were to become no less important than spectator sports.

To a large degree travel had traditionally shaped the features of modern leisure and it was to be expected that the changing travel patterns of the post-war years would slowly transform the nation's leisure pursuits. Between the wars the car had already pioneered the way towards new kinds of recreation, and after 1945 a growing proportion of people took to the roads (deserting the trains) in search of pleasure in the summer. Initially the changes took the form of a proliferation of motor-coaches, with consequent problems of congestion and parking. Henceforth municipalities, particularly at the seaside, were forced to invest considerable sums to cope with parking problems. But perhaps the most peculiar feature of leisure in the first fifteen years of peace-time is that it seems so much at variance with the bleak image of economic troubles and post-war austerity with which we. associate those years. It was as if the more obvious national pursuits of pleasure took place *despite* prevailing circumstances. Whereas in the last twenty-five years of the nineteenth century, the revolution in mass leisure, particularly among working people, had taken place because of the upturn in economic fortunes; the situation after 1945 was quite the reverse. Mass enjoyment, nurtured as a consumer product in better times, was by mid-century able to survive despite the circumstances. Nothing shows more clearly the degree to which leisure had become a part of national life, a right to which everyone felt they had a legitimate claim. If pleasure is an indicator of good times, then clearly the history of the immediate post-war years suggests that life was not as bad as it appears at first sight.

Many of the changes which have in retrospect came to be associated with the greater prosperity of the late 1950s and 1960s were in fact, in evidence in the immediate post-war years. York, which since 1900 has yielded an abundance of important evidence for social investigators, again pointed the way towards major changes. By 1950, for example, the children of that town were heavier and taller than they had been in 1936 (in itself unusual testimony to the nutritional benefits of carefully regulated and judicious war-time diets). There seems little doubt that for the great majority of the population the 1950s witnessed an accentuation and diffusion of the changes already in train in the war years and immediately after. It seems equally beyond doubt that many of these changes were a direct result of state intervention in securing a fairer and more equitable diet and health for the bulk of the people. Looking back it is hard to deny that the British people emerged from the dark days of war-time and post-war austerity in a better physical condition than ever before.

The most fundamental change of the 1950s was the unleashing of an unprecedented consumer power throughout most levels of society; this in turn dramatically reshaped the social face of Britain. The British began to enjoy the longest and most continuous boom in the nation's recent history. Unemployment, for example, which had so pockmarked the inter-war years, effectively disappeared during the war and remained scarcely significant throughout the 1950s, a decade when consumer spending almost doubled. Companies boomed, with an occasional but rare falter in a generally upward economic swing. The rare voice of gloom, pointing out weaknesses in the system or illustrating the even greater advances being made in Europe, was unheeded by a nation intent on enjoying the fruits of its bonanza. For men and women who remembered the 1930s and war-time, the 1950s seemed like the promised land which perhaps made all the sacrifices of the past twenty years tolerable. These were the years when material hardware, so familiar today, became the commonplace. Electronic gadgetry, irons, television sets, washing machines, refrigerators, motor-cycles and cars, transformed the lives of millions of people. One has only to remember how the acquisition of these items was such a major event to appreciate their individual and collective significance. The words of Eric Hobsbawm, again, express the phenomenon perfectly: 'It was an unquestionable fact that most people "had never had it so good" in material terms, and if this was due not only to technological revolution and higher incomes but to the increasing spread of hire purchase, it was still a fact.'

There was a major change in the British industrial base which lay behind many of these social changes. There was a relative decline of older, heavier industries and the emergence of a wide range of new light and electrical industries which fed the nation's insatiable appetite for consumer goods. People were able to buy these goods in vast quantities largely through the growing acceptance of HP which, though originating a century before and developing between the wars, (particularly in the retailing of the wireless sets), was only fully accepted by a financially cautious nation in the 1940s. It was HP (and its corollary, the people's capacity to pay the instalments) which fuelled the consumer revolution.

While it is relatively easy to state the bold facts of the history of HP, it is more complex to assess the degree to which the new national interest in consumer goods diverted interests and money away from more traditional pursuits. There seems to be strong evidence that at the time the British people were being seduced by HP-financed material goods the amounts of money they spent on other, older leisure pursuits began to decrease, relatively. Cinema-going went into a major decline, as did attendances at professional football matches. On the other hand, as 'good times' set in, consumption of alcohol began to rise – largely, perhaps as a result of a growing acceptance of social drinking, and a determined effort to provide a more congenial environment, and more varied drinks, in English pubs. Cinemas were not alone in their decline and frequent conversion to other industrial purpose. Churches of most denominations suffered a similar fate and growing numbers of them, particularly in the inner cities where the population declined through urban redevelopment, became derelict, or were converted into storage buildings or warehouses; some even became night clubs and bingo halls. This triggered off an ecclesiastical urge to seek new ways of reaching the people, including the more bizarre, populist approaches by ministers who thought the problem was merely one of style. It was, and is, something much more fundamental, for church-going was, among other things, a leisure activity which changed simultaneously with other leisure pursuits. Moreover many of the traditional pastoral cares of the church had, since the Second World War, passed to the new agencies of the state. It seemed indisputable, as Rowntree and Lavers discovered in 1951, that while the Christian ethic was deeply impressed on the British people at large, the nation remained generally unreceptive to the formal teachings of the churches.

One product more than any other epitomised the change in leisure patterns; the TV set came to dominate both the front room and also the nation's wider recreation habits. After the initial establishment of ITV (Independent Television) with its powerful commercial lobby, most other forms of recreation were obliged to use television advertising to promote their interests. Its social impact at many levels was incalculable, and it was particularly important in redefining the nation's attitude to leisure. TV hastened the decline of the cinema and drove entertainment away from the public place, back into the home. There had been, as we have seen, a great deal of traditional domestic entertainment, particularly musical, but even this was transformed by the TV which, unlike sound broadcasting, tended to drive out other entertainments.

As ownership of sets spread, the quality of the programmes

improved and the hours of broadcasting lengthened, TV came to exercise an increasingly formative role. Not only do the great majority of people now enjoy TV as their major source of entertainment, dwarfing all others, but in many respects there is no longer even a clearcut line between non-leisure and TV watching. People eat, talk, do homework and housework under the flickering glare of the screen. Surveys indicate that TV has resulted in housewives spending less time on domestic work and it has been suggested that 'so great has been the impact of television that it would appear to have resulted in a reallocation of what is conventionally defined as "leisure" and "work" within the home.' Yet in some respects the impact has been paradoxical. While there has, for example, been a marked decline in live football attendances (falling by some twenty million from its peak of the later 1940s) many more people today watch matches on TV (ten million each Saturday night). The spread of global TV, made possible by technological change associated with space exploration, has enabled hundreds of millions of people to watch major sporting events. World Cup soccer and the Olympic Games are now watched by upwards of a quarter of the world's population. If TV has undermined attendances at particular sporting events, it has beyond question provided some games with unimaginable audiences, creating in the process boundless commercial possibilities. Consequently it is difficult to estimate the impact of TV for, while it had contributed substantially to the decline of cinema and theatre, it has stimulated other forms of leisure and in some cases has converted minority and rather expensive sports, such as show jumping and golf, into major spectator events.

A major indication of the post-war change in leisure has been the diffusion of holidays with pay and the extension of longer holidays. In 1951 66 per cent of manual labourers were entitled to two weeks paid holiday, but by 1974 54 per cent were entitled to between three and four weeks; there has also been a consequent development of second holidays particularly among the better-off. Before 1939 it was commonplace for people to spend their holidays at home, even when receiving holidays with pay, but the last quarter of a century has seen a firmer commitment to enjoying a holiday away from home; thirty million Britons take their holidays in the British Isles, about three-quarters of them travelling to the coast. Even more significant perhaps is the fact that millions of Britons now go to Europe, particularly to Spain, for their holidays – a revolution forged from consumer power, the development of cheap air travel and the evolution of international holiday companies. While the most dramatic social and economic consequences of tourism are to be seen in Spain, Britain has not remained untouched by the unleashing of millions of local and foreign visitors; by 1959 some 5 per cent of the working population was employed in the tourist trade. Tourism and holiday-making have become major economic concerns in their own right, more recently having profound economic repercussions for the national drive for foreign currency.

An increasing proportion of English holidays away from home are now taken by car. Widespread car-ownership, like that of the TV set, entails social change of great significance and its ramifications for leisure were incalculable. The car has changed the physical face of the seaside resorts (where railway stations were even converted into car parks), undermined traditional patterns of holiday-making at the resorts (making long-stay visits less popular), and opened practically every quarter of the nation's shore line and countryside to the penetration of motorists. Coping with the car has become a major problem for the authorities and planners at the coast and country, and motorways have been built specifically to cater for holiday traffic. In 1970 almost 70 per cent of the 34.5 million people who took their holidays away from home travelled by car. And one survey after another has confirmed the fact (observable to the naked eye) that millions of motorists make regular weekend trips into the countryside, and perhaps nine million day trips are made each weekend in summer. Seaside resorts have long experience in, and are ideally suited to cope with, hordes of day-trippers (Southport for example can take 300,000 a day) but country retreats are less capable of handling such crowds. Caravan and camp sites, rural car parks and knots of people unleashed onto an often unwelcoming countryside – these are among the car's more obvious consequences. How does one set the social cost of such developments against the undoubted personal and collective benefits which car ownership has brought? Whole regions of the country, now developed as tourist areas (particularly in the West Country, Wales and Scotland) were, until the coming of the motor car, remote and inaccessible.

In recent years foreign travel has been perhaps the most dramatic change in national leisure habits though still dwarfed by the millions who enjoy themselves at home. The airlines are able to whisk millions of people to the Mediterranean sun, while the growth of shipping lines specialising in carrying cars from Britain to Europe provides parallel evidence of the growth of foreign holidays. The lure of Europe is of long-standing, and could be found in its most famous form in the eighteenth-century Grand Tour. On the eve of the First World War some one million Britons visited Europe annually, but this figure now seems insignificant compared to the developments since the 1950s.

Much of the appeal of foreign travel is the work of complex and sophisticated pressure groups working on behalf of the airlines and travel agencies, and this commercial pressure is fundamental to most forms of modern leisure. This was also already apparent in the late nineteenth century, but today the commercialisation of leisure has reached an unprecedented peak. Leisure pursuits constitute a major industry which employs large groups of workers and which can provide the dizziest of salaries.

Sports in particular have experienced an amazing transformation.

Non-team games, golf, tennis and show-jumping, for example, are now large international concerns involving multi-millions of pounds. Such funds have been attracted not simply (or even largely) through attendances: spectators now provide a relatively small part of the income many games, the lion's share coming instead from advertisements, sponsorship, and related TV coverage. A brewery pays a king's ransom to persuade a tennis star to wear its name on his headband, football teams haggle for thousands of dollars in return for wearing a particular brand of boots, advertisements in every conceivable language festoon the world's sports stadiums, their messages directed not at the crowd but towards the TV cameras. English schoolboys have abandoned their traditional satchels in favour of bags with famous commercial names on the side; leisure shoes have given way to multi-coloured sports shoes, while sports shirts, shorts and track suits with commercial insignia have become items of daily wear. Moreover such dress is now international, helping to blur national distinctions (once so marked within Europe at least) at the sartorial level. There are few clearer indications of the successful penetration of the recreation industries into western society than the way in which their products – in modified form – have been absorbed into the mainstream of everyday life.

Related to this exploitation of sporting life, reflected in most big towns in the increase of local sports shops, is the degree to which the principal sports have become professional and international. Soccer, rugby, cricket, tennis, show-jumping, athletics depend for their excellence upon jet travel and the ease with which sportsmen and women can compete with each other across the world. It is now commonplace for British football teams to play in the remoter regions of Europe in mid-week. Horses and racing cars have their own jet cargo planes to deposit them at distant venues. One result has been that individual sports as well as team games have developed into international cults. Golf and tennis stars, racing drivers and motor cyclists are often famous in their own right, their faces and voices well enough known to launch a commercial product.

Through all these changes it might seem at first sight that the highly commercialised sports have, by emphasising the very best in the professional games, presided over the death of the amateur. In fact the reverse is true for, beneath the glossy veneer of the professional sporting circuses there are millions who, possibly spurred on by their professional peers, play simply for enjoyment. Leisure facilities in Britain today – football fields, tennis courts, golf clubs, swimming pools – are sorely taxed by unprecedented numbers keen to enjoy their facilities. While it may be true that an even greater proportion of the British people fail to avail themselves of these facilities (which in most cases are inaccessible to poorer people), the overall picture is remarkably healthy. Many of the more recent municipal investments in sporting facilities have been designed for individualistic games (squash being perhaps the best example) and cannot attract very large groups, but it seems likely that horizons have been widened by the proliferation of sports in most major towns. It is also significant that many of the more recently popularised sports involve costly equipment and clothing. Although children continue to play their own sports and games, with the usual improvisations, many people are now anxious to set aside substantial sums for expensive sports. Equally, the main spectator sports, including those, like football, which were traditionally cheap, have been forced by economic circumstances substantially to raise their admission charges. In many respects the playing and watching of sports often involves considerable cost to the player or spectator.

Much of this phenomenon is a result of the wider problem of inflation which has so transformed the industrial world in the course of the 1970s. Equally, however, much of it is the result of commercialisation which sees the sporting world as an area for easily garnered riches. In such a world, success means all; losers, no matter how gallant or skilled, are not commercial propositions. With the stakes so high, and the commercial pressures so intense, the will to win has transmuted many games and sports into combats of gladiatorial proportions (quite literally the case with international car racing) and the outcome is often inflated by the rhetoric of popular journalism and TV coverage.

Many older forms of leisure and entertainment have begun to falter under the financial burdens. Ballet, live music and theatre have often been kept alive solely by a massive infusion of state or charitable money. Moreover the years since the late 1960s have witnessed a rich flowering of local musical and theatrical talent (some of it politically inspired) anxious to reach a wider audience, though this has survived largely by the refusal of its young practitioners to demand more than a marginal living from its meagre income. Travelling groups, workshops and collectives have undoubtedly brought a new element of richness and diversity into the nation's cultural life but only time will tell how this phenomenon will survive in a society which begrudges a living wage to the bulk of its actors and musicians. Many such groups perform in schools or in small theatres, which themselves survive largely by subsidy and, again, the heroic work of a small band of ill-paid activists. However much we bemoan the corrosive effect of commercialisation on the nation's leisure pursuits, it seems unquestionable that, culturally, the scene is more varied than it was twenty years ago – and this includes the world of broadcasting.

Broadcasting, both television and radio, is a pervasive source of political and cultural controversy. In its amazing diversity it provides a source of entertainment, education and culture (both high and low) which is cheap and unusually varied, and as often excellent as it is sometimes banal. Its weaknesses are manifest, but its peaks of achievement provide entertainment of the highest order. There must be few viewers of modern British TV who, in the space of a single week, fail to find satisfaction for even their most esoteric tastes. This is clearly the case also with sound broadcasting. Criticisms of the more popular aspects, inescapable in an age of cheap transistor sets, are apt to ignore the positive sides of broadcasting.

Few areas of leisure have remained unscathed in the social revolution of the past quarter of a century and much of that revolution is due primarily to the unleashing of a new consumer power which has widened many people's choice as to how to spend their free time (which has also increased). The most obvious, institutional pursuits – from colour TV to sporting occasions – demand relatively high expenditure from the spectators. At the amateur level the major games and sports (individual and team) demand even greater funds and time from participants. Even the physical face of English recreations has changed to suit the public's insistance on a more comfortable environment – better food, drink and toilet facilities. Organisations unable to afford the heavy costs of such improvements often find themselves in a downward economic spiral; unable to pay for attractive facilities, they are unable to attract the crowds and hence the necessary income. Perhaps the most salutary tale of the past decade involves cricket. Once slowly dying as a county game, cricket has been revived and is now in a resurgent mood, thanks predominantly to the innovation of shorter contests with large commercial backing (though much of that backing, particularly from the cigarette companies, is designed solely to penetrate the now forbidden world of TV). Sponsorship alone will not provide all the financial answers for ailing games (as soccer has discovered in its over-proliferation of sponsored contests), and once commercial sponsorship intrudes itself into a game, that game tends to alter beyond all recognition. The levels of athletic excellence in, say, tennis and golf are unprecedented, yet the style, tenor and ethos of those games have changed past recall.

The overall result has been that most forms of organised sports in Britain have become obsessed with improving their immediate physical environment. Dog and speedway tracks even provide restaurant facilities for the more prosperous customers; eating out while watching sport coincide – a telling comment on the merging of English leisure habits. Eating out itself has become a major form of entertainment. Many towns which in, say 1960, had virtually no café or restaurant can now offer an amazingly cosmopolitan range of eating houses where the cuisines of Europe compete with those of Asia. Pubs too have taken on a new role (though in some senses reverting to their traditional role) of providing meals. In the process they have changed from basically beer-drinking saloons into sumptuously though often garishly decorated palaces, offering an unusual range of exotic drinks, many of them inventions of the fertile minds of brewery marketing men. Pubs which in the 1950s sold only mild, bitter and bottled beers, can now offer Pernod, Scandinavian lagers and American liquor. There are few pubs, even in poorer districts, which have been able to resist this change. And it stems, not from an unaccountable desire of beer drinkers in, say Oldham, for Pernod instead of mild, but from an emergent consumer power which, directed by commercial pressure (much of it through TV) demands new tastes and enjoyments.

The combination of consumer power and commercial pressure has been primarily responsible for the physical changes in recent English leisure habits. Few popular seaside holiday resorts, for instance, even resemble their former selves of the 1950s. Piers, theatres, stations, boarding houses, these and much more, have been modernised or replaced. The same is true of the more successful sports stadiums, pubs, eating houses and surviving theatres and cinemas. Whether the public 'demands' such improvements is not clear; but that is certainly what they have got, in return for their money.

There remains, as always, the other side of this image of a prosperous and increasingly indulgent nation. A substantial and apparently unchanging proportion of the population remain locked into desperate economic and social circumstances which prevents all but physical survival. The poor with large families, the sick and the old, the under- or unemployed, rarely get the chance to enjoy the nation's rising expectations. It may be true that many of the poor, for example, now possess a TV (a sign that yesterday's luxuries become today's essentials), and that in many respects they seem better provided for than the poor of a generation ago. But such relativity is of no consequence; what matters is the contrast between their own lives and aspirations and the immediate world around them. Such contrasts can only confirm their deprived condition. For those without spare money to enjoy the pleasures they see around them, it is of little comfort to hear they are living in an affluent society.

A dramatic change in recent years has been the swelling invasion of tourists from countries with more buoyant economies, for whom a visit to Britain is a relatively cheap holiday. The need to cater for these visitors, with their badly needed foreign currency, has become a major preoccupation, as witnessed by the seductive efforts of British travel firms, cities and government agencies in Europe and North America. The result, in 1975, was the spending of some £1,000 million by foreign tourists, with all the ramifications that involves. Large sections of the community (and of certain towns in particular) depend for their livelihood on this foreign invasion and the explosion in varied leisure pursuits has in large measure been designed to cater for these visitors. Despite the expansion in modern leisure and despite the oft-repeated platitudes about the emergence of a leisured-society, the future of leisure in this country is obscure, to a large extent because of prevailing economic conditions. The demands of leisure occupations will doubtless survive, if only to keep alive the large industries concerned, but it is uncertain whether the rate of change of the past quarter of a century can be maintained. Who in 1952 could have predicted the levels of prosperity and material consumption which, depression not withstanding, have come to dominate British society today? The right to free time with pay is an unquestioned fact of modern western society, yet this right is of very recent vintage and is the result of a combination of historical tradition, commercial interest and government involvement. The struggle to secure free time in modern industrial society was hard and long; new industries have sprung up which concentrate on occupying the nation's leisure as fruitfully and enjoyably (and profitably) as possible. Anyone able to afford the price of this book and with the free time to read it, has in fact fulfilled this historically-rooted formula perfectly.

12 Summary

The leisure occupations of the English people were fundamentally transformed in the nineteenth century by the process of urbanisation and industrialisation. A comparison between, say, 1870 and 1780 shows a qualitative shift in the way people enjoyed themselves. In general the older, turbulent and often bloody games and sports had died, giving way to more ordered and disciplined recreations. The new industrial society demanded – and got – entertainments which were consonant with the wider social and economic interests of contemporary society. But this 'purging' was neither manipulated (though it was encouraged by those who saw the old pastimes as inimical to the new economic order) nor complete. Many habits survived in transmuted form, nowhere more obviously than among children who continued to enjoy the games and songs of the predecessors. But in the early years of the nineteenth century, industrial people in particular found themselves denied the time, the space, and the money to enjoy many of the established enjoyments.

The upper classes continued to complain of the lower orders' addiction to excessive drinking and promiscuous sex, and throughout the century, in greatly different social situations, alcohol and the place of drink occupied pre-eminent positions particularly among the men. Moreover the face of urban England seemed to be equally disfigured by armies of prostitutes in search of a precarious living. Apart from drink, perhaps the most obviously pre-eminent leisure pursuit was the enjoyment of music which, unlike so many other leisures, united sexes and classes.

Few activities can be divorced from their immediate economic context, and the greatest of all influences on nineteenth-century leisure was the fluctuation in economic fortunes. As people of all classes secured more free time and spare money, they found themselves with the wherewithal for enjoying it. There was moreover an undoubted process of assimilation at work whereby social groups tended to follow the recreational leads of their betters, though as soon as a pastime or custom become too 'bourgeois' or 'plebeian' the class above moved on to more distinctive (i.e. isolated) pursuits. Nowhere was this process clearer than at the seaside resorts which emerged from their origins as spas to become attractions for the emergent middle class and (after the railways with their excursion trains) for the working class. In the process certain social groups (often from specific regions) stamped their own social tone on a resort. The lure of the sea became a national obsession, made possible by train services and fledgling consumer power, while at the resorts entrepreneurial efforts were directed towards providing commercial entertainment on a lavish scale.

By the last quarter of the century many of the nation's major enjoyments were orchestrated by large commercial enterprises. Leisure had become an industry requiring heavy capital investment and astute management. But it depended ultimately on consumer power and as such its growth in the years 1870 to 1914 provides a telling insight into the expanding finances of contemporary English people. There remained of course ranks of the poor and the dispossessed, but by the turn of the century the pursuit of commercial enjoyment (seaside trips, music hall, brass bands, drinking and spectator sports) had become commonplace among people whose parents and grandparents could scarcely have dreamed of such treats. Time and again, in the 1890s, contemporaries remarked on the widespread commitment to enjoyment even among the poor.

In those same years the nation seemed to be obsessed with sports; millions of men (and sometimes, though less commonly, women) played and watched a variety of organised games, most of which had flowered since the mid-century. In the evolution of those games, the public schools were crucial and from those schools the new codified games emerged to become the passion of millions who had never even heard of a public school – a process greatly helped by a competitive spirit. Athleticism was implanted in the new state schools and was thus enhanced and passed on from one generation to another. But the peaks of sporting achievement were best represented by the new professional athletes in highly commercial games which, increasingly, were played at international level. From small beginnings, the major sports of the English people had by the end of the century become global phenomena.

Compulsory education was also important in helping to disseminate literacy which, though tracing its roots back to pre-industrial society, and greatly promoted by the Sunday schools, became particularly important in the late nineteenth century, Popular journalism, cheap comics, weeklies and booklets flooded the market, satisfying the most esoteric of reading tastes. Reading for pleasure slowly became a feature of English society, and reading of course helped to encourage interest in other forms of leisure, yet even reading was dominated by powerful commercial interests which saw leisure as a highly profitable venture. On the eve of the First World War there were few leisure activities which remained untouched by commercial interests.

During the First World War there was a powerful resistance to organised leisure, which was thought to be contradictory to the war effort. Yet, despite that resistance, people continued to enjoy themselves, more especially those whose earnings were increased by work in the war industries. Similarly, during the slump years of the 1920s 1930s, there was no relaxation in the commitment to organised pleasures, despite the harsh times. But there were fundamental changes in those years, for the wireless and cinema added a new dimension to people's lives, in the process undermining some of the older recreations. Certain forms of leisure, which had been born of improving conditions in the late century, survived and in some cases flourished in the harsh times of depression.

During the Second World War the state took a different approach and (unlike 1914–18) encouraged entertainment in order to complement the people's industrial and military efforts. Indeed the provision of war-time leisure opportunities became a government concern for the first time. The austere peace of the late 1940s saw a massive upsurge in the nation's pursuit of leisure interests despite (or perhaps because of), the continuing hardness of daily life. When economic conditions began to improve in the 1950s people turned eagerly to the consumer durables pouring from the new light industries, a process which reshaped many of the nation's leisure occupations. Most seminal of all these durables were the television and the car. In essence however, it was but a reprise on a more massive and fundamental scale of a process already clearly defined in the last quarter of the nineteenth century, of leisure emerging in response to demands created by consumer power, and commercial interests taking advantage of new opportunities. Of course the sheer scale of modern leisure interests is qualitatively different from anything known before – but even that is more revealing of the economic context than it is of leisure itself. In the past twenty years, the emergence of television has created the largest of audiences (and hence of markets) for a range of recreations. Television – the most seminal form of leisure in its own right – is crucial for many other forms of mass recreation. In the process, many of the nation's leisure habits have developed a wider setting: many of the public school games of a century ago are now the passion of a global community.

Sources and further reading

Introduction

Dumazedier, J. *Towards a Society of Leisure*, trs. J. S. McClure, Collier-Macmillan, 1967.

Harrison, B. *Drink and the Victorians*, Faber, 1971.

Riesman, D. *The Lonely Crowd*, Yale, U.P., 1950; (abr. edn. 1969).

Riesman, D. *Individualism Reconsidered and Other Essays*, Free Press, Clencoe. Ill., 1954.

Veblen, T. *Theory of the Leisured Classes* (1899), n.e. Allen and Unwin, 1925; paper, 1971.

Walvin, J. *The People's Game: a social history of English football*, Allen Lane, 1975.

Walvin, J. *Beside the Seaside: a social history of the popular seaside holiday*, Allen Lane, 1978.

Chapter 1. Leisure in an urban society 1830–1870

Aiken, J. *A Description of the Country from 30 to 40 miles Round Manchester*, London, 1795.

Ayton, R. *A Voyage Round Great Britain, Undertaken in the Summer of the Year 1813*, 1814.

Baker, J. A. *The History of Scarborough from the Earliest Date*, London, 1882.

Brooke-Smith, M. *The Growth and Development of Popular Entertainments and Pastimes in the Lancashire Cotton Towns, 1830–1870*, University of Lancaster, M.Litt. thesis, 1970.

Census for 1851, *Parliamentary Papers vol. 1xxxv*, 1852–53.

Checkland, S. G. *The Rise of Industrial Society in England, 1815–1885*, Longman (1964), illus. edn., 1971.

Edinburgh Review, 13 (1809), January.

Engels, F. *The Condition of the Working Class in England in 1844*, Panther, 1968 edn. (also ed. W. O. Henderson and W. H. Chaloner, Blackwell, 1971).

George, M. Dorothy. *Hogarth to Cruikshank, Social Change and Graphic Satire,* London, 1969.

Grossmith, George and Weedon. *The Diary of a Nobody* [Mr Pooter] (1892), Penguin Books, 1975 edn.

Hammond, J. L. and B. *The Age of Chartists, 1832-54* Longmans, 1930.

Hay, D., Linebaugh, P. and Thompson, E. P. eds. *Albion's Fatal Tree: Crime and Society in Eighteenth Century England,* Allen Lane, 1975.

Hinderwell, T. *The History and Antiquities of Scarborough and the Vicinity,* 1798.

Hobsbawm, E. J. *Industry and Empire: economic history of Britain since 1750,* Weidenfeld and Nicolson, 1968.

Home, T. (Ms). Thomas Holme to Home Office, 8 September 1826, H.O. 40/21, fol. 209-10.

Hutton, T. *A Tour to Scarborough in 1803.*

Malcolmson, R. W. *Popular Recreations in English Society, 1700-1850,* Cambridge U.P., 1973.

Manners, Lord John. *A Plea for National Holy Days,* London, 1843, edn.

Royston Pike, E. *Human Documents of the Industrial Revolution,* Allen and Unwin, 1966.

von Raumer, F. *England in 1835,* London, 1836, 3 vols.; rev. edn. Irish U.P., 1972.

Reid, D. A. 'The decline of St Monday, 1776-1876', *Past and Present* (1976), no. 71.

Richard, H. *Memoirs of Joseph Sturge,* London, 1864.

Strutt, J. *The Sports and Pastimes of the People of England,* 1802.

Thompson, E. P. *Whigs and Hunters: the making of the Black Act,* Allen Lane, 1975.

Tocqueville, Alexis de. *Journeys to England and Ireland,* trans. G. Lawrence, Faber, 1958.

Ward, J. T. *The Factory Movement, 1830-55,* Macmillan, 1962.

Chapter 2. The railway age

Altick, R. D. *Victorian People and Ideas,* Dent, 1974.

Aspin, C. *Lancashire, The First Industrial Society,* Helmshore Historical Society, 1969.

Barnes, D. 'The opposition to Sunday rail services in North Eastern England, 1834-1914', *Journal of Transport History,* 6, no. 2 (1963).

Birch, J. W. *The Isle of Man: a study in economic geography,* Cambridge, U.P., 1964.

Bridges, J. *The Sabbath Railway System Practically Discussed,* London, 1847.

166

Carr, R. *English Fox Hunting. A History,* Weidenfeld and Nicolson, 1976.

Carter, E. F. *A Historical Geography of the Railways of the British Isles,* Cassell, 1959.

Chesney, K. *The Victorian Underworld,* Penguin Books, 1972.

Cooper, D. D. *The Lesson of the Scaffold,* Allen Lane, 1974.

Delgado, A. *The Annual Outing and Other Excursions,* Allen and Unwin, 1977.

Eardly, S. *The Lord's Day; is it a holy day or a holiday?,* Birmingham, 1838.

Granville, A. B. *The Spas of England and Principal Sea-Bathing Places,* 2 vols., London, 1841; Adams and Dart, 1971.

Hoskins, G. *Devon,* London, 1964; n.e., David and Charles, 1972.

Lickorish, L. H. and Kershaw, A. G. *The Travel Trade,* Practical Press, 1958.

Malcolmson, R. W. *Popular Recreations in English Society, 1700–1850,* Cambridge U.P., 1973.

Marchant, P. 'Early excursion trains', *The Railway Magazine,* **100** (1954).

Ottley, G. *A Bibliography of British Railway History,* Allen and Unwin, 1965.

Patmore, J. A. *Land and Leisure,* Penguin Books, 1972.

Perkin, H. *The Age of the Railway,* David and Charles, 1970 edn.

Pevsner, N. *The Buildings of England. Derbyshire,* Penguin Books, 1953.

Pevsner, N. and Hubbard, E. *The Buildings of England. Cheshire,* Penguin Books, 1971.

Pollard, S. *A History of Labour in Sheffield,* Liverpool U.P., 1959.

Remarks on the Regulation of Railway Travelling on Sundays . . . by a Railway Director, London, 1836.

The Times, 2–3 June 1865.

Vamplew, W. *The Turf: a social and economic history of horse racing,* Allen Lane, 1974.

Ward, J. T. *The Age of Change, 1770–1870: documents in social history,* A. and C. Black, 1975.

Williams, B. *'Piers Closed. An Account of the Development of the Pleasure Piers',* Thesis, Institute of Architectural Studies, University of York, 1974.

Chapter 3. Sinful recreations

Burton, E. *The Early Victorians at Home,* Longman, 1972, Arrow Books, 1974.

Burnett, J. *Plenty and Want,* Nelson, 1966.

Chesney, K. *The Victorian Underworld,* see Chapter 2.

Harrison, B. *Drink and the Victorians,* see Introduction.

Harrison, B. 'Pubs' in H. J. Dyos and M. Wolff, *The Victorian City,* 2 vols., Routledge, 1973, vol. 1.

Harrison, B. 'Underneath the Victorians', *Victorian Studies,* **10** (1967).

Harrison, J. F. C. *The Early Victorians, 1832-51,* Weidenfeld and Nicolson, 1971.

Heasman, K. Evangelicals in Action, London, Bles, 1962.

Marcus, S. *The Other Victorians,* Weidenfeld and Nicolson, 1966.

Mayhew, H. *London Labour and the London Poor,* 4 vols., New York, Dover edn. (repr. Cass, 1967), Vol. 4.

Nield, K., ed. *Prostitution in the Victorian Age,* Gregg International, 1973.

Pearsall, R. *The Worm in the Bud,* Penguin Books, 1971.

Royston Pike, E. *Human Documents of the Victorian Golden Age, 1850-1875,* Allen and Unwin, 1967.

Seymour-Smith, M. *Sex and Society,* Hodder and Stoughton, 1975.

Seymour-Smith, M. *Fallen Women,* Nelson, 1969.

Stafford, Ann. *The Age of Consent,* Hodder and Stoughton, 1964.

Thompson, E. P. *The Making of the English Working Class,* n.e. Penguin Books, 1968.

Chapter 4. Useful pleasures

Altick, R. D. *Victorian People and Ideas,* see Chapter 2.

Aspin, C. *Lancashire. The First Industrial Society,* see Chapter 2.

Bamford, S. *The Autobiography of Samuel Bamford,* ed. W. H. Chaloner, 2 vols., Cass, 1967.

Engels, F. *The Condition of the Working Class in England in 1844,* Panther, 1968.

Harrison, J. F. C. *The Early Victorians, 1832-51,* see Chapter 3.

James, L. *Fiction for the Working Man, 1830-1850,* Penguin Books, 1963.

James, L. ed. *Print and the People 1819-1851,* Allen Lane, 1976.

Lacqueur, T. W. *Religion and Respectability. Sunday Schools and Working Class Culture, 1780-1850,* Yale U.P., 1976.

Morning Chronicle 15 November 1849.

Royle, E. *Radical Politics, 1790-1900:* Longman (Seminar Studies in History), 1971.

Royston Pike, E. *Human Documents of the Victorian Golden Age,* see Chapter 3.

Turner, E. S. *Boys will be Boys, History of Sweeney Todd, Deadwood Dick. etc.,* n.e. Penguin Books, 1975.

Chapter 5. Leisure and material improvement 1870–1914

Avebury, Lord. *Essays and Addresses, 1900–1903,* London 1903.

Booth, C. *Life and Labour of the People in London,* vol. 5, Poverty (1903), repr, Kelley, U.S.A., 1970.

Booth, W. *In Darkest England and the Way Out* (1890), repr. of 6th edn. C. Knight, 1970.

Chambers, J. D. *The Workshop of the World: British economic History from 1820 to 1880,* Oxford U.P., 1968.

Court, W. H. B. *British Economic History, 1870–1914: commentary and documents,* Cambridge U.P., 1965.

Duff, A. G. *The Life and Work of Lord Avebury,* London, 1924.

Hobsbawm, E. J. *Industry and Empire,* see Chapter 1.

Hutchinson, H. G. *The Life of Sir John Lubbock,* 2 vols., London, 1914.

Mathias, P. *Retailing Revolution,* Longmans, 1967.

Pollard, S. and **Crossley, D. W.** *The Wealth of Britain 1085–1966,* Batsford, 1968.

Rowntree, S. *Poverty. A Study of Town Life,* London, 1903.

The Saturday Half Holiday Guide, London, 1868.

Saturday Half Holidays, London, 1856.

Stevenson, J. *Social Conditions in Britain between the Wars,* Penguin Books, 1977.

Webb, S. and **B.** *Industrial Democracy,* London, 1898.

Whitaker, W. B. *Victorian and Edwardian Shopworkers and the Struggle to Obtain Better Conditions and a half holiday,* David and Charles, 1973.

[**Wright, T.**] 'A Journeyman Engineer', *The Great Unwashed,* London (1868), 1970 edn.

Chapter 6. Down to the sea in droves

Ayton, R. *A Voyage Round Great Britain,* see Chapter 1.

Bagwell, P. S. *The Transport Revolution from 1770,* Batsford, 1974.

Bailey, F. A. *A History of Southport,* Southport 1955.

Gilbert, E. W. 'The growth of inland and seaside health resorts in England', *Scottish Geographical Magazine,* 55, 1939.

Gilbert, E. W. 'The growth of Brighton', *Geographical Journal,* 114, 1949.

Gilbert, E. W. *Brighton: Old Ocean's Bauble,* London, 1954; repr. Flare Books, 1975.

Gilbert, E. W. 'The holiday industry and seaside towns in England and Wales', *Festschrift Leopold G. Sheidl zum 60 Geburtstag,* vol. 1, Vienna, 1965.

Granville, A. B. *The Spas of England,* see Chapter 2.

Kilvert, F. *Kilvert's Diary,* ed. W. Plomer, 3 vols., Cape, 1956.

Lennard, R. 'The watering places', in R. Lennard, ed., *Englishmen at Rest and Play,* Oxford U.P., 1931.

Musgrave, C. *Life in Brighton: from the earliest times to the present,* Faber, 1970.

Perkin, H. 'The "social tone" of Victorian seaside resorts in the North West'. *Northern History,* 11, 1975-76.

Pimlott, J. A. R. *The Englishman's Holiday,* London (1947), repr. Harvester Press, 1976.

Russell, R. *A Dissertation on the Use of Sea-Water in the Diseases of the Glands,* London, 1752.

Walton, J. 'Residential amenity; respectable morality and the rise of the entertainment industry in Blackpool', *Literature and History,* 1 (1975), March.

Walton, J. 'The Social Development of Blackpool 1788-1914' University of Lancaster, Ph.D. thesis, 1974.

Walvin, J. *Beside the Seaside,* see Introduction.

Chapter 7. The rise of organised sports

Alcock, C. W. *Football, the Association Game,* London, 1890.

Alcock, C. W. *The Book of Football,* London, 1906.

Arlott, J. ed. *The Oxford Companion to Sports and Games,* Oxford U.P., 1976.

Betts, J. R. 'The Technological Revolution and the Rise of Sports, 1855-1900', *Mississippi Valley Historical Review,* XL, 1953.

Dunning, E. ed. *The Sociology of Sport,* Cass, 1971.

Edwards, C. 'The new football mania', *Nineteenth Century,* 32, 1892.

Mandle, F. W. 'Games people played', *Historical Studies,* April 1973.

Mason, R. 'History of the Game in England', in E. W. Swanton, ed., *The World of Cricket,* Michael Joseph 1966.

Meller, H. E. *Leisure and the Changing City, 1870-1914,* Routledge, 1976.

Molyneaux, D. D. 'The development of physical education in the Birmingham district from 1871-1892. M.A. thesis, University of Birmingham, 1957.

Owen, O. L. *The History of the Rugby Football Union,* Playfair Books, 1955.

Rees, R. 'The development of physical education in Liverpool during the 19th century', M.A. thesis, University of Liverpool, 1968.

Ritchie, A. *King of the Road: an illustrated history of cycling,* Wildwood House, 1975.

Robertson, M. *The Encyclopaedia of Tennis,* London, 1974.

Strutt, J. *Sports and Pastimes,* see Chapter 1.

Walvin, J. *The People's Game,* see Introduction.

Chapter 8. The sound of music

Ehrlich, C. *The Piano: a history*, Dent 1976.

Gamble, G. *The Halls*, London, 1899.

Nettel, R. *Music in the Five Towns, 1840-1914*, Oxford U.P. 1944.

Nettel, R. *Five Centuries of Popular Music*, London 1956.

Osborne, D. F. *Music Hall in Britain*, David and Charles, 1974.

Pearsall, R. *Victorian Popular Music*, David and Charles, 1973.

Pearsall, R. *Edwardian Popular Music*, David and Charles, 1975.

Roberts, R. *A Ragged Schooling, growing up in the classic slum*, Manchester, U.P., 1976.

Russell, D. 'True blues stand to your guns. An analysis of the social and political content of music hall song and sketch, 1880-1914', unpublished paper.

Scholes, P. A. *The Mirror of Music, 1844-1944*, 2 vols., Oxford U.P. and Novello, 1947.

Sutcliffe, J. *The History of Music in Birmingham*, Birmingham, 1945.

Young, K. *Music's Great Days in the Spas and Watering Places*, Macmillan, 1968.

Young, P. M. *The Choral Tradition*, Hutchinson, 1962.

Young, P. M. *A History of British Music*, Benn, 1967.

Chapter 9. Treats and children's games

Booth, C. *Life and Labour of the People in London*, 1st series, vol. 3.

Delgado, A. *Victorian Entertainment*, David and Charles, 1971.

Delgado, A. *The Annual Outing*, see Chapter 2.

Dore, G. and Jerrold, B. *London: a pilgrimage*, 1872, New York, Arno Press, 1976; David and Charles, 1971.

'Education and maintenance of pauper children', 1896, *Minutes of Evidence, Parliamentary papers*, 1896, vol. xliii.

Horn, P. *The Victorian Country Child*, Roundwood Press, 1974.

Kilvert, F. *Kilvert's Diary*, see Chapter 6.

Kynaston, D. *King Labour: British working class 1850-1914*, Allen and Unwin, 1976.

Lickorish, L. J. and Kershaw, A. G. *The Travel Trade*, see Chapter 2.

Lowndes, G. A. N. *The Silent Social Revolution*, Oxford U.P., 1969.

Malcolmson, R. W. *Popular Recreations*, see Chapter 1.

Opie, I. and P. *Children's Games in Street and Playground*, Oxford U.P., 1969.

Reports of the Assistant Commissioners on the state of popular education in England, *Parliamentary Papers*, 1861, vol. xxi.

Final Report on the Commissioners on the Working of the Education Acts, 1888, *Parliamentary Papers*, 1888, vol. xxxv.

Roberts, R. *A Ragged Schooling,* see Chapter 8.
Stickland, I. *The Voices of Children 1700-1914,* Blackwell, 1973.
Thompson, F. *Lark Rise to Candleford,* Oxford U.P., 1954, 1959.

Chapter 10. The Great War and after 1914-1939

Briggs, A. *History of Broadcasting in the United Kingdom:* 1. *The Birth of Broadcasting,* Oxford U.P., 1961; 2. *The Golden Age of Broadcasting,* Oxford U.P., 1965.
Brunner, E. *Holiday Making and the Holiday Trades,* Oxford, Nuffield College, 1945.
Conference on Workers' Holidays, Industrial Welfare Society, London, 1938.
Dougill, W. 'The British coast and its holiday resorts', *The Town Planning Review,* **16**, no. 4 (1935).
Graves, R. and Hodge, A. *The Long Weekend,* Four Square, 1961.
Hoggart, R. *Uses of Literacy,* Penguin Books, 1958.
Marwick, A. *Britain in the Century of Total War,* Penguin Books, 1968.
Mowat, C. *Britain between the Wars,* Methuen, 1959.
Minutes of Evidence before the Committee on Holidays with Pay, HMSO, 1937.
New Survey of London Life and Labour, London, 1935, vol. 9.
'Report of the Committee on Holidays with Pay', April 1938, Cmnd 5724, *Parliamentary Papers,* xii, 1937-38.
Roberts, R. *A Ragged Schooling,* see Chapter 8.
Rust, F. *Dance in Society,* Routledge, 1968.
Stevenson, J. *Social Conditions in Britain between the Wars,* see Chapter 5.
Taylor, A. J. P. *English History, 1914-1945,* Oxford U.P., 1965.
Turner, R. and Palmer, S. *The Blackpool Story,* Blackpool, 1976.
Vamplew, W. *The Turf,* see Chapter 2.

Chapter 11. Austerity and after 1939-1950

Board of Trade White Paper, *Staggered Holidays,* Cmnd 2105, July 1963.
British Tourist Authority, *Research Newsletter,* no. 13, Summer 1974.
British Tourist Authority, *Digest of Tourist Statistics* no. 5, April 1975.
Calder, A. *The People's War: Britain 1939-45,* Cape, 1969.
Hobsbawm, E. J. *Industry and Empire,* see Chapter 1.
Hours and Holidays, Labour Party Research Dept, London, 1974.
Let Us Face the Future, Labour Party, London, 1945.
Lavey, P. *Recreational Geography,* David and Charles, 1974.
Patmore, J. A. *Land and Leisure,* Penguin Books, 1972.

172

Pearson, R. E. 'The Lincolnshire Coast Holiday Region', University of Nottingham, M.A. thesis, 1965.

Rowntree, B. S. and **Lavers, R. R.** *English Life and Leisure,* Longmans, 1951.

Rowntree Papers, Borthwick Institute, University of York.

Smith, M., Parker, S. and **Smith, C.** eds. *Leisure and Society in Britain,* Penguin Books, 1973.

Walvin, J. *The People's Game,* see Introduction.

Walvin, J. *Beside the Seaside,* see Introduction.

Index

Themes in British Social History

This major new series will cover the most important aspects of British social history from the renaissance to the present day. Topics will include education, poverty, health, religion, leisure and popular protest, some of which will be treated in more than one volume.

These studies will provide standard works in the rapidly developing field of social history. The books are written for undergraduates, postgraduates and the general reader; and each combines a general approach to the subject with the primary research of the author.

The General Editor is Dr John Stevenson of the Department of History, University of Sheffield.

Titles already published:
Religion and Society in Industrial England A. D. Gilbert
The Gentry G. E. Mingay
A Social History of Medicine F. F. Cartwright
The Press and Society G. A. Cranfield
Leisure and Society 1830-1950 J. Walvin

The story of leisure in modern British society is of increasing interest to historians and sociologists, but there has not hitherto been a general survey of the evolution of leisure, and leisure-time activities, as we know them today. The topic is an attractive and lively one; but it is also important: for not only are the games and pastimes which characterised mature industrial Britain a fascinating study in themselves, they also provide a new insight into the fundamental social and economic changes which transformed British society during the nineteenth and early twentieth centuries.

James Walvin's book is thus not simply a collection of histories of different sports and amusements, but also an investigation of the extent, significance and changing nature of leisure during the period. It shows how the first industrial society came to grant ever more free time (and spare cash) to growing numbers of the population; how leisure was transformed from a minority privilege to an ambition, and expectation, of the majority, and hence to a commonplace fact at every level of society. And it reveals how industrialisation, while initially destroying the leisure activities of many, nevertheless enabled people ultimately to enjoy themselves on a scale unimagined by their ancestors.

Leisure and Society is a serious contribution to the study of an important topic, and it will be welcomed by students and academics in a number of related disciplines; but it will also appeal to a far wider readership since, engrossing and intriguing and full of good things, it explores a subject which dominates the thinking of many of us, and intimately concerns us all

James Walvin is Senior Lecturer in the History Department at the University of York.

Longman Group
£2 95p net